HARVARD HISTORICAL STUDIES

Published under the direction
of the Department of History
from the income of the
Henry Warren Torrey Fund

Volume CIII

Wills and Wealth
in Medieval Genoa,
1150–1250

Steven Epstein

Harvard University Press
Cambridge, Massachusetts, and London, England
1984

Library of Congress Cataloging in Publication Data

Epstein, Steven, 1952–
    Wills and wealth in medieval Genoa, 1150–1250.

    (Harvard historical studies, v.103)
    Bibliography: p.
    Includes index.
    1. Wills—Italy—Genoa.   2. Genoa (Italy)—Social
life and customs.   3. Genoa (Italy)—History—To 1339.
I. Title.   II. Series.
LAW   929′.345182   84–9133
ISBN 0–674–95356–8

Preface

This study of wills and wealth in medieval Genoa concentrates on two important aspects of social history—the family and charity—the study of which has too often depended on prescriptive sources. This is particularly true for the period before the fourteenth and fifteenth centuries, when European bureaucracies began to survey their countries and cities with increasing rigor. Concerning the central Middle Ages, the law and religious teaching provide a framework for examining how people ordered their personal and spiritual lives, but by themselves these sources leave many questions unresolved. Documents of practice illuminate individual lives, but in aggregate they are merely a rough and undigested mass of random facts. Social history written from prescriptive sources often reflects the qualities of the material; it generalizes in a didactic way. Personal documents yield an assortment of desultory vignettes that demand of the reader an imagination skilled in reaching its own conclusions. Some way should be found to combine the benefits of both approaches; a legal framework with copious individual examples would be ideal. Wills are well suited for this task. They were bound by law and custom, but not excessively so, and they offer the most complete available portraits of individual lives and concerns.

One can reasonably assume that a last will and testament reveals what a person, and collectively a society, deems important. Charity and the family emerge as principal concerns. The history of the family is necessarily in part the history of property. The will was designed to facilitate the conveyance of wealth from one generation to the next, but there was still ample scope for individual preference. Studying these personal decisions gives a more complete view of the medieval family in a period when it experienced the stresses of active urbanization and a commercial revolution, and endured. Charity, or philanthropy, did not represent some sort of alternative to the family but rather was inextricably bound to the family and its destiny. At the moment of approaching death the next world seemed to merge imperceptibly with this one. Charity might take a number of forms—many of which benefited the whole family or specific members in this world as well as the next. Charity was a spiritual attribute, and yet it also worked to preserve social harmony. After taking care of their own family, testators tried to bolster the social framework in which the family had to exist. Charity pleased God and hence resulted in divine favor. Often, pious deeds took on a practical cast; for example, freeing a slave had both spiritual and social consequences, or providing dowries for poor women benefited the soul while supporting the institution of marriage. Charity and the family and the many connections between the two are the focus of this book.

As we shall see, Genoa and this period offer favorable ground for this study. This century of Genoese history, from roughly 1150 to 1250, encompassed Genoa's rise to importance in Italy and the Mediterranean world. Four themes dominated the political life of the city in this century. The first concerns the internal consitution of the city, which was a free commune. The Genoese experiment in self-government went through three phases: consuls of the commune to 1191, when the city began to rely on a *podestà* for executive functions; a *podestaria*, which suffered a loss of control in the 1240s and 1250s, when the city was wracked by factionalism; and the election of Guglielmo Boccanegra as captain of the people in 1257, which for our purposes marks the end of the classic medieval commune. The constant struggle with nearby Pisa for supremacy in the Tyrrhenian Sea is the second theme, and here the century witnessed the gradual extension of Genoese naval power in the region, culminating in the complete defeat of the Pisans at Meloria in 1284. Third, Genoa was in a very disputed way subject to the German emperor. Around 1150 the city was in conflict with Frederick Barbarosa, and in 1250 it was part of the alliance that rejoiced at the death of Frederick II. Occasional supporters of the emperor in Italy, especially when they thought it would do them some good in Corsica and later in Sicily, the Genoese were in an isolated corner of Italy and could usually afford to remain aloof from the struggles between the empire, the papacy, and the Italian communes, except when involvement was profitable or their native son Innocent IV required help. Finally, the eastern Mediterranean trade and the Crusades increasingly involved Genoa in the East, where the city played an important role in commerce, and in the Latin Kingdom of Jerusalem. In the East, however, Genoa ran into another Italian rival—Venice. Just at the end of this period Genoa's relations with its new and ultimately insurmountable rival were deteriorating rapidly. The growth in trade, described by Robert S. Lopez as a "commercial revolution," itself owed much to advances in the arts of war and shipbuilding, as well as to the city's contacts with the more advanced societies in the Byzantine East and Islamic North Africa.

This book concentrates on a social portrait of urban life in this key century of Genoese history. Wills are superb documents for social history, but their proper use requires a close examination of the way in which they were produced and preserved, and their formal character. Chapter 1 addresses these problems, and also looks carefully at the will as a historical source. The technical discussion has been kept to a bare minimum, but it is necessary to consider the legal conventions that surrounded the making of a will. Looking at the will in this way casts the issue of medieval record keeping in a new light. Chapter 2 explores the circumstances and motives behind the decision to make a will. It is important to know who made wills, and when, where, and why they made them, in order to understand their strengths and weaknesses as sources. Chapters 3 and 4 discuss the mention of family members in wills, beginning with children and branching out to other relatives and voluntary associates such as friends. The funeral as a ritual provides a useful start for looking at the intentions behind philanthropy, and Chapter 5 examines Genoese charity with an eye toward the funeral and burial. Chapter 6 discusses the wide range of social and spiritual charities that the Genoese patronized. After looking at how the Genoese bequeathed their wealth, in the last chapter I attempt to show by investigating estate inventories how they accumulated property. The study concludes with remarks on some general trends and interpretations concerning the period. Some readers might prefer to read a sample will at the outset, and there is one in Appendix A. All the sums of money that appear in this book, unless otherwise indicated, are in Genoese lire (see Appendix B on money and prices).

I would like to thank, first and foremost, my thesis adviser David Herlihy. He set me on the path of social history that led to Genoa, and at every step his help and example made the way possible. Robert Lopez provided me with a kind introduction to his Genoese colleagues and Genoese historiography. Angeliki Laiou and James Given read the entire manuscript and offered many useful suggestions. I would also like to thank the History Department of Harvard University, which twice made it possible for me to do research in Genoa. The Archivio di Stato of Genoa gave unstinting help and a friendly atmosphere for working. Gabriella Airaldi and Geo Pistarino of the Institute of Paleography and Medieval History of the University of Genoa extended deeply appreciated courtesies to someone far from his native habitat. I would also like to thank Elizabeth Suttell of Harvard University Press for her careful reading of the manuscript and her many useful suggestions. Finally, the interest and support of my wife, Jean, survived the whole project and are worth more than I can acknowledge here.

Contents

Wills and Wealth in Medieval Genoa

It may seem strange that of all men sailors should be tinkering at their last wills and testaments, but there are no people in the world more fond of that diversion. This was the fourth time in my nautical life that I had done the same thing. After the ceremony was concluded upon the present occasion, I felt all the easier; a stone was rolled away from my heart. Besides, all the days I should now live would be as good as the days that Lazarus lived after his resurrection; a supplementary clean gain of so many months or weeks as the case might be. I survived myself; my death and burial were locked up in my chest. I looked round me tranquilly and contentedly, like a quiet ghost with a clean conscience sitting inside the bars of a snug family vault.

Herman Melville, *Moby Dick*

1 / The Sources

Genoese wills survive as a historical source because they were written down in notarial cartularies, or notebooks. These notarial cartularies are bound books of paper sheets arranged in folios and contained in a cardboard cover sometimes wrapped in parchment. The cartularies, together containing 632 usable wills for the period 1155–1253, have survived time, war, and neglect; they exist today in the Archivio di Stato of Genoa.[1] In 1684 the French fleet of Louis XIV bombarded Genoa and scored several direct hits on the Archivio di Stato, destroying many cartularies and damaging and scattering others.[2] The work of restoration was entrusted to two novices, who, despite their dubious training in paleography and diplomatics, did a reasonable job of restoring some semblance of order. If the title page of a cartulary was missing, they attempted to identify the notary from internal evidence. If a fragment was too short to be bound up separately, they combined fragments from different notaries and bound them together in units of two hundred to three hundred pages. The cartularies that had emerged unscathed were usually about this length. The notaries would carry these books around the city, consulting them frequently, and this practice had dictated the maximum size of the cartulary in both its original form and in the seventeenth-century compilations. Because of these and subsequent efforts to preserve them, most cartularies contain acts of business by several notaries. This has resulted in some confusion over citation, since the name of the first notary is the title of the cartulary.

Historians first made use of these cartularies by editing and publishing them. The pioneer in this work was Arturo Ferretto, who in 1906 published his edition of the notary Maestro Salmone's acts from 1222 to 1226.[3] Ferretto evidently chose this notary's cartulary—not the earliest one to have survived—because Maestro

Salmone had had a diverse clientele and worked for some of the city's most prominent families. Ferretto supplied full transcriptions for about one-half of the acts, and summaries for those he thought were less important. One generation's interests are not another's, and his successors have generally published complete records, not summaries. Ferretto also edited several collections of acts from different cartularies that had the common theme of relations between Genoa and other Ligurian towns.[4] While his transcriptions are not perfect, Ferretto set a high standard of diligence that found few immediate imitators. Economic historians such as Eugene H. Byrne began to use these cartularies as sources for studying medieval trade and shipping. These two interests, quite natural given Genoa's important role in both, began to dominate Genoese historiography, and in turn generated a need for reliable printed texts. In 1935 Mario Chiaudano and Mattia Moresco published an edition of the earliest notarial cartulary—that of Giovanni Scriba—whose acts covered the years 1154 to 1166.[5] Meanwhile, the Wisconsin School of economic historians were also working in the Genoese archives, and a fruitful collaboration soon developed. American and Italian scholars worked out a plan for publishing complete texts of all the twelfth- and early thirteenth-century cartularies. No other city in Italy was able to claim as substantial a body of source material for this period. This series of texts, known as *Notai liguri del sec. XII,* first appeared in 1938.[6] By 1940 various teams of editors, including Robert L. Reynolds, Margaret W. Hall, Hilmar C. Krueger, Mario Chiaudano, and others, had published editions of the notaries Guglielmo Cassinese, Oberto Scriba de Mercato, Bonvillano, and Giovanni di Guiberto.[7] The war disrupted this project, but Fascist race laws had already cast a shadow upon it when in 1940 one edition's title page omitted the name of C. Jona, one of the editors.[8] After the war Krueger and Reynolds published the last text, that of the notary Lanfranco, and they turned their efforts to microfilming some of the remaining cartularies.[9] Altogether the project published the greater part of six cartularies.

At the same time that these editions appeared, another scholar, Robert S. Lopez, began to demonstrate how to use notarial cartularies in conjunction with other sources, including other cartularies. Beginning with his biography of Benedetto Zaccaria in

1933, Lopez mined these cartularies by pursuing such topical themes as the wool trade and Genoese colonies. He also went beyond traditional economic concerns to lay the foundation for medieval Genoese social history, and he began the useful habit, which most Genoese historians have continued, of appending relevant notarial acts to articles and books. The American students of the Wisconsin School, which eventually included Lopez himself, have continued to use the cartularies as a whole to answer many different questions rather than taking up the task of compiling editions. In Genoa itself, some editions of notaries who worked in the Levant and in other Ligurian towns have appeared, as well as a few monastic cartularies.[10] The present study is based on wills taken from twenty-six cartularies and one manuscript, and includes all the extant wills written in the city between 1155 and 1253.[11]

The range of business conducted in the presence of and recorded by notaries is enormous. The common activity was commerce; the well-known Genoese *societas* and *commenda* contracts made up the bulk of business of all notaries until around the middle of the thirteenth century, when some specialization occurred. Sales of land and goods, dowry contracts, apprenticeships, testaments, inventories, and anything else that required a written record with legal force, appear in the cartularies. An act recorded in the cartulary and not subsequently vacated by one or both of the parties had legal validity. Notarial acts are not sworn documents; rather they are promises or ratifications made in front of witnesses. The acts acquired legal force because the law granted it, and because the individual or parties stipulated penalties for failure to comply with the terms of an act. For example, a testament was a public declaration of record recognized by both Roman and Lombard law; the legal force also resulted from the executors' obligations. For the reason that the notarial cartulary had legal force, it became customary for notaries to arrange for their cartularies to be deposited, upon completion or the notary's death, with the commune, so that they might be preserved and consulted. The depositing of the cartularies became habitual sometime between 1150 and 1250. The making of copies of old but relevant business during the course of the thirteenth century proves that some sort of archive had been established.

Testaments, documents of enduring relevance, were often copied out for descendants. An early instance concerns a dispute between the Monastery of San Andrea de Sestri Ponente and Simona, daughter of the late Guglielmo Picamiglio, in 1232.[12] The dispute centered on certain disagreements in the way the parties interpreted the wills made by Enrico Picamiglio in 1210 and Giovanna, wife of Guglielmo Murta, in 1231. The earlier documents survived, and the notary copied them into his record of the present controversy. As we shall see, it is improbable that the family preserved copies of these testaments. The copies were presumably made from the cartulary of Jacopo, the notary who wrote the original wills. The notary Filippo da Sori wrote a testament for Simone Silvagio on December 8, 1252.[13] At the bottom of the page containing this will is a note dated November 9, 1279, stating that the notary Giovanni de Pona copied out this testament for Bertolino Silvagio. The city government or the guild of notaries preserved these cartularies. However, the date when this custom began is uncertain. Giovanni Scriba's cartulary covers the years 1154 to 1166. The next surviving fragment of a cartulary belonged to Oberto Scriba and covers a portion of 1179. Not until the thirteenth century are there significant remains. Giovanni Scriba served for some time as an official scribe of the commune, and the governmental records contained in his cartulary may have provided the reason for preserving it. Once the process of preserving some cartularies began and the volume of business conducted in Genoa grew, it made sense to require the deposit of all cartularies. The advantages of such an archive are obvious, but one can only speculate about its development.

It is useful to clarify some terminology at this point. The Italian literature refers to the acts a notary recorded in his cartulary as *imbreviatura*.[14] A *carta* or *instrumentum* was a formal presentation copy of an act in parchment, made for a party to an act of business or some other interested person. When the word *act* is used here, it means *imbreviatura*. The period 1150–1250 exhibits a wide variety in contemporary terminology. In his own testament the notary Giovanni Scriba listed sums that clients owed him for his *cartula* at a price of six denarii each.[15] These *cartulae* were almost certainly acts and not instruments. At the end of a will Pietro Rufo made for one Mabilia in 1213, he wrote the brief note "dedit

denarios VI."[16] Presumably this sum was the fee for the act. Notaries made their living by writing up these acts, and most of the
time there was no need for an additional copy.

Notaries usually vacated or canceled an act in one of two ways.
One was simply to cross it out; occasionally the notary would write
cassa in the margin to indicate that a party to or author of an act
had vacated it. An agreement that had been fulfilled, completed,
or transferred to another notary might be crossed out. Acts were
also canceled when the testator wanted a formal copy. Some notaries used two or three styles of cross-outs to distinguish the
reasons. None of these methods generally apply to wills, and in
fact the great majority of them were not canceled. Since most
people did not have copies made of their testaments, the act in
the cartulary was the legal record of a person's last wishes. Religious institutions preserved a handful of exceptional parchment
copies of wills. In most of these cases the institution benefited
substantially from the terms of the will, and so the document was
saved as the legal title to the bequest. The Monastery of San Siro
had in its archives a parchment copy of the will of Giacomo de
Turcha, dated August 6, 1205,[17] which had been specially made
for his wife, Giulietta. In his will Giacomo gave his wife the right
to give away her share of his goods if she decided to enter religion,
or for her soul. San Siro may have acquired the document because
she chose one of these alternatives. Still, most people did not have
copies made of their own wills. As we shall see in the next chapter,
most testaments seem to have been sickbed declarations, and so
making a copy for the testator may not have been a pressing need.
Or perhaps, more important, many testators were unable to read
the document anyway; in this case, reliance on the notary's record
would have been natural and unavoidable.

Formal Character

What is a testament? "The term testament is derived from two
words which mean a signifying of intention."[18] Thus the authors
of Justinian's *Institutes* introduced beginners in the law to the subject. The testament, or last will (*ultima voluntas*), was the legal way
for a person to settle his affairs in this world. As Marc Bloch
points out for a later period, in words which apply to this one as

well, a will "was a work of piety as much as of wise provision and was intended above all to ensure the salvation of the soul by devout bequests."[19] Many testators considered the salvation of the family to be of equal importance. A person contemplating his own death necessarily relied on trust, custom, and the law, for the individual did not expect to see his intentions realized. In the early Middle Ages testaments usually consisted of just a few deathbed utterances, which the kin honored and no one committed to writing. Local customs determined the principal forms of inheritance within the family; remnants of Roman law and the barbarian law codes provided a general framework when one was necessary. The city of Genoa preserves its silence on the subject until the mid-twelfth century, when notarial cartularies began to be preserved and, by a haphazard process of transmission, have survived to the present day. In the earliest extant cartulary are testaments written by the notary Giovanni Scriba.

In order to clarify the discussion that follows, I present below an outline of a standard Genoese testament. Naturally, not every document contains all these sixteen units, or has them in the same order, since notarial style was often individualistic. A certain amount of evolution must also be kept in mind; in general, the testaments written before 1200 are simpler than the later ones.

1. Name of the testator. A cognomen was infrequently used before 1250, and occurred only at the top levels of society. Patronymics, toponymics, relationships to other persons, and occupations were almost always linked to the first names.

2. Reason for making a will. Unfortunately, formulaic statements predominated, but common reasons, in order of frequency, were illness or plans for a pilgrimage or journey.

3. Burial site. This was absent in those wills made for reasons of travel.

4. Bequests for the soul (*pro anima*). This type of bequest was usually made in cash, but occasionally the testator left property or goods for his soul.

5. The division of the charitable bequests. Typical kinds of bequests are a tithe to the Cathedral of San Lorenzo; bequests for funeral and burial expenses; endowment of masses; bequests to religious institutions, pious causes, and the poor; manumission of slaves; bequests to servants, friends, and family members.

6. Nomination of distributors. The testator named the relatives or friends responsible for disbursing the charitable bequests.

7. Dowry statement. A man acknowledged his wife's dowry and provided for its return, or claimed that he had already done so. Women rarely mentioned this subject, instead leaving their husbands a legacy.

8. Legacies to family and friends.

9. Provision for the rest of the goods. Having finished the specific bequests, the testator named his principal heirs to everything left. The scale of the remainder depended on how much had already been bequeathed.

10. Nomination of tutors. A person with minor children named tutors, or guardians, and outlined the nature of their responsibility.

11. Legal formulas. These ratified the testament, gave it the force of law, reserved the right to add codicils, and canceled any previous will. Every notary had his own favorite phraseology.

12. The place where the will was made. The notary identified the town, neighborhood, or village and the building or spot where the act transpired.

13. Date. All testaments were dated, and around 1200 it became customary to give the time of day as well.

14. The witnesses. The law required the presence of five witnesses who were not kin or heirs.

15. Cancellation of the will. If the notary drew lines through the will, we know that the testator had vacated it or had had a copy made.

16. The notary. The document by itself does not identify the notary, but with a few exceptions the cartulary or the handwriting establishes his identity.

These sixteen points are discussed in detail in subsequent pages, but it is useful to have this general plan of the testament clear from the beginning.

The Law

How did the testament come to take on this form? For three reasons: the law required a testament to conform to a prescribed set of rules; traditional social behavior suggested that the testator act in an acceptable way; and individual needs and desires prompted an expression of personal will in the face of the other two strictures. In other words, a person had to do certain things, he ought to do others, and above all he wanted to work his own will.

Most of this book is devoted to studying social behavior and personal desire; but the first stricture, the law, must be the point of departure. The law supplied a framework, the *ius testamenti*. As late as the eleventh century, Genoese commonly claimed that they lived by the Roman or Lombard law. The Lombard law disappears from the sources by the mid-twelfth century, but it may have continued to exert a lingering influence.[20] Genoa could not claim a continuous Roman tradition, yet many Genoese called themselves Romans, and Lombard law conceded them this privilege. In the early Middle Ages the "Roman" population governed itself according to whatever fragments of vulgar Roman law it could muster. By about 1150 the study of Roman law had revived and made available in Italy the fruits of the jurisprudence of Justinian's era. Giovanni Scriba possessed a copy of the *Institutes*, and the testaments he wrote, as well as subsequent ones by other notaries, all reveal the influence of Roman law.[21] The arrival of Roman law did not obliterate earlier tradition, but Lombard law had never established a rigorous procedure for making wills. Significantly, this law first mentioned wills when it allowed oral testaments to be considered valid.[22] In some matters, such as the status of women and the age of majority, centuries of custom would not vanish quickly or without a struggle. This tension between the law and actual social circumstance is a familiar one. Most notaries were not lawyers; neither were their customers nor the city officials charged with hearing disputes. Given these conditions, let us first explore how notaries were trained in the law and their profession.

The most common way to acquire notarial training was to be apprenticed to a notary. A young man looking over a skilled notary's shoulder by day and going over the day's work at night would receive an excellent introduction to the profession. A handbook would also be very useful, especially for understanding the legal framework. A wide range of guides was available in the thirteenth century, and they provide us with an idea of what a notary was expected to know about the law. For convenience one may call these handbooks formularies, because at a minimum they include sample forms of all those documents that a notary might have to draw up. The authors of these formularies also explained and analyzed, to varying degrees, the sample documents included in the texts. A systematic study of the surviving formularies would greatly enhance our knowledge of the notarial and legal professions, but at this stage of scholarship even the relationships between the various texts are unclear, and the topic seems to have attracted little attention in recent years. I shall briefly consider four formularies in order to ascertain the scope of legal knowledge that the notary brought to the testator. They are the *Formularium Tabellionum* by an anonymous notary of Bologna, written circa 1205; the *Ars Notariae* of Rainerio da Perugia, written from 1224 to 1234; the *Ars Notariae* of Salatiele, the first version dated 1242, revised sometime before 1254; and the *Ordo Iudiciorum* of Martino da Fano, written circa 1264 but reflecting a career going back to the 1220s.[23] All four texts reveal the influence of the University of Bologna; only Martino wrote his text elsewhere, and he was certainly trained at Bologna. If these particular formularies were not available in Genoa, similar works were. No Genoese formulary from this period survives, but this city, without a university, was used to turning to Bologna, or perhaps Pavia, for such works.

A useful way to explore how these texts instructed notaries is to look at their answers to a basic question: who was not capable of making a will? A primer on this subject is the *Institutes* of Justinian, where in Book II, Title XII, are listed seven basic categories of persons incapable of making a valid will: those absolutely in the power of others (except for soldiers on duty), minors, lunatics (except in lucid intervals), spendthrifts, deaf-mutes, the blind (with some qualifications), and prisoners. The Anonymous of Bologna followed this list exactly, employing the language of the *Institutes* and revealing his dependence on that work for his own legal framework.[24] The text of Martino da Fano is more discursive and assumes rather than teaches a knowledge of the law.[25] Copious citations of other legal works direct the reader to more detailed commentary. Martino's text is limited to five general topics in his discussion of persons who cannot make a will. He first explains the special circumstances of a soldier's will, and he proceeds to give quite a detailed analysis of how a blind person might make

a will. Martino next makes the important but in this context irrelevant point that a person must explicitly either name or disinherit every son, or else the will is not valid. After noting that
women can make wills, Martino concludes by observing that rural
folk needed only five witnesses for their wills. The advice provided
here is useful, but again this work presumes much and perhaps
was not intended for novices.

Salatiele provides the most complete discussion of this question.[26] He begins by considering the seven exceptions outlined in
the *Institutes,* although he devotes less time to soldiers and more
to the question of prisoners—a matter of some interest to the
contentious Italian city-states. Salatiele explores the *Code, Digest,*
and *Novellae* of Justinian for more information about those not
capable of making a will and discovers seven more categories:
slaves; those condemned to death or exile; anyone whose free
status was uncertain; hostages; those condemned for defamatory
verse (a nice touch of erudition here, but this must have perplexed
some medieval notaries); monks or canons regular (because they
were dead to the world already); and heretics and traitors. Other
authors were perhaps content to omit these categories because,
except for the scabrous poets, these people all fall into the general
class of those in the power of others. Salatiele's formulary is the
most comprehensive guide a notary might hope for; indeed, it
may have told notaries more than they needed to know. The
glosses included in this work provide a real commentary on the
law, and indicate that a notary might possess as much legal knowledge as a lawyer. Finally, Rainerio da Perugia presents as complete
a list of exceptions as Salatiele, but without the latter's extensive
legal apparatus.[27]

There were a variety of formularies in circulation, providing
notaries with legal instruction. The last will was not unique to
Genoa, and it would be helpful to look briefly at what the formularies suggested about the form of a will. The Anonymous of
Bologna includes comments in his sample will that indicated alternatives or proper legal usages.[28] For the most part Genoese
practice conformed to the sample will he provided, but there are
important differences. His introductory statement is more verbose
and ornate than that of almost any Genoese notary. He devotes
some time to explaining how to return the fruits of usury, despite

the fact that even though the church taught that this was desirable, and notaries were explicitly taught how to include returns of usurious gains in a will, only about one percent of Genoese testators mention usury at all in their wills.[29] Similarly, Rainerio da Perugia notes in his discussion of *pro anima* bequests a way to return tithes, although no Genoese returned a tithe by will.[30] All the authors discuss at length how a testator could disinherit a child and for what reasons, yet not one Genoese will records a disinheritance. Salatiele considers only sons as principal heirs, and he even excludes wives from the list of potential tutors.[31] There are many more ways in which the formularies are not sure guides to contemporary practice; but one may nonetheless conclude that individual notarial practice dictated the basic shape and order of a testament, even though the authorities themselves often differed.[32] No sample will was as detailed or comprehensive as the general scheme presented earlier in this chapter. However, practice among Genoese notaries differed to an extent that suggests that informal methods of training played a key role in preparing novices for their craft.

The body of Roman law and the formularies established a set of rules concerning inheritance about which there was no dispute. Roman law stated that a testament was a public act to be witnessed by five men, or seven in the case of a nuncupative (oral declaration) will.[33] The law's principal impact was on the one hand to acknowledge the testator's right to dispose of his property in any way he wished, and on the other hand to place reasonable restraints on this right. The effect of these restraints was to protect the rights of the family, especially children. Sons were emancipated at age twenty-five at the latest, but Genoese society was prepared, perhaps because of Lombard influence, to recognize adult responsibility at eighteen or nineteen. Daughters were never emancipated, only transferred from father to husband. The law permitted a person to exclude emancipated sons and married daughters from the testament, and this exclusion was assumed when the will made no explicit mention of them. Roman law raised the question of the testator's soundness of mind, and so all testators claimed to be sane. The *Institutes* distinguish carefully between unsound mind and actual insanity. A child could claim that he was wrongfully disinherited because the testator was not of sound mind. "This does not mean that he [the parent] was really insane, but that the will, though legally executed, bears no mark of that affection to which a child is entitled from a parent."[34] The law permitted a person to disinherit children or favor one over the others, but it also indicated that the desire to disinherit them was not necessarily sound or legal.

The testaments frequently mention the *lex falcidia,* which is the only law the wills specifically cite. All legacies remained in the testator's free disposition, but this law required that the heirs inherit at least one-quarter of the estate unencumbered by debts or other bequests.[35] The formularies and Genoese practice reveal a more complicated situation. The word *falcidia* itself came to mean the one-quarter share of the heirs, and by the twelfth century the definition also included a sense of any minimum share, regardless of size, that a person was legally obliged to leave his children. The testators most commonly used the expression *pro falcidia* in connection with tiny bequests that in no way consumed one-quarter of the estate. For example, Giovanni Calcantra left his daughter Giovanna ten solidi for *falcidia* and named as principal heir his other daughter, Dolcolina.[36] The use of the term *pro falcidia* indicates that he left ten solidi to Giovanna because he recognized an obligation to leave her something. The testament of Montanaria Taraburlo clearly states that her daughter Floria had received a dowry for *falcidia* and should be content.[37] Daughters were not the only relatives dismissed with a *pro falcidia* legacy. Giovanni Lavagnino, unmarried and without children, left twelve denarii to his sister Giulia for *falcidia* and named as principal heir a certain Lucia, perhaps his fiancée, but not a relative.[38] The use of the term *falcidia* argues against any attempt to construct a general picture of Genoese testaments from Roman law. Nor, if Roman law itself had disappeared, could we reconstruct it completely from the extant wills.

Roman law carefully delineated the concepts of legacies and heirs and opened up the testament to a variety of types of gifts to relatives, friends, and charities. Manumission of slaves by will was also accepted Roman practice. As I have noted, the law placed limits on the ability of some people to make wills at all. Perhaps most important, Roman law introduced the ideas of succession and substitution. Naming heirs by degree, or succession, offered the testator the opportunity to allocate his property well into the future. Having named an heir, the testator would often direct what should happen to the bequest if the heir died without issue or failed to carry out a reasonable condition. The naming of an heir in the second degree was sometimes qualified by a further statement concerning a third heir, who would inherit if the second likewise defaulted in some way. The reasonable conditions to bequests which the law allowed often reveal the most personal aspects of a will, and in subsequent chapters I shall discuss them in detail.[39]

These examples illustrate the kind of structure the law created for testaments. Doubtless the notaries possessed at least a minimum competence in the law, and the testators themselves may have picked up a few scraps of legal knowledge by having witnessed the dictation of wills. Women were not permitted to be legal witnesses, but their presence at the sickbed of relatives afforded them the chance to learn something about the process of making a will. Familiarity with the law provided the notary with a legitimate reason to impose restrictions or conditions on testators who had a slender grasp of the legalities. What person would have used the expression *pro falcidia* to describe small gifts to relatives without a notary's suggesting it? It is necessary to remember the scene of the dictation, to imagine a notary telling his client that he ought to save everyone trouble and leave close relatives something rather than omit them altogether. Or perhaps the notary might mention that it was a good idea to have secondary heirs in case the principal ones died. (Any discussion of how the notary may have intervened in this way is best deferred until I take up redaction in detail.) The importance of the law and the notary's knowledge of it explain the broad areas of uniformity in testaments. The notaries were able to ensure that a person's intentions were impervious to subsequent legal dispute, and hence the notary reinforced the testator's existing predispositions. (However, Martino da Fano set forth the proper legal ways to mount court challenges to wills.)[40]

The will was not the only legal way to convey property within the family. Parents provided their daughters with dowries, and fathers settled property on their sons when they emancipated them. The most common form of pure gift was the *donatio inter vivos* (gift between living persons). By using this form of gift, a person could give wealth away during his lifetime and be certain that the gift would take place under whatever conditions he chose to make. The testament, in most instances, represents a decision by the testator not to give away the bulk of his wealth before he died. The *donatio inter vivos* appears less frequently in the cartularies than wills do. A rare type of testament is known as a *donatio causa mortis* (gift because of death). Minors—children still under the authority of parents or tutors—used this form to make gifts. Minors were not legally able to make a will, since they did not have the right to relinquish property without consent. But if a parent or tutor consented, a minor was able to make a last bequest. In most cases minors made testaments with consent; only a few very legally minded notaries insisted on the *donatio causa mortis* as a proper form.

The law, transmitted to the notaries by the formularies, decisively shaped the will. It is worth pausing to consider the Genoese will in a broader context. As I have already noted, Genoa has the best collection of the earliest notarial records, but there are some documents from other cities that, while not nearly as numerous as the Genoese examples, nevertheless reveal contemporary Italian practice. Venice and Amalfi are important places to examine because they remained in communication with Byzantine practice and hence preserved a more continuous tradition of making wills. An Amalfitan charter of 1087 routinely recorded a donation to a monastery made by the executors of a will, and it is only a matter of chance that the earliest known will from Amalfi is dated 1099 and not earlier.[41] This will, and a few others from the early twelfth century, betray no Norman or Northern Italian influence but seem to reveal a separate and older tradition of making wills, one combining Lombard and Roman practices.

Sporadic Venetian testaments are known from the early Middle Ages, but not until the twelfth century are there significant remains. The will of Romano, a priest of San Marco, dated February 1151, again reveals a separate tradition.[42] The form and structure of this will have almost nothing in common with the surviving work of Giovanni Scriba in Genoa some five years later. In Venice several priests combined their office with that of notary, and they included in their thirteenth-century wills, in place of the Roman legal formulas used in Genoa to conclude a last testament, anathemas damning to a fiery hell with Judas anyone who might presume to break or corrupt the will.[43] As in the case of Amalfi, the Venetian wills survive not in cartularies but as isolated parchment documents. During the thirteenth century the Venetian testaments began to show more signs of legal knowledge and practice, yet their formal structure continued to lag behind that of the Genoese wills. In Siena the earliest notarial cartulary dates from 1227 and contains wills that resemble Genoese practice in form and phraseology. The editor of this text noted that this Sienese notary seemed well versed in Roman law and the most modern notarial style.[44] The earliest sizable collection of Sicilian documents comes from the small town of Erice in western Sicily. A Jew made the first known testament in this town in 1299.[45] While the principal Italian cities preserve commercial records concerning Jews, I know of no other place where Jews made formal public testaments or even served as legal witnesses to acts by Christians, as they did in Sicily. This island had an ethnic mix unknown to Northern Italy, and here Roman law competed with even older traditions.

Venice and Genoa had quite different commercial and legal heritages, and the structure of the notarial profession and the documents notaries redacted reveal few common features. While it is not the purpose of this study to survey what appears to be a quite diverse Italian experience, the point here is that Roman law provided only a general framework that local tradition and needs (in Genoa a strong Lombard influence and an active commercial environment), as well as notaries, shaped in different ways. A study of the zones of these different practices would be most useful; here I shall concentrate on Liguria. The volume and sophistication of the Genoese notarial record and this brief comparison to other regions suggest that Genoa's notaries were among the best trained and most legally minded notaries in Italy, but also that their work remained typical of a local area and was not necessarily affected by universal practice. Let us turn to the cartulary itself and see how the will was actually drawn up—the process known as redaction.

Redaction

Since formal copies of testaments are very rare in Genoa, the question of how the notarial will came into being is fundamental to this study. I shall leave to the next chapter the specific circumstances of time, place, and motive in individual wills. The point to concentrate on here is that the notary was in the business of taking dictation. The testators would state their intentions in the Ligurian dialect of the time (only a few rare examples of this language are left to remind us that the Genoese did not speak Latin). The notary would then transform the oral declaration into a Latin document drawn up in an increasingly strict legal form, replete with formulaic statements which had nothing to do with the testator's language or intention. It is necessary to know as much as possible about how the notarial will was produced—the process of redaction—in order to determine what compromises of intention were made because of the law, language, or indeed the style of particular notaries.

Marc Bloch was one of the first to point out the problem of mode of expression, when a language known to a select few preserved and recorded everyone's thoughts. "Thus every Latin charter or notarial record is the result of a work of translation, which the historian today if he wishes to grasp the underlying truth, must put back, as it were, into the original."[46] The Latin testament, at least to some extent, imperfectly echoes the wishes it contains. Furthermore, in translating a will back into the original oral declaration, one should drop the legal formulas and perhaps change the order of statements. Looking closely at how the will was redacted should illuminate this mode of expression so foreign to the people compelled to use it.

The Genoese testaments of the mid-twelfth century represent a stage in an evolutionary process which had been going on for some time. A few charters of the tenth century survive; the church and the rudimentary city government of the eleventh century generated a small but growing number of written records. The earliest document that resembles a testament is a *carta iudicamenti* of Amico Calvo, dated April 1110.[47] This document, which is not a true testament, concerns a gift that Amico Calvo made to the Monastery of Santo Stefano for the good of his soul. As such, this charter conforms to the usual pattern of a pious benefaction. However, Amico Calvo also gave his nephew Oberto a house in the city, on condition that Oberto give the monastery L.20 for Amico's soul. Oberto was away on a journey to Jerusalem, and the gift was made contingent upon his safe return. If Oberto died without a legitimate son or daughter, the house would revert to the monastery. Amico also left to some other nephews, sons of Giordano Longo, another house in Genoa. This last clause is important for two reasons. The word *iudico* ("I leave") is used for the gift to the nephews. This word, replacing the *dono* ("I give") employed earlier, emerges later as a favorite with testament writers. The last gift had no connection with the monastery; why then did Amico mention it in this act? This charter has elements in common with the general pattern for a testament outlined earlier, yet at the same time it is not called a testament, and it lacks several key ingredients. If the testamentary form had been fixed and well known, Amico Calvo would have united these disparate intentions in a testament. The *carta iudicamenti* disappeared over the course of the twelfth century. Fifty years later Amico's intentions might very well have taken the form of a will. If this line of reasoning, based as it is on a single document, is correct, then between 1110 and 1155, when Giovanni Scriba's cartulary begins, the citizens of Genoa became familiar with the testament and began to use it. (Amalfi was, not surprisingly, ahead of Genoa in this development.) This conclusion considerably narrows the period of the process of development, and coincides with other changes in Genoese society. The commercial revolution of the twelfth century, the increased importance and activity of the communal government, and the return to the study of Roman law all argue for the increased importance of the written word in Italian society. Genoa was in the forefront of the first two developments, and was not slow to take advantage of the third, as we have seen.

A cursory examination of most notarial cartularies reveals that they are far too neat in general to be the copy made directly from dictation. However, the cartularies of Guglielmo Cassinese and Oberto Scriba occasionally demonstrate so much variety of usage and so many signs of haste in writing that these may sometimes represent the original dictation. Since the law and notarial formularies supply little hard evidence about how notaries created their cartularies, only by physically inspecting the cartularies can one learn how they were redacted. There are loose slips of paper, known as *notulae,* found between the pages of the cartularies. These brief notes are thought to represent the jottings the notaries made while they transacted business. It is thought that from these notes, usually discarded, the notary would later write the act contained in his cartulary. By examining these notes one can gain some insight into the redaction process and acquire some feeling for the differences between the cartulary copy of the testament and a person's oral declaration. One *notula,* containing the testament of Oberto de Bogi, is found between folios 118 and 119 in one of Oberto Scriba's cartularies.[48] Oberto Scriba was an active notary for many years. Having drawn up thousands of business agreements over his career, he was doubtless capable of taking down acceptable drafts of routine matters directly into his cartulary. But testaments tended to be somewhat rare acts, so even an experienced notary who was good at dictation may have preferred, as Oberto evidently did, to make notes. There is every reason to believe that notaries did what was convenient at the time, working with or without a draft as the situation warranted.

Oberto de Bogi's testament lacks all the usual formulaic statements contained in a will, but the order of the notes follows the order of a complete will. For example, the simple beginning of the *notula,* "Obertus de Bogi," would appear in the formal cartulary copy as something like "Obertus de Bogi de ultima voluntate sic me et mea ordino." The next words in the note name the burial site, and the rest of the note amounts to little more than a list of names and sums which are very difficult to interpret (a problem one might expect when reading someone else's personal shorthand). The principal fact learned from this *notula* is that the order of statements is the same as for a formal cartulary copy, down to the witness list. Again, particular circumstances and the whims of individual notaries created some variety of method. Notaries, at least at the beginning of their careers, or faced with a long and difficult transaction, may have chosen to work from notes. In other matters where form was habitual, or in simple acts (and not all testaments were complicated), confidence may have prevailed, and the notary may thus have copied an oral declaration directly into his cartulary. The press of business may also have necessitated immediate redaction, such as, perhaps, in the case of deathbed declarations.

A second *notula,* inserted between the pages of Jacopo Taraburlo's cartulary for the year 1227, tells a similar story.[49] Taraburlo's cartulary is notable for its fine, almost manuscript quality handwriting, which could not possibly have resulted from dictation, and which indicates Taraburlo's unusual carefulness. For these reasons his *notula* is much more comprehensible than Oberto Scriba's, though it too lacks several concluding formulaic statements. The note in this case may have been taken from dictation, and then served as the draft from which Taraburlo made the cartulary copy. These *notulae* tell us something very important about the redaction process. The notary would have read the draft to the testator and witnesses to check the accuracy, and he may have subsequently brought the cartulary back in order to read the complete formal act to the witnesses again. The witnesses, if not the testator, thus intervened twice in the evolution of the document—once after the testator dictated it and again after the notary drew up the formal act in his cartulary. We have no way of knowing how much time transpired between these two interventions. Since many, if not most, testaments were sickbed declarations, the time was probably short, perhaps a day or two. However, even the notes do not represent a complete return to the original oral statement.

Another kind of notarial act sheds some light on just what happened when a person stated his last wishes. Sometimes the notary was not summoned or did not arrive on time, and a potential testator died without a written will. He was not considered to have died intestate, however, for if five witnesses had heard his wishes, they could go to court and testify to the deceased's intentions. The court, the parish consuls of pleas (civic judges chosen annually), would register this testimony, and this proceeding conferred legal validity on the deathbed declaration. Some notaries, such as Oberto Scriba and Guglielmo da Sori, specialized in recording these oral wills, either because they worked part-time for parish courts (Oberto for Molassana, Guglielmo for Sori) or, less likely, because the witnesses brought their own notary. This kind of will enables us to see to some extent the testator without the notary. An act in Oberto Scriba's cartulary records that on

November 11, 1186, some witnesses appeared before the parish consuls of pleas.[50] Ingone de Berzile declared that he knew and was certain that he had been in a house in Plazo when Ingeza, the wife of Ravano, was suffering from an illness that killed her. Before she died, Ingeza bequeathed her goods; the woman's last thoughts naturally centered on how she wanted her property to be divided among her children and husband, and nothing else. Four other people turned up in court to agree exactly with Ingone's memory of this event. (More often than not, the witnesses produced at court all agreed with the first witness.) Together they were a sufficient number to have this will recorded and given legal validity.

Another document of this type describes a more complicated situation. Giordano and his mother-in-law, Altilia, appeared before the consuls of the parish of Nervi on November 26, 1198, with suitable witnesses, to testify to the last will of Adalasia, Giordano's wife.[51] Here again the first witness offered the complete account, but this time he provided more detail, and the order of presentation closely resembles a normal testament. Someone may have coached the first witness, because the others remembered Adalasia's deathbed statements very differently. Adalasia had left numerous small bequests for masses and to churches and priests, and there was some understandable confusion over these legacies. More to the point, Adalasia had been married before, and had a daughter, Aeleta, from the first marriage. The witnesses disagreed whether this daughter alone or all the children were committed to Adalasia's mother or to her husband. This problem had serious implications for family structure and ties, a subject that will be considered later.

Several conclusions emerge from these and other cases. Perhaps most important, the testators were primarily concerned about family matters; when time was short, they dispensed with every other aspect of the will save the family. The notary's presence was a definite advantage to anyone making a will. The comparative rarity of the oral wills indicates that families or individuals preferred to summon a notary in order to avoid the possible confusions of collective memory and a court appearance. It was also advisable that the notary read the final draft of the testament to the witnesses while the event was still fresh in their minds. The wills in the cartularies are more structured, and this argues for a certain give and take between the notary and his client. The notary may have informed the testator what he was supposed to do, or the notary may have asked some questions while the testator declared his will in order to fill in omissions or the predictable lapses in a sick person's concentration. However, the formularies specifically direct the notary to follow the wishes of his client. At the end of his sample will Rainerio da Perugia states, "And thus you write, whatever the testator shall have said about the above [the testament] or about whatever else, because the will of the testator is law."[52] Nevertheless, these oral wills indicate that the possibility of interference or influence by the notary, or someone else for that matter, needs to be considered. There is potential for distortion or imposed uniformity of language. I shall return to this point again, because it is important to know if the wills supply the testator's authentic voice or the notary's conventional phrases and legalisms.

So far we have seen that the act of making a testament required a person wishing to make one to summon a notary and the appropriate witnesses. The testator would declare his intentions verbally, and the notary would take down as notes or directly into his cartulary. After the notary had drawn up a formal version of the act, he would return shortly to check the testament with the witnesses. The cartularies of the thirteenth century often contain some blank space on pages; presumably these spots were reserved by some notaries who routinely took dictation directly into their cartularies but made notes, and hence saved space, for complicated transactions. Alternatively, not all notaries preserved strict chronological sequence in their acts but rather made notes and then drew up the formal acts later. This method of working would break up the exact chronological sequence of dictation. In general, one can distinguish notaries as either primarily note takers or writers from dictation. Individual practice might have depended on the notary's age or experience, as I have observed. The redaction process applies to all types of notarial acts, not only testaments, though they were among the most complicated kinds of business that a notary conducted.

Let us now turn to the wills themselves for more hints about what happened when a testator declared his intentions. Giovanni Scriba wrote all his wills in the first person, but the majority of the twelfth-century wills were written in the third person. Giovanni di Guiberto, whose extant acts cover the years 1200 to 1211, switched from third to first person during that time. Most of the later notaries used the first-person pronoun, but the formularies split evenly on this question. The wills in the first person preserve the testator's own voice. A clear example of this individuality occurs in a codicil to Giulietta Zacaria's will. She made her will on May 28, 1248, and on June 1 she clarified a few points in a codicil, in which she introduces an addition to her husband's bequest with the words *quod dicebam* ("what I was saying").[53] Giulietta recalled her will verbally; she referred to part of a document not by reading it but by remembering her words or by listening to the notary translate and read her words back—hence the "what I was saying." Moreover, occasionally a testator would use the second-person pronoun ("to you") while making bequests. Rubaldo the tailor addressed his cousin Aimelina this way, from which one infers that she was present in the room when Rubaldo made his will.[54] The witness lists do not contain the names of beneficiaries or women, so only the pronoun *you* applied to them reveals that they were present. Since, as we shall see in the next chapter, most people made their wills at home, immediate family members and even neighbors might be in attendance. The use of the second-person pronoun is one of the few rare echoes of actual speech. Even the notary Raimundo Medico, who usually used the third person, sometimes fell into the first person when writing testaments; probably he found adjusting the entire document back to the third person to be a needlessly complicated operation. Eventually most notaries abandoned the awkward third-person wills.

The fact that the notaries added and deleted words in the testaments in their cartularies poses several problems. Changes are rare, and their small number demonstrates that notaries prepared these documents skillfully. There are four main categories of changes. First, the notaries corrected mistakes of the ear, the principal drawback of dictation. These were errors that had slipped in at the time of the oral declaration, and the notary might catch these when he read the act back to the testator or witnesses. Second, the notary himself would introduce some changes that did not affect the will's content but that concerned the notary's metier.

This type of change usually occurred in the formula. Third, if the notary worked from notes, any changes made after the oral declaration would appear in the notes and not in the cartulary. Since there are comparatively few changes, one might assume that an intermediate first redaction—the notes—existed. In the case of a notary who did not work from notes, changes in the text may reflect changes in the testator's intentions, or errors immediately caught. Fourth, when the notary read the cartulary copy of the testament to the witnesses and perhaps the testator, their memories might prompt changes, or the testator might simply have changed his mind. Any mistakes made in copying the notes into the cartulary would also appear there but would be corrected in the same manner.

The first category can be discussed briefly and then put aside. An example of a mistake of the ear occurs in the will Pietro Rufo wrote for Sofia in 1213.[55] Buried in a long list of bequests is a L.10 legacy to Sofia's niece Fineta. Originally the notary wrote the name "Vigneta"; later he crossed it out and inserted the right name. When was the error noticed? Since Pietro Rufo worked from notes, the witnesses or the testatrix herself presumably caught the error.

The second category of changes, the alterations introduced by the notary, would most likely have occurred when he examined the cartulary text. For example, when the notary Azo de Clavica wrote a testament for Maria, the wife of Landulfo in 1247, he neglected to repeat the word *iudico* ("I leave") in most of the bequests, so he later inserted the word above the line every time it was required.[56] This type of change has little to do with the oral declaration. Similarly, changes in formulaic statements were the notary's concern. Bonovassallo de Cassino forgot to include in the will of one Rubaldo the very traditional and nearly universal tithe of the pious bequests to the Cathedral of San Lorenzo, so he attached a mention of the tithe to the testament.[57] For reasons that will be discussed later, the notary, or perhaps the confessor if one was present, was the most likely person to notice this omission. A last example of this type of change is the correction made by the notary Urso, who changed the reference to the place where a testament was made from in the city of Genoa to outside the

walls. The date, time, and place of an act were the notary's business
to note, and any alteration here is likely a result of his own ini-
tiative, or perhaps the witnesses'.

Examples of changes in the notes are few, since only two wills
exist in that form. Jacopo Taraburlo, a tidy and careful notary,
made no changes in his notes, whereas Oberto Scriba's notes are
confusing precisely because he did make so many alterations.
However, it is not possible to reconstruct the process of correcting
errors from the notes. The great majority of changes in the cartulary text consist of substantive alterations.

The fourth category of changes requires close analysis. These
are the additions or deletions presumably made when the notary
read the will back to the witnesses or the testator. Maestro Salmone, for example, did not work from notes but instead wrote the
oral declarations directly into his cartulary. Aidela's testament of
June 5, 1222, proves that this was Maestro Salmone's usual procedure.[58] Aidela began her will by leaving forty solidi for her soul,
with the tithe to the Cathedral of San Lorenzo, which she selected
as her burial site; the rest of her money was to be spent for masses
and her funeral. The notary at this point crossed out the whole
will and began again. This time Aidela left forty-five solidi for her
soul, the tithe, and twelve denarii each to four churches and one
bridge (as we shall see, bridges and other public works were frequent beneficiaries). The remainder, forty solidi, was to be expended as above as her son-in-law might determine. The only
reasonable explanation for the first version's appearance in the
cartulary is that Aidela changed her mind while dictating her
testament to the notary. She increased the amount left for her
soul and, more important, expressly chose some recipients of her
pious donations. As a rule, people did not diminish or eliminate
religious bequests but instead fundamentally altered existing ones
or imposed new conditions.

A striking change occurred in Mabilia's will.[59] She first left everything to her husband, to do with as he wished. Then this was
crossed out, and Mabilia proceeded to leave all her goods to her
daughter Richeldina, making her husband heir in the second degree; that is, he would inherit if the daughter died without a
legitimate heir. This is no simple substitution, for the succession
clause directly follows the naming of a principal heir. Mabilia

seems to have changed her mind literally between sentences. Simone Barlaria added a slave to the property he left his wife;
Delomeda made a legacy to her sister contingent upon the sister's
marrying.[60] As a last example, Jacoba, the wife of Giovanni Portonario, excluded two of her daughters from succeeding any of
her sons if they should die without an heir.[61] The significance of
the apparently spontaneous changes of intention is often elusive;
doubtless those on the scene knew the reason, or may even have
suggested the changes. In their opening sentences everyone claimed
to be of sound mind. These changes all fall within the bounds of
custom and the law, and arouse no suspicions of insanity or vi-
ciousness. The changes that add clarity merely amplify existing
intention and do not represent complete changes of heart. The
process of redaction allowed the testator at least a second chance
to reverse a bequest; when Mabilia substituted a new principal
heir, she did exactly that.

The redaction process thus shows how the Genoese made their
wills. These were oral declarations to notaries. The process allowed the notary, testator, and witnesses to correct any errors.
Most people did not have a copy of their own will but trusted the
notary and his cartulary copy. The law permitted witnesses to
testify in court if no written will existed, but this procedure was
cumbersome, and most Genoese successfully avoided it by making
a will. I shall shortly return to the question of just what kind of
influence a notary was able to exert on his client. Finally, a testator
was able not only to correct his errors but also to introduce complete changes when the notary read the will back to him. These
changes are important because they show the testator, no doubt
buffeted by various pressures, making decisions. It was possible
for the testator to change his mind at any time.

Second Wills

Redaction did not exhaust the opportunities to express a change
of intention or correct an error. If time and money were no ob-
stacle, the testator could simply make a new will, which would
vacate any previous one. The random nature of the surviving
source material offers no certainty that any given testament is the
last one an individual made. Continuous runs of documents are

an isolated phenomenon; the great bulk of the notarial record for the century has disappeared. Some people may have preferred a particular notary or may have had professional ties of long duration with one or another of them, but there is no reason to assume that anyone would have returned to the same notary to make a new will. Fortunately, there are six cases of repeaters to consider. Ogerio Vento made wills on November 19, 1162, and May 11, 1163; Giulia, the wife of Guglielmo Balbo de Castello, on August 16, 1201, and July 27, 1237; Antonio Rapallino on August 24 and November 5, 1213; Guirardo de Verzellato on May 4, 1228, and February 12, 1248; Contessa, the wife of Oberto Balbo, on December 16, 1232, and April 27, 1233; and finally Stefano the shopkeeper on February 3 and March 9, 1236.[61] All of these people at least lived to make second wills, though only Ogerio Vento stated that he was ill when he made the first one. All of the paired wills, and particularly the ones made thirty-six and twenty years apart, contain significant differences. Since there is no reason to doubt that the first testament was valid, in each case a change in circumstances or intentions explains the necessity of making a new will rather than simply adding a codicil.

Ogerio Vento was one of the wealthiest people in Genoa, and his family was prominent in communal affairs in the mid-twelfth century. In the November 1162 will he said that all his male and female slaves should be freed "if the Lord shall have called me on account of this sickness."[62] He lived through the winter, and in May he dictated another testament. This time he did not mention any illness but ordered his slaves freed after his death, although specifically denying them any *peculium,* or private property. It is unlikely that his family would have thrust these slaves out of the Vento household with nothing. Ogerio's seeming harshness is unusual, especially since in his first will he made no mention of *peculium.* There are some minor differences in the two wills, which by themselves did not require the making of a new act. The main difference concerns a clause Ogerio Vento added to the second will to clarify the bequest to his sons. In the first will he made the sons the principal heirs in equal proportions, with the condition that if one died without an heir, the others should succeed to whatever remained at that time. This provision was the same in the second will; however, he added a condition that his house should always remain with his sons, grandsons, and great-grand-sons (*pronepotes*), and if any of the descendants and their wives wanted to split off their share, they were to receive the just value less L.200.[63] Ogerio wanted his sons to stay together and keep the tower within the family, and he provided a financial incentive for them to do so. Over the winter he obviously contemplated the future of his family, down to the third generation.

Giulia, the wife of Guglielmo Balbo, provides us with two wills spaced almost two generations apart. In 1201 she had already been widowed, by the late Sorleone Pevere, with whom she had two sons, Rubaldino and Guglielmino; she had one son with her second husband. By 1237 her extreme old age (by contemporary standards) alone accounts for the new will. Now she was again a widow, and two of the sons mentioned in the previous will were dead. Giulia had had another son, Alberto, by her second hus-band, who in turn had eight children, and she was a generous grandmother. Giulia named as heirs her sons, Alberto and Gug-lielmo Pevere, and the children of her late son Rubaldo. Thirty-six years is a long time in a family's history, and while Giulia's intentions had remained basically the same, the pool of available heirs had not.

Antonio Rapallino, in contrast to Ogerio Vento and Giulia, was a humble citizen of very modest means. On both occasions his testaments were brief acts which primarily concerned his family. On August 24, 1213, Antonio named as heirs his son Marchesino and his granddaughter Bonadonna, daughter of his late son Rai-naldo. By November 5 Antonio had changed his mind and dic-tated a new will in which he left everything to Marchesino. Perhaps Bonadonna had died in the intervening period; or more likely she had married and received a dowry, which Antonio would have supplied, representing her claim to family wealth. Once it had been paid, only Marchesino's rights remained. Whatever caused this change in family circumstances, when Antonio wanted to alter such a fundamental part of a will as the principal heir, he canceled his old will and made a new one.

Guirardo de Verzellato also provides us with two wills, written by different notaries twenty years apart. At neither time did Guirardo have a wife or family, but there is no sign that he was a cleric. The bequests for his soul are the important aspect here. Guirardo left in 1228 pious donations totaling L.548 s.10, a huge amount of money, to a wide variety of churches and causes. He also directed that anything left of his property after the other bequests were paid should be distributed for his soul. His favorite charities were the Dominican order and the poor. Guirardo wanted to be buried at the Church of Santo Spirito, if he died in Genoa. (His anticipating that he might not die in Genoa suggests that he may have been an immigrant or a merchant.) In 1248 Guirardo's esteem for the Dominicans was undiminished, but he had changed his mind about a burial place, now favoring the Church of San Domenico in Genoa. His charitable bequests amounted to only L.40. However, he states, "I have given away goods in my lifetime for my soul as it pleased me."[64] In the absence of any known relatives, nothing prevented Guirardo from making gifts *inter vivos,* and he may very well have distributed his property in the way suggested by the 1228 testament. Very little had changed; Guirardo's intentions and religious impulses had endured. Twenty years later Guirardo's second will tells us almost nothing we did not know from the first. Of course, since he had no family, the continuity between the two wills may not be particularly remarkable.

Contessa, the wife of Oberto Balbo de Sampierdarena, made her first testament in December 1232, with the consent of her father, Oberto de Campi. Here again, the main difference between this will and the one she made the following April concerns the family. In the first will she left the rest of her goods—that is, the bulk of her property—to her children, Obertino, Bergognone, Guglielmo, Rollandino, Roseta, and Giovannina. Contessa wanted them to succeed one another if any died without an heir. If they all died childless, she wanted her husband to succeed; but if he did not survive, her property was to go to her father's relatives. Four months later Contessa left L.100 to her two daughters and bequeathed the rest of her goods to her four sons, who were still to succeed each other. Furthermore, Contessa directed her sons to give their sisters L.50 each upon marriage, but if they married without consent, the daughters were to receive nothing except *falcidia*.[65] The daughters had obviously lost ground: their original equal shares with the brothers had been reduced, and they were no longer to succeed their brothers either. Why would a mother do this? Recall that Jacoba Portonario's will similarly treated her daughters. Interestingly, Contessa's second will does not mention her father's consent.

The final instance, that of Stefano the shopkeeper, confirms the emerging patterns. The changes from February to March of 1236 all refer to Stefano's wife, Lombarda. In fact in this case the notary, Bonovassallo de Cassino, copied over the old will in its entirety, and in March he used the symbol •/• at the bottom of the page to footnote the new details.[66] In February, Stefano left his wife all his bed furnishings on the condition that she remain a widow. He also left Lombarda her clothes and the house in which they lived. In the second testament all this remains the same, but he adds that she should also receive L.20 to eat and dress at his expense so long as she stays with their children. These changes hardly seem to justify the effort and expense of making a new will. Stefano's intentions are worth considering. Clearly he was preoccupied with the idea of Lombarda's remarrying after his death, and in order to induce her to stay at home with their children, he offered cash, room, and board.

In all the cases in which there was a family the testators designed a second will to accommodate changes of intention that affected the family. Family circumstances and needs develop over time; any particular testament is merely a glimpse of family life on one day. The six cases of repeat testaments presented here, together with the types of changes previously discussed, indicate that a person carefully blended a mix of calculation and emotion in making a will. Since not every Genoese expired shortly after executing a testament, we must hesitate to assume that the dispositions of any document were irrevocable and final.

Testators were able to change their wills, and there are demonstrable reasons for their occasionally doing so. The law was beyond their personal control, and limited to some extent the will's individual character. One last aspect of redaction, notarial style, permeated the whole process and hence may have affected the will's content as well as its form.

Notarial Style

What role, if any, did notarial style and usage play in the making of a will? The work of some thirty-five notaries survives for this period. In some cases only one or two testaments exist, or none at all; for others there are dozens of examples. Generalization is therefore perilous, yet some facts emerge from examining the cartularies. Like all professional people, a notary built up a clientele during the course of a career. When a cartulary often repeats a particular family name, such a professional tie is indicated. For example, Guglielmo Sapiente was frequently involved in the Doria family's business, and when Simona Doria wanted to draw up a will, he was the natural choice for the task. He was also the official notary for recording the acts of Niccolò della Volta when he was *podestà* (governor) of the Val Polcifera in 1210.[67] Pietro Rufo had some of his regular customers in the Della Volta, Doria, De Nigrone, and other prominent families. By contrast, Oberto Scriba found no business too humble for his pen; many of his testament customers are among the poorest people known to have made wills. Wealthy people, whose activities often required the presence of a notary, seem to have relied on "their" notary to write a testament. Some commercially active persons saw a notary almost every day, and so they were able to make comparisons and find a congenial one. Many people, average citizens, are known only from their testaments, and they may have selected a notary from the neighborhood or simply on the basis of availability. Finding a notary was not hard in Genoa.

Notaries as a rule did not conduct business in their own homes. Some notaries installed themselves for the day in a shop or in front of a church or some other well-known spot, and waited for the clientele to come to them. Other notaries might work a circuit during the day, spending the morning in one place and moving on as the day progressed. A few notaries, perhaps novices, spent their time hunting up business. A few institutions had favorite notaries and would summon them when required. Niccoloso Beccaira had such a relationship with the Hospital of San Giovanni in Capo d'Arena, where he turned up to write wills for patients when necessary.[68] All of these variables helped to determine how a person who needed a notary selected one.

As outlined earlier, all testaments follow a general pattern, but each notary varied slightly from this pattern. Lantelmo tended to jumble up bequests for the soul with legacies to the family, perhaps reflecting the actual way the testator spoke. Bonovassallo de Maiori's clients habitually included in the will's first sentence statements about their health—more so than any other notary's clientele. This is an example of how a notary's style could affect the will; Bonovassallo must have asked his clients how they were. Other examples are numerous, but they are of interest here only where the kind of bequest varies by notary rather than by individual. In other words, did some notaries suggest to testators what they ought to do in their will? This important question is examined in future chapters, where I consider specific types of bequests. I have already explored how notarial language and the law shaped a testator's will but have found no evidence that language distorted intentions. For present purposes it is enough to consider how the notaries employed formulas. Formulas are statements required for legal form or by custom. These standard clauses appear in all testaments, with some variations, and some formulas occur in all other types of acts. They are worth examining because they do not represent the testator's own words. The notary would contribute the formula's style; sometimes, but not always, the meaning was still the testator's.

The formulas of the testament fall into two basic categories— the introductory and concluding sentences.[69] The introductory statement usually states that the act is a testament, or as it was normally called a last will (*ultima voluntas*). Over the period 1150– 1250 the formula tended to become more complicated and exact. Giovanni Scriba often varied his first sentence from the simple "I, Raimundo Pictenado, leave . . ." to his most elaborate "I, Leda di Guidone, with contemplation of my last will leave . . ."[70] Oberto Scriba favored two or three standard opening sentences, with no discernible pattern. Guglielmo Cassinese customarily used the plain "Gisla de Castello by her last will leaves . . ."[71] Cassinese's student Giovanni di Guiberto followed his master's formula for the first few years of his cartulary, but around 1203 switched the first person and adopted as his usual first sentence, "I, Simone Buferio the Elder, wishing to make a disposition of my goods, by my last will leave . . ."[72] However, Giovanni switched back and forth between these two alternatives for some time. Lanfranco, active from

1203 to 1225, used a simple formula reminiscent of Giovanni Scriba's. As the thirteenth century progressed, conventional statements of piety, health, or travel plans were added to the standard repertory. The notary Enrico de Bisagno phrased his beginning sentence, "I, Stefano Scriba, son of Giovanni di Guiberto, fearing the judgment of God, make disposition of my goods thusly."[73] As legalisms continued to develop, everyone began to claim as a standard condition that they were sane: "I, Simone Silvagio, sick in body, sound in mind and intellect, and being of good memory, fearing the divine judgment of God, with contemplation of my last will, make disposition of my goods thus."[74] This last example, from 1252, indicates that the testators may have had a heightened sense of individuality. On the other hand, the contemporary notary Giovanni Vegio carried the evolution of the introductory sentence to its logical conclusion when he adopted the formula, "I, Adalasia, daughter of the late Bonovassallo de Nolasco, et cetera."[75]

The concluding formula is less interesting. Giovanni Scriba varied his statements, but the general sense is that if the act is a last will or testament, and if by any law the act is not valid or is withdrawn, the testator reserves the right to make a codicil or another testament. Each notary had his own particular way of expressing these ideas. The right to alter a testament is the key reservation here. As the custom of making wills spread during the thirteenth century, the concluding formula began to contain a clause that vacated any previous testament and declared that the current one should be valid forever—that is to say until another will was made. Maestro Salmone was one of the first notaries to include this declaration, but at the outset it seems to have been reserved for those who actually needed to revoke a previous will. Soon, however, everyone was waiving any previous testament; legally this was a sound move, since the date of the act etablished a will's precedence. In the 1240s one further refinement in the formula protected the commune's rights to any loans or obligations. The commune, in the last years of the wars against Emperor Frederick II, was almost bankrupt, and it was forced to borrow extensively from its citizens.[76] The right of the city to exact forced loans was such a serious matter—the very survival of Genoa was at issue—that even the solemn testament could not interfere with the city's right to borrow the property of its inhabitants.

The notaries had various formulaic styles, and occasionally style alone tells us something about the testator. It is easy to overlook how basically similar the formulas are, especially the concluding ones. The formulas partially represent what the law contributed to the process, to the extent that the notary understood and applied the law, but they tell us little about the testator or his intentions.

Wills of Notaries

The wills of notaries are significant because they enable us to look at the document from another angle. There are four such wills: Giovanni Scriba made some notes for his own will on March 13, 1157; Niccolò Ferrario went to Maestro Salmone to draw up a will on June 15, 1226; Stefano Scriba went to Enrico de Bisagno on November 4, 1231; and Oberto de Marzano went to Matteo de Predono on March 30, 1251.[77] Three of the four notaries went to colleagues for their wills, perhaps on the theory that a notary who drew up his own will had a fool for a client. Giovanni Scriba's notes were not a final draft; he may have intended to go to another notary for the official record. This notary wrote many wills, but it is hard to compare those final drafts to his personal notes. We can compare Niccolò Ferrario's will, written by Maestro Salmone, to the five the testator himself wrote between September 1220 and August 1221, to see if Niccolò's will resembles his own work or Salmone's.[78] None of Stefano Scriba's notarial acts survive, so no comparison is possible. He was, however, the son of Giovanni di Guiberto, whose extant cartulary contains numerous wills. Only a few pages of Oberto de Marzano's cartulary survive, and he wrote no wills in this fragment.[79]

Apart from lawyers, notaries were most suited to dictate a will to another notary, and therefore least likely to be influenced by another notary's style or legal expertise. The three complete wills betray no signs of notarial experience; they are normal wills for three moderately well-to-do citizens. Most important for present purposes, these wills are no more individualistic than the rest of

the sample. In other words, notaries were typical clients, and Niccolò Ferrario's will establishes this conclusion in detail. He had his
own formulas and style of writing, which he employed when he
wrote a will, and none of these characteristics appeared in his own
testament. Instead, Maestro Salmone's style predominated: the
first and last sentences, the order of the bequests, the use of typical
phrases. In his will Niccolò noted that he had several commercial
agreements in progress, and Maestro Salmone had drawn up some
of these too. The habit of patronizing another notary was evidently
not limited to wills. Yet Niccolò must have benefited from his own
experience when he was the client of another notary. Notarial
style helped to determine the will's format, and the law tried to
protect the rights of blood relatives. The notarial wills reveal that
notaries were willing to consign their intentions to another style
and method. While various influences helped to determine the
will's structure, there appears, at this stage, to be sound reason
for assuming that the will spoke for the testator and not his notary
or lawyer. To the extent that professionals offered advice, they
seem to have reinforced existing intentions. Although it is important to continue to look for signs that notaries intervened in
or influenced clients' wishes, so far there is no such evidence.

Inventories

This study of wills and wealth in medieval Genoa relies on
various kinds of source material. Another type of document that
plays an important role in this analysis is the inventory, and I shall
briefly consider some of this source's strengths and limitations.

In comparison to wills, the inventory as a document has a short
and simple history. Inventories are found in notarial cartularies;
they are, when complete, lists of the deceased's possessions made
by the executors in order to protect the heirs, and themselves.
Robert Lopez was the first to point out the significance of inventories in his essay on the composition of personal patrimony.[80]
Before his work, inventories were mainly of interest to historians
of language and dress, since they contain many rare words describing household items and clothes. Inventories begin with a
formula stating the names of the administrators, heirs, and the

deceased. Another introductory formula commonly found in the standard inventory states that the administrators have undertaken an accounting of the deceased's goods in order "to take advantage of the benefit of the most sacred emperor Lord Justinian's constitution, and to avoid penalties set for those who do not make an inventory."[81] The inventory was of value to the administrators as well as the heirs: the former could free themselves from any accusations of fraud, and the latter could have a list of the property which would facilitate any division of the estate. Occasionally a testator would exempt his heirs or the executors from the responsibility of making an inventory. This course was frequently taken when there were only one or two heirs. What must have seemed a bothersome chore was unnecessary under such conditions. When Fulcone de Castello requested that his wife be free from any obligation to account for his goods, it might have been because the great wealth of this family called for discretion, or even secrecy.[82]

Inventories survive in small numbers beginning in the 1230s. The notary Enrico de Bisagno seems to have specialized in this type of business, which sometimes took the greater part of a day to transact. There are a few interesting cases of testaments that subsume an inventory. Some people, for whatever reason, wanted to make an item-by-item list of their possessions during their lifetime. These lists, though rare, exist almost from the beginning of the extant record. The value of such lists is obvious, and the need for them preceded the habit of formally taking advantage of Roman legal practice. Another sign that a list of possessions existed is the notarial act by which the heirs divided up the estate. Also, sometimes a person might parcel out property during his lifetime. In both cases some sort of informal inventory would have been helpful and probably existed. The division aimed to create equal shares, and this did not require a minute analysis of personal property. Instead, the division was meant to distribute fairly the land and cash on hand. These acts of division, whether accompanied by an inventory or not, are important because they indicate the approximate value of the estate. The "rest of the goods" clause in the will, which named the principal heirs, specified only the share and not the actual amount of the bequest. The division of an estate, whether done by a living person or after his death, emphasized landed wealth, and hence usually related to the highest levels of Genoese society.

The main problem of drawing up an inventory was that the act of making a list of goods often degenerated into apparent drudgery for the administrators as well as the notary. After the formulas discussed above, and perhaps mention of one or two other items such as a house or land, there is often a large blank in the document. The next sentence states that the space was left for writing in anything else the administrators might later find or remember. Then the inventory concludes with the place, date, and witnesses to the act. There are more examples of this type of perfunctory list than there are reasonably complete inventories, which also include a space for later additions. Some richly detailed inventories give a complete list of all the documents contained in the deceased's strongbox. These inventories present a more complete view of a person's wealth than a will does. However, the increased emphasis on the legality and necessity of making a formal inventory coincided with a tendency to treat the process as a pro forma obligation. This tendency produced uninformative inventories. In cases where there was only one heir, the pro forma inventory is understandable.

A final problem of the sources is that there are only a few inventories for which the original testament survives. Oberto Barleta, for one, made his will with the notary Niccolò Ferrario on October 9, 1220,[83] and his children's tutors and the administrators of his goods conducted an inventory of the estate on December 31, 1220, with the same notary.[84] Although Barleta in fact died sometime shortly after he made his will, this is a rare case. In general it is not wise to assume that the death of a testator occurred soon after a testament was drawn up. Lopez cites the case of Giulietta Zaccaria, who was sick and made a will on May 28, 1248.[85] A search for her inventory would turn up nothing, however, since she was still alive in 1280. We have also seen that Giulia Balbo outlived the making of her first will by thirty-six years. There is also no reason to assume that the executors would employ the notary who wrote the will to do the inventory as well, for the executors might have developed ties with a notary of their own. The surviving cartularies are too small a fragment of the total

volume of business to ensure any sizable number of link-ups between wills and inventories. Some notaries seem not to have done
any inventories, and may consciously have avoided this kind of
time-consuming business. (The notary had to be present during
the inventory, and a proper one could take a long time.) Oberto
Barleta thus represents an exceptional and fortuitous case. As a
rule, the inventory's value is somewhat diminished for the purposes of this study.[86]

Having looked at the sources and some related problems, let
us now examine the testament more closely and ask who made
testaments, and why, when, and where they made them.

2 / The Testament as an Act

The testament was an act made by an individual at a specific time and place, for personal motives. Let us first consider who made these wills.

Testators

No question about the writing of wills can be considered in isolation from the others, but we might look first at the names and identities of the testators themselves. From 1150 to 1250, 632 Genoese—323 men and 309 women—made wills. Their names combine elements of design and custom. As a rule, parents would choose the first names for their children. Although the habit of naming children for their grandparents fostered a certain conservatism in naming, after the first few children, parents relied on local fashion, the inspirations of piety, or whim. Benjamin Z. Kedar's study of the frequency of use of first names demonstrates a shift in favor of saints' names from the twelfth to the fourteenth century.[1] Using the lists of citizens who swore to uphold various agreements made by the commune, Kedar established the frequency of use of male names—lists that conveniently bracket the period of this study. (See Tables 1 and 2.) In addition to indicating a shift to saints' names, data from both dates reveal the great variety of first names used in Genoa. The top eight names account for only about 40 to 60 percent of the total during this period. The rich collection of first names indicates that they were the principal means of identifying people. By 1251, when surnames were becoming more common, the decline in the "others" category reveals that the variety of first names was just starting to contract. Unfortunately, no comparable source of information exists for female names. The most common names among female testators for the period 1155–1253 are listed in Table 3. Here again the

Table 1. Frequency of use of male names in Genoa, 1157.

Name	Number of persons	% of total
Guillielmus	49	15.7
Obertus	15	4.8
Ansaldus	13	4.1
Bonusvassallus	11	3.5
Bonifacius[a]	9	2.9
Gandulfus	9	2.9
Iohannes[a]	8	2.6
Ogerius	8	2.6
Others	190	60.9
Total	312	100

Source: Benjamin Z. Kedar, "Noms de saints et mentalité populaire à Gênes au XIVe siècle," *Le Moyen Age* 73 (1967): 433.

a. Names of prominent saints.

Table 2. Frequency of use of male names in Genoa, 1251.

Name	Number of persons	% of total
Guillielmus	17	9.9
Iacobus[a]	14	8.1
Enricus	12	7.0
Iohannes[a]	12	7.0
Nicolaus[a]	11	6.4
Lanfrancus	10	5.8
Obertus	7	4.1
Petrus[a]	6	3.5
Others	83	48.2
Total	172	100

Source: Benjamin Z. Kedar, "Noms de saints et mentalité populaire à Gênes au XIVe siècle," *Le Moyen Age* 73 (1967): 433.

a. Names of prominent saints.

richness in the variety of names is clear, for women even more so than for men. It is not possible to examine any shifts in feminine names, for the sample covers the whole century. The presence of Iohanna, Iacoba, and Maria is no suprise; the first two are fem-

Table 3. Frequency of use of female names in Genoa, 1155–1253.

Name	Number of persons	% of total
Iohanna[a]	21	6.8
Adalasia	20	6.5
Alda	14	4.5
Iacoba[a]	13	4.2
Maria[a]	12	3.9
Giulia	11	3.6
Aidela	10	3.2
Aimelina	8	2.6
Contessa	8	2.6
Agnese	8	2.6
Sibilia	8	2.6
Others[b]	176	57
Total	309	100

Source: Archivio di Stato di Genova, Cartolari Notarili.
a. Names of prominent saints.
b. Includes sixty-four names that appear only once.

inine forms of popular male names, and the popularity of Mary requires no explanation. No Giulio—which would be the counterpart of Giulia—appears in any of the Genoese records of the period, nor do any of the other popular female names have a masculine form. Remarkably, out of the 309 female names, sixty-four appear only once. It might be argued that this great variety of female names suggests that daughters were not as important as sons to the family's sense of social identity and continuity. The smaller pool of male names may have provided an incentive to develop the surname in the urban environment, since the male first names were not by themselves guarantors of a personal identity. One also needs to know more about whether naming the child was in this period left to the godparents or the family before concluding that daughters simply mattered for less. Parents had a wider choice of names to give daughters, and perhaps this wider choice resulted from a need for individuality. Women did not often use last names or occupations to identify themselves. Since women in a sense had to rely on their first names for a public identity, there were consequently more feminine names. Also, there were two large sets of potential names for women—feminine forms of male names, and names unique to women.

One prolific couple, Simone and Richelda Buferio, had twelve children—eight sons and four daughters. The names they chose for their children were Ansaldo, Amico, Enrico, Guglielmo, Corradino, Buferetto, Ottolino, Anselmino, Aimelina, Carenzona, Isabellina, and Iacobina.[2] Only five of these names appear in the list of popular names. The Genoese favored the use of diminutive names for their children, and in this case the Latin certainly reflects the spoken language. During adulthood the sons and daughters seem to have dropped the suffix; they were not little anymore, and so they shed their childhood names. The name Buferetto completes a circle of sorts: when pushed to invention, the Genoese often made a first name out of a surname.

Only thirteen people who made wills were content to give solely a first name and no other name or form of identification. The rest were able to choose among a wide assortment of ways to name themselves. For women the range was rather circumscribed. Most women referred to themselves as someone's wife, even if they were widows. Marchisia even called herself the wife of the late Girardo da Bisagno, even though she was at the time married to a certain Andrea.[3] Presumably most people did not know her as Marchisia, the wife of Andrea, and her social identity remained tied to that of her deceased husband. In the next most common name pattern a woman claimed to be her father's daughter. Although some women from prominent families used the surname, even in cases where the father had a surname, the daughter often did not use it. Frequently a married woman would still refer to herself as her father's daughter, though most women who claimed this relationship were unmarried. These two name forms—either wife or daughter—account for over 80 percent of all female names. A few women identified themselves by other relationships, such as the niece, sister, or mother of a certain man. Here again the relationship was always to a man, another sign of the status of women in the community.

In an article on surnames and places of origin, Robert Lopez writes, "In Genoa the larger part of the prominent bourgeois families, whether of noble origin or not, received their surnames during the eleventh century, and transformed them into hereditary family names during the twelfth, but the process was far from complete even at the end of the thirteenth century."[4] The middle and lower classes lagged at least a century behind in acquiring permanent family surnames. These surnames were used primarily by men. The process of transforming a sobriquet, occupation, place of origin, ancestor's name, and so on into a family name provides ample room for uncertainty about the real source of these names. The Avvocato family may have acquired their name as the result of being advocates for a religious institution, but not every *advocatus* was a member of this family. The Bancherio family has long confused some historians. They were evidently bankers; but again, not every *bancherius* was a banker, or a member of this family. It is tempting to associate the Pevere (pepper) family with the trade in this precious commodity, and perhaps they took their name from being the chief local suppliers. However, this kind of speculation can easily become fanciful.

Patronyms, another form of identification, frequently evolved over time into surnames. The most famous example of this was Zaccaria de Castro, who lent his name to the well known Zaccaria family. Young people were especially likely to use patronyms, for the purpose of a name is to identify its owner, and fathers were better known in the city than their children. Sons and daughters were equally likely to use a patronym, even though the father might have a surname or some other way of identifying himself. When the son acquired an independent role in society, he probably began to use the family surname, if one existed, instead of the patronym.

Toponyms, if used, generally succeeded a patronym—for example, Altilia, the daughter of Guglielmo da Domoculta. Names derived from a place fall into two categories—those referring to Genoa and its immediate environs, and those referring to Liguria. For the city, certain *Compagne* (wards) often appear as part of a name—Soziglia, Piazzalunga, and Santo Stefano. Given so many Giovannis and Guglielmos, city toponymics were often associated with common first names. In all such cases the person in question lived in the area that formed part of his name. Villages and small towns close to Genoa, such as Sampierdarena, Rivarolo, Zimignano, and others in greater Liguria, from potential rivals like Rapallo and Savona to tiny hamlets up in the mountains, all appear as parts of names. Lopez has argued that by and large people had some connection with their toponym, and when this tie became tenuous, the toponym either developed into a surname or more often simply disappeared.[5] We cannot assume that everyone in Genoa with a Ligurian toponym was a first-generation immigrant. The nature of the connection must be determined for each person. Testaments are useful in this matter because people mention churches or land they owned in the place whose name they carried; this notice confirms the tie even if the family had arrived in Genoa some time earlier. As we shall see, the habit of spending summers outside the city was engrained in Genoa, at least for those able to afford it. The wealthy families retained ties and dependants up in their mountain retreats, and even the moderately well off hoped to own a farm or house in some village where they had their roots. The powerful Genoese families who claimed to be noble often had small principalities outside the city.

The clergy was the most distinctive group to be known by occupation. The rest of the people who gave a job as part of their name generally belonged to the artisan classes. Blacksmith (*faber*), shoemaker (*calegarius*), baker (*furnarius*), and the various types of employment in the cloth business—weaver (*texitor*), cutter (*affaitor*), wool merchant (*lanerius*), and draper (*draperius*)—all appear in Genoese wills. Only males used their occupations as names, except for a very few women who identified themselves as nurses (*baiula, nutrix*) or weavers (*texitrix*). It is difficult to give frequencies for each type of name because people so often combined different types. For example, Pietro, who made a will in 1239, called himself "Pietro, the son of Oberto batifoglio and Riccarda, daughter of the late of Riccardo, the furrier of Montpellier."[6] No one would call Pietro all of this, but just "Pietro" did not suffice. Here we have the use of every type of name—patronym (son of Oberto), a very rare matronym (son of Riccarda), occupation (a kind of jeweler or metalworker, and a furrier), and even a toponym (the distant city of Montpellier). People used enough identifiers to avoid being confused with anyone else, and to display filial affection or marital deference. The use of surnames as the most com-

mon form of identification increased during the thirteenth century, but was by no means universal. As late as 1251 two brothers,
Rufino and Aimerico, who were both wool merchants and had no
surname, used only a toponym to identify themselves, and in fact
lived in two separate places, Lodi and Rivoturbido. Since they did
not have a surname, only the fact that they mentioned each other
in their wills, and the fortuitous survival of these wills, proves the
relationship.[7]

The analysis of names allows for some preliminary answers to
the broad question raised earlier: who made wills? By 1250 anyone
who could afford the small sum to pay a notary could make a will.
The destitute had no need for a will; the few possessions of the
poor were passed down in legal silence. Women had the right to
dispose of their dowries and any other personal property by will,
and they were inclined to do so, especially in the early years of
marriage, when their fathers were keenly interested in this wealth.
Unmarried men and women had more choices to make and needed
a will if they hoped to have any influence on the eventual distribution of their property.

Some women of very modest means were among the poorest
people to make wills. One Giovanna was the second wife of Bosio
da Lunesana, and the couple had no children together. Giovanna's
total bequests, amounting to L.1 s.18, were ten solidi for her soul,
ten solidi to one of Bosio's daughters by a previous marriage and
five solidi to another, ten solidi to Bosio, and one soilidus each to
three goddaughters.[8] An ironworker earning seven denarii a day
would have made Giovanna's store of worldly treasure in sixty-
four days.[9] She had about 25 percent of a slave's price, around 4
percent of the cost of a house. Giovanna's L.1 s.18 places her at
the bottom of the scale of testators' wealth; special circumstances,
in this case having no children of her blood, may explain why she
made a will at all. The poor do not appear in the Genoese cartularies, and an unknown number of people may have preferred
to do what they wanted with their goods while they were alive
and able to oversee the distribution. The great diversity of wealth
among the Genoese testators supports the idea that most people
with any property at all unassigned to heirs made wills. By 1250
more people were making wills than in 1150. The comparative

rarity of oral testaments brought to court with witnesses suggests that of the class of potential testators (and Giovanna's will indicates that this was a broad group), more people made wills than either gave deathbed declarations or died intestate.

Motive

Why did people make wills? For most of the individuals under study here the answer to this question will always be unclear. There were two pervasive motives presumably applying to everyone: a desire to take care of the family, and the fact that the church encouraged the faithful to make a last act of charity in order to benefit the soul.[10] Sometimes a testator would give a specific reason. The notaries Guglielmo Cassinese, Maestro Salmone, and Lanfranco, who together wrote 130 wills, or virtually one-fifth of the sample, never included a reason why a client made a will.[11] Yet Raimundo Medico, who wrote forty-two extant testaments, included a reason in twenty-two of them.[12] Thus the inclusion of a reason why the will was made seems to have depended mainly on notarial habit. Whether a person dictating a will would have spontaneously stated his reason, or whether the notary observed the situation, reached his own conclusion, and included the reason in his introductory formula, are open questions.

The seventy-eight cases of a testator's giving explicit reasons for making a will shed some light on this issue. The testaments of four people form a special category, for they were entering religion and wished to dispose of their worldly property. In 1229 Ponzio de Bellegarda, perhaps a native of Provence, made a will in favor of his mother because he was about to enter the Dominican order.[13] He made the will in the order's chapter house in Genoa, and seven friars witnessed the act. Giovanna, the wife of Guglielmo de Murta, made her will in 1231 because she wanted to become a *conversa* (lay sister) at the Cistercian monastery of San Andrea de Sestri Ponente.[14] She left the bulk of her property to the monastery, and she had the consent of her husband to do this. Montanaria, the wife of the late Vassallo Safrano, wanted to enter the Convent of Sant' Eufemia of Tortona, and for this purpose she made a will in 1239 giving the convent L.30 after her death and usufruct of this sum immediately.[15] She made her son Filippino heir to the rest of her goods. Giovanni de Tera made his will on November 19, 1245, behind the Cathedral of San Lorenzo, but he gave no details beyond his desire to enter religion.[16] Entering a monastery, a type of departure from the world considered to be like death, required the making of a will to dispose of property. The secular clergy did not follow this procedure.[17]

A journey or pilgrimage provided another reason for a will. Twenty-six people state that they intended to travel. Almost all of these statements occur after 1200, another sign of the rich detail in thirteenth-century wills. Seven testators supply no destination, although Maestro Giovanni de Cucurno mentioned that he was going by sea. The Genoese were no strangers to sea travel, and its uncertainties prompted some people to provide for catastrophe. One person, Adalasia Cagnola, supplied the destination for her trip: Sicily.[18] Seventeen people were specifically traveling on pilgrimage, and thirteen of them were going to Santiago de Campostella in Spain ("volens visitare limina beati Iacobi apostoli").[19] Two enterprising couples, Baldoino and Margarita, and Martino and Asteraria, intended to make the journey together.[20] The first pair, in a gesture of either togetherness or parsimony, created a very rare document, a single testament containing the last wishes of two people. Baldoino and Margarita decided that if they both died on the journey, their slaves, Corzo, Vera, and her son, Simonetto, should be freed, but if only one died, then only Corzo would be manumitted. (Genoese piety was often practical; so too, one suspects, were the prayers of slaves.) The well-traveled shipping lanes between Genoa and Barcelona, which reduced the amount of travel to Galicia, may have influenced the popularity of Santiago. The first known pilgrimage there was in 1179, so far as the wills state, but most were in the thirteenth century. In 1212 two ladies made wills because they were going on pilgrimage to Rome.[21] Pietro da Pavia made a will in Genoa in 1244 while en route to the Holy Land, and in 1248 two men, who joined the Crusade contingent assembling in Genoa at the request of King Louis IX of France, also made wills.[22] The king had arranged shipping through his Genoese agent, Ugone Lercario, and more than the two whose wills survive participated in this venture. Genoa had been active in the crusading movement since its inception, and the hazards of this particular armed pilgrimage offered the clearest incentive for making a will.

The last category of reasons for making a testament is illness. The oral wills discussed in Chapter 1 fit this case, but for the time being I shall consider only explicit claims of sickness. The introductory formula or the notary's statement concerning where the act took place contain these claims. The notary Bonovassallo de Maiori included such statements in the will's first sentence—for example, "I, Giacomo d'Alba, infirm in body and of sound mind . . . ," or "I, Viride, the wife of the late Simone de San Donato the notary, placed in a very bad illness, fearing the judgment of God, and in my right mind . . ."[23] Raimundo Medico, in noting where the act transpired, would often put down something like, "Done in Genoa in the house of the said Giovanni, in which he was lying sick."[24] Another notary, Lantelmo, used the verb *iacebat* (was lying, was in bed) to describe the condition of some of his clients. There are forty-nine explicit claims of illness, many of which Raimundo Medico mentioned. The temptation to associate this notary with the medical profession is strong, since he also wrote wills at the Hospital of the Crociferi in Bisagno. Other notaries wrote wills in hospitals; but since the testators were not necessarily patients at the time, such wills are not counted as explicit statements of illness. These hospitals were religious institutions, and people often wanted to be buried at them, particularly at the distinguished Hospital of San Giovanni in Genoa. Consequently, a wish to be buried there, rather than illness, may account for the fact that some of the wills were drawn up in hospitals. The Hospital of the Crociferi was connected to the Church of Santa Maria, and all four of the people who made their wills at the hospital wanted to be buried at the church. Only eleven people made their wills at hospitals; counting them as guaranteed cases of illness would still increase the number of known cases only to sixty, or about 10 percent of the total sample.

A presumption of illness is warranted if the testator died shortly after drawing up the will. Antulo della Croce made his will on January 24, 1192, and another act of January 31 refers to him as the late Antulo.[25] Finding this later reference is a matter of chance. Only in a few instances is it possible to ascertain the approximate date of death. As the case of Giulietta Zaccaria reminds us, a statement of illness need not imply mortal illness.[26] In the entire sample only two people explicitly claim to be healthy. One of them, Giulia, the wife of Guglielmo Balbo de Castello, offers a reason for making a will. The notary wrote in the concluding formula of her testament, "This is her last will which she made in health because of the various and sudden perils which always make human life difficult."[27] The healthy Giulia may have conceived some need to explain her will, and the normal vicissitudes of life were reason enough for her. This explanation suggests that it was unusual for a healthy person to make a will. In 1212 another individual stated, "I, Bertolino de Leo, although I am sound in body, yet thinking of the future since men quickly fall away on account of human fragility . . ."[28] Bertolino was concerned about the rights of two natural sons, whom he freely admitted were his by a woman he called his concubine. If he had died without recognizing these children as his own—and the will accomplished this—the boys' position in Genoese society would have been very precarious. In general the Genoese manifest a sense of life's uncertainties and seem aware of how quickly good health could change.

Thus far four principal incentives for making a will have been discovered: illness, departure on a journey, entering the religious life, and a desire to make provision for the future. Only a small number of wills provide concrete reasons. What about the intentions of the other testators, whose wills give no explanation? Nearly every will had a legal formula at the end that names the spot where the act took place. Unfortunately, the bottom of the page in the cartularies is often damaged. Since notaries tried to use only one side of a page for a will whenever possible, they squeezed in the date and place at the bottom, inadvertently condemning some of these notations to destruction. When one or more acts occurred at the same time and place, the formula says so, and if the original reference is missing, a whole series of acts is rendered imprecise. Almost six hundred wills indicate the place where the act transpired. Let us examine these places and times to see if they help clarify the reasons why these wills were made.

Place

There are four types of places to consider, apart from those wills that lack a subscription. The most common place for a person to make a will was in the house he lived in; about 60 percent of the testators did just that. However, the Genoese clearly distinguished between those who owned homes and those who rented. "The house of Giovanni" belonged to him; neither of the expressions "the house in which Giovanni lived" or "the house of Ansaldo where Giovanni lived" indicates ownership of the house by Giovanni. The first phrase suggests a boarder or renter, and the second is ambiguous. Giovanni may have rented Ansaldo's house, or may have been his friend or relative. Often the notary simply states that Giovanni made his will in Ansaldo's house, and we must try to find out what Giovanni was doing there. Was he lying sick in his own home, or had he gone to someone else's house to find a notary? Notaries commonly conducted their business in homes, shops, churches, public spots, and even on street corners. The testator's health must have influenced his choice of the place where the will was made.

There are tests that help to differentiate the two principal places where notaries wrote wills—the house of a sick person and the place where the notary himself usually worked. Some notaries did most of their business at fixed locations. Raimundo Medico and Giovanni Scriba spent much of their time in the arcade (*volta*) of the Fornari family, Oberto Scriba at the house of Bonifazio della Volta or the Pediculi warehouse, Lanfranco at the house of Lanfranco Rosso, and Bonovassallo de Cassino at the *entrepôt* that once belonged to the Fornari. Anyone who made a will at any of these places can be assumed to have gone to the notary. The same holds true for public spots, such as the steps of the cathedral or the city streets. Usually a notary did not remain in one place for the whole day. On September 18, 1203, the busy notary Giovanni di Guiberto wrote twenty-one acts in eight different places—eight acts on two separate occasions during the day at one of his favorite work sites, the arcade of the Fornari.[29] If a person made a will at some house where the notary was conducting other business, and if there is no indication that the testator lived in this house, we can assume that he had left his own house to find a notary. One hundred forty-four testaments, 24 percent of the total, were made at a place where the notary usually conducted business.

The other two types of places are the house of a friend, relative, or business associate, and a church or hospital. In the former case, I have separated these wills from the larger category of wills made in houses because of doubt whether the testator lived there or not. When found at the home of friends or business associates, the testator had probably gone there to conduct some other business and taken advantage of the opportune presence of a notary to make his will.

Of all the wills considered in this study, 353 were drawn up at the home of the testator, 36 at a church or hospital, 54 at the home of someone other than the testator, and 144 at the notary's work site. Among the wills drawn up on account of the testator's illness, 41 were made at the testator's home, one at a church or hospital, seven at another person's house, and one at a notary's place of business. Among those drawn up for a testator who was about to travel, ten were done at the testator's home, 14 at the notary's work site, and none at either a church or hospital or the home of another person.

Obviously, most people made their wills where they lived. Although the numbers were small in the case of wills made because of illness or travel, it is nonetheless possible to conclude that illness confined a person to his home; significantly, only one person who said he was ill, except for the one who was in a hospital went outside of a home to find a notary. The pattern suggests that most of the people who made their wills at home, and hence the great majority of all testators, were ill. The picture concerning travel is different. Some people who planned to make a trip drew up their wills at home, but a bare majority found a notary at his usual place of business. These wills warn us against assuming that all wills written at home were the result of illness.

Time

When, by the month, day, and hour, did people make their wills? An analysis by year is not useful, because in any given year the number of extant wills depends on the cartularies, so for some years there are no wills. The Genoese began their year on December 25, so their year coincides with the modern style except for the days between Christmas and January 1, when their year is one ahead. Table 4 summarizes the drawing up of all extant wills by month. The list reveals two peaks, in April and August, and a slight falling off from October to January. David Abulafia has noted that for commerce, "the great concentration of business occurred well before October, in the late spring and summer when long-distance trade to the east Mediterranean . . . was planned."[30] The stay-at-home months created a decline in travel, and thus in wills made for that reason. The few known cases of such wills support this conclusion, especially concerning the last three months of the year. The spring months suggest an increase in the writing of wills because of commercial travel plans. For what it is worth, illness seems to have been spread fairly evenly throughout the year with a slight increase in the summer. The climate of Genoa is generally salubrious because of its proximity to the sea and the absence of swamps. August, even in the Middle Ages, was a slow business month in Genoa. Contracts for local autumn sailings, much less frequent than spring travel, were usually made in September. Winters are mild in Genoa, but sea travel in the Mediterranean in winter was always perilous and was avoided whenever possible. It is interesting to note that the making of testa-

Table 4. Number of wills drawn up per month in Genoa, 1155–1253.

Month	All wills	Wills of travelers	Wills of sick persons
January	40	1	2
February	46	1	4
March	59	6	6
April	88	5	2
May	53	6	4
June	49	1	6
July	67	2	7
August	77	2	7
September	50	1	5
October	45	0	4
November	33	0	2
December	25	0	2

Source: Archivio di Stato di Genova, Cartolari Notarili.

ments did not slump, as did everything else, in August, which would likely have been the most trying month for ill persons in the city.

Every notary included the day of the month in the date, but only one, Federigo da Sestri, noted the day of the week for all his acts, which include two extant testaments.[31] Another notary, Tealdo da Sestri, who worked at Bonifacio, Corsica, in the 1230s, also routinely supplied the day of the week.[32] Only these two notaries, who were perhaps trained in the same way and may have been related, ever gave the weekday. All the other notaries were prepared to give the hour of the day, even occasionally the indiction, but they did not include the day. To find this obvious omission in the midst of so much precise dating is at first glance puzzling.

Giovanni di Guiberto only once mentioned a day's name. The witnesses of the will of Anselmo de Ferraris appeared before the consuls of the parish of Bavari on April 23, 1206. The principal witness stated that Anselmo had made his will in the month of March just past, on a Sunday at the hour of terce.[33] None of the witnesses knew the date, but they did remember that it was a Sunday and that the time of day had been around 9:00 A.M.[34] There is a split here between notarial usage, which depended on the calendar, and the way the populace reckoned time, by the day or week. It seems more likely that people knew what day it was than that they knew the date. Then why did notaries not record the day? The month and its multiples (sixty or ninety days) and the year were the important commercial units of time. The Genoese who needed to plan ahead thought in these terms. In a loan agreement, for example, the date was crucial because the repayment was ordinarily fixed at some number of months, or on a certain date, in the future. In this scheme the actual day of the week did not matter, since time was measured in large blocks.

If we know the day of the month and the year, it is easy to calculate the day of the week. From Saturday, May 19, 1201, to Friday, August 17, 1201, the notaries Giovanni di Guiberto and Oberto Scriba were both working in the city.[35] Between these two dates were thirteen Sundays, one of which was the important feast of San Giovanni, on June 24. Giovanni di Guiberto worked on five of these Sundays, and so did Oberto Scriba. Neither worked on June 24 or on the feast of Corpus Christi, which fell on Thursday, May 24. Sunday was the day of the week when people were least likely to work at business requiring a notary's presence. That the activity of buying and selling considerably diminished on Sunday constituted a partial victory for the church. Apart from Sundays, the notaries' work habits seem to have been almost random. They worked at their own pace, but they did not take off more than two days in a row. The busiest day of the week was Tuesday (probably the main market day); Oberto worked every one, Giovanni all but one. The other days of the week, including Saturday, did not fall far behind Tuesday as working days. Giovanni di Guiberto's Sundays saw the usual range of business—*commenda* and *societas* contracts, land sales, wills, and even the sale of a slave. On August 19 he wrote up a fitting act for a Sunday: in the presence of five witnesses a former slave named Giovannino, from Tunis, petitioned to be admitted to the Christian religion and hence abandon the "Saracenic error."[36] The chaplain Oberto baptized him, and the notary recorded the deed. After the ceremony the notary went to some familiar business haunts and drew up three *commenda* contracts. Whatever scruples prevented people from working on Sunday did not always apply to making agreements; how the notaries justified their own behavior is another matter. Writing was not physical labor, and Sundays may have been a convenient time for people whose normal weekly activities kept them apart to see each other and come to terms. Because notaries had a light work load on Sunday, they had time for complicated affairs such as transcribing court sessions. For testaments Sunday was an average day.

The canonical hours and the ringing of bells provided the Genoese with a way to measure their day. Genoa was filled with churches, and no one was far from a campanile. Sundials must also have been a common sight in medieval Genoa before the city acquired its municipal clock in 1353.[37] The Romans had divided up the day and night into units of twelve hours each, and the canonical hours derived from this practice. In winter the daylight hours, still twelve, were shorter than the nighttime ones; the opposite was true in summer. Not until the invention and widespread use of clocks did a day consist of twenty-four equal hours. The seasons, and the shifting times of sunset and dawn, became the measuring sticks used to determine the hour of the day. The original units of the church day were[38]

Matins	three hours after midnight
Prime	six hours after midnight (around dawn)
Terce	nine hours after midnight
Sext	noon, or midday
Nones	three hours after noon
Vespers	six hours after noon (around dusk)
Compline	nine hours after noon (after sunset)

By the thirteenth century these hours had evolved into[39]

Prime	beginning of the day, first hour
Terce	middle of the morning
Nones	midday
Vespers	middle of the afternoon
Compline	around the end of the day
Evening	first few hours after sunset
Night	after normal bedtime

The eye could observe noon with practice, but no one knew exactly when midnight was. So in practice prime tended to be shortly after dawn, and terce was more precisely three hours after prime, and so forth. The laity did not share in the rigors of the religious life; no notary conducted business at matins or even mentioned this time. Around 1200 notaries began to include the time of day in the dates of all their acts. Oberto Scriba never wrote down the time of day in his work of 1186 and 1190, but after a gap in the surviving record, we find him in 1200 routinely giving the time.[40] Every thirteenth-century notary included the time of day as standard procedure. One notary, Guglielmo da Sori, on February 15, 1201, noted the act's time of day for the first time.[41] From this day forward Guglielmo always recorded the hour. So universal was this habit that it suggests a guild regulation or a communal ordinance.

One feature of the canonical hours requires a word of explanation. By the thirteenth century the canonical hours no longer conformed to their original times, as the two sets of hours above indicate. In his truly pioneering work on the medieval hours, the

German historian Gustav Bilfinger points out that by the central Middle Ages these hours had shifted. He observes that the name *sext* had largely disappeared from the historical record, and that the later hours had all moved up in time.[42] Nones, originally the ninth hour, was associated with midday (hence our *noon*), vespers had moved to the middle of the afternoon, and so forth. The reasons why these hours shifted are complicated, and in fact not generally accepted. Most standard works on time still hold to the original canonical hours and dismiss Bilfinger's proposals. Bilfinger suggests that since on fast days the clergy was not supposed to eat until nones, they moved the service up so that they might eat sooner.[43] Since the laity were also obliged to fast, particularly during Lent, he plausibly explains how changes in ecclesiastical habits eventually influenced the laity. All that is at stake here for present purposes is that the names of the hours had changed, and this early evidence from Genoa, unknown to Bilfinger in 1895, generally supports his conclusions. Two pieces of interesting evidence weigh heavily in his favor. Several hundred thousand Genoese documents were dated to the hour in the thirteenth century, and not one of them mentions sext. The name had in fact disappeared.

There is one absolute way to check time measurements in the past; all that we need is an event that we can calculate as to time, and then we can compare the time at which contemporaries said it occurred. The total eclipse of the sun on June 3, 1239, is an ideal test case. This eclipse began at 11:58:09 A.M. (G.m.t.), and Genoa was in the center of its path across Europe. The Genoese chronicle for that year notes that the sun was obscured and night became day just a little after the middle of the day. The chronicle includes a short poem written to commemorate the subject, and one verse observes that "God sent this sign of fear in the ninth hour."[44] In Genoa at least, nones was midday, and this fact is important because we may now accurately fix the times when the Genoese made their wills.

Why did the Genoese require such exactitude in dating? Giving the time of day helped witnesses recall one act of business out of many on the same day. The thirteenth century saw an enormous increase in the volume of business conducted in Genoa, and the rapid pace of commercial life may have confused someone who found himself being a witness several times a day. Even without the aid of a personal timepiece such as a watch, or even the municipal clock, people in the thirteenth century were beginning to measure their day not by the amount of time a task required but by arbitrarily fixed units of time. The notaries recorded the hour to aid the witnesses' recollections, and perhaps also because they were inclined to be precise. Any new way of being precise would appeal to the notarial mind and would quickly spread. More likely, the Genoese hours reveal a rather widespread preoccupation with time and its passage. Commerce had changed the way people thought about time, and although the Genoese day lacked the discipline of the factory, it had already left behind the familiar rhythms of rural life.

Jacques Le Goff has proposed a distinction (at base quite nebulous) between "merchant's time" and "church's time."[45] According to him, the merchants were in the process of rationalizing, and hence also "secularizing," time. Yet the church had its own calendar, which followed the principal religious holidays, and its own cosmic sense of eternity. As I have noted, in the thirteenth century mercantile life appropriated the canonical hours for its own purposes. Even the principal feasts—the nativity of San Giovanni, Michaelmas, Christmas, and Easter—became convenient benchmarks for measuring a contract's duration. To take Genoa as an example, people viewed time in various ways. Merchants thought in terms of the sailing seasons or the time required to travel to the fairs of Champagne. Artisans worked for a daily wage, or were prosperous enough to employ others at that rate. The Genoese churches followed a different rhythm, punctuated by the liturgical day, Sunday, and the principal feasts. The clergy's life followed this course, and yet the laity were supposed to attend services and participate in fasts, and the Genoese clergy were no strangers to commerce. The church also conveyed to the laity certain eschatological themes. The testaments indicate that the average Genoese was capable of thinking about eternity at least once. The church as an employer imposed a schedule on monks, nuns, and priests. It also tried to persuade the laity to think about an ultimate judgment, and not to work on Sunday. Secular tasks also required a pace of work, and daily life doubtless incorporated the canonical hours as a handy convenience which the Church bells provided for free. One might propose many "times": merchant's, church's, artisan's, agricultural. For as long as people had worked, they had been rationalizing time. To fix the feast of Saint John as the day a contract would expire does not secularize time. Church and secular time intersected at so many points that any distinction between the two obscures more than it reveals. Instead, let us consider how the notaries worked during the day, and the hours when their clients made wills.

The cartularies reveal the rhythm of work of one occupational group—the notaries themselves—and therefore also say something about how the clients passed the day. Notaries usually began their working day around terce, and sometimes dawn found them on the job. On September 13, 1203, Giovanni di Guiberto wrote twenty-one acts in his cartulary, which illustrate a typical if rather busy day.[46] He started the day around terce at the shop of the Fornari, staying there long enough to record one loan and four cloth sales. He then moved to the portico of Guglielmo de Castello's house sometime after terce (perhaps about 11:00 A.M.) to write up a loan recovery, and then he went back to the Fornari. The next piece of business occurred after nones, after which he took some sort of break for lunch and a rest. From the time when Giovanni resumed work to after vespers, he spent an active afternoon and early evening; he drew up twelve *commenda* contracts at five different places. The next day, September 19, he maintained the pace by doing twenty pieces of business before lunch, when he quit for the day.[47] This was the schedule of an extremely busy notary. Niccoloso de Beccaira's cartulary contains fewer commercial transactions, and there are days when he seems to have had no business at all.[48]

To some extent the notary's availability and schedule determined the timing of a will; the testator's own rhythm of work and health were also important factors. A person wanting to make a will because he intended to travel could take care of this bothersome detail at his own convenience. If illness intervened, however, and disrupted the normal pattern of life, the timing, both by day and hour, was subject to new considerations. As we have seen in the analysis of sites, a notary was prepared to go to a person's home, perhaps at some tacit risk to his own health, to write down the last wishes of those too sick to travel to a normal place of business. How strongly did notaries acknowledge an obligation to leave their usual haunts for this chore? A close examination of the hours of the day provides some answers to this question.

The list below gives a breakdown of 464 wills according to the time of day at which they were written. The divisions of the day appear in the left-hand column.

Before daybreak	2	Nones (midday)	7
Around dawn	1	After nones	35
Before prime	3	Between nones and vespers	66
Around prime	1	Before vespers	4
Prime	1	Around vespers	21
After prime	5	Vespers	6
Between prime and terce	20	After vespers	39
Before terce	46	Between vespers and compline	31
Around terce	19	Before compline	4
Terce	4	Around compline	4
After terce	31	Compline	3
Between terce and nones	68	After compline	20
Before nones	1	Night	6
Around nones	16		

Thus we see that of the 464 wills, eight were drawn up in the hours before prime, 94 in the morning between prime and terce, and 123 between terce and nones. One hundred thirty-two wills were drawn up between midday and vespers, 81 between vespers and compline, and 26 after compline.

In the cartularies the term *sext* never appears, but the expression "middle of the day" does. In order to simplify matters, some times are grouped together. For example, "before vespers" includes such qualifiers as "a little before vespers." Vespers also signifies the ringing of vespers (*pulsante ad vesperas*), which some notaries used to indicate an exact moment. When a notary states that an act took place "around" a certain hour, he might mean either before or after that time, but in fact in almost all cases "around" the hour meant before it to the notaries who used the phrase. Since the notary knew the time by listening for bells or looking at a sundial, he would know it was after terce if he had heard the bell or marked the shadow. "Around terce" might simply have indicated that it was a long time since prime. The notaries who used the word *circa* (around) placed it chronologically later than *ante* but before the hour itself; thus the normal sequence was before nones, around nones, nones. Finally, the phrase "between terce and nones" causes some problems because it is vague and covers about half the morning hours. One can only assume that business recorded at this time was not conducted close to either hour.

Wills were virtually the only form of business that the notary conducted before or around dawn. Extraordinary circumstances such as illness or approaching death seem to be the only possible reasons for such early activity. Of equal importance and even greater numbers are the wills done after vespers, already night-time in winter. Notaries preferred not to work after vespers, and certainly not after compline, when much of the city slept. The same extraordinary circumstances must have applied when they did. There is the expected lull in the early afternoon, but otherwise between prime and vespers the pace of testament writing was brisk and constant. The pace remained the same after vespers, which is unusual, given the normal working habits of notaries, and only after compline did the activity of making wills abate. Would the reason why the will was made determine the time of day it happened? Those wills made on the fringes of the normal day— before dawn or well after sunset—without explicitly giving a reason, seem to be wills made by the sick. However, most people made their wills between prime and vespers, so one must look more closely at these wills for clues about their origins.

To plot the number of wills drawn up for a specific reason against the hours of the day would be fruitless, since only seventy-eight wills state a reason. Table 5 uses the breakdown by canonical hour to show at what site wills were dictated at each time of day. Four basic sites appear in the record: the testator's home, the notary's workplace, a church or hospital, and the house of a relative or friend. Table 5 illustrates some of the points made above about illness, although it covers only the post-1200 wills, because they are the only ones that give the time and the place. The overwhelming majority of wills made before terce were dictated at home. This situation changed after terce, when the commercial day began, and the number of wills made at home, and for that matter all wills, diminished considerably. Once the Genoese fin-

Table 5. Breakdown of 431 wills by hour and site.

| | Number of wills drawn up— | | | |
Hour of day	At testator's home	At notary's workplace	At church or hospital	At home of relative or friend
Before day	2	0	0	0
Around dawn	1	0	0	0
Before prime	2	0	0	0
Around prime	1	0	0	0
Prime	0	1	0	0
Subtotal	6	1	0	0
After prime	6	0	0	0
Between prime and terce	14	2	4	2
Before terce	23	12	3	4
Around terce	12	1	1	0
Terce	2	0	0	0
Subtotal	57	15	8	6
After terce	16	8	3	1
Between terce and nones	34	19	4	4
Before nones	1	0	0	0
Around nones	10	5	1	0
Nones	3	3	0	0
Subtotal	64	35	8	5
After nones	15	7	1	6
Between nones and vespers	37	13	6	5
Before vespers	4	0	0	0
Around vespers	13	4	0	3
Vespers	3	2	0	0
Subtotal	72	26	7	14
After vespers	25	7	0	4
Between vespers and compline	21	7	2	4
Before compline	2	0	0	0
Around compline	5	0	0	0
Compline	2	1	0	0
Subtotal	55	15	2	8
After compline	15	1	1	3
Night	7	0	0	0
Subtotal	22	1	1	3

Source: Archivio di Stato di Genova, Cartolari Notarili.

ished their midday break, which lasted for an hour or two after noon, business activity and testament making again increased. One of the refinements of Table 5 is that it shows that people made their wills closer to vespers than nones. After vespers the situation reverted to what it had been early in the morning: again the great majority of wills were made at home. The wills made in hospitals or churches follow the same time pattern as those made at the notary's work site. Those people who dictated their wills in the house of a relative or friend might very well have been ill, but we cannot be sure of this; nor do we know whether the testator normally lived with this individual. To sum up, then, the notaries were willing to break their daily pattern and go to the homes of the sick to write wills. The notaries preferred to do this either before or after the busiest times of the commercial day. The wills written at the notary's normal work site may be the ones made for reasons such as travel. The time of crisis for grave illness is generally in the early morning. Perhaps people who survived a difficult night were encouraged to dictate their last wishes early the next morning, while fears about a person's ability to endure another night may explain the increase in testaments made in the early evening. It seems clear that most, but not all, wills were made by people who were afraid that they were dying. The fear of sudden death from other causes could result in much the same frame of mind. Knowing something about the testator's mental state will be important when we look in subsequent chapters at bequests to charity and the family.

We have learned something about the daily routine of notaries, but not much direct information about the ordinary citizen's daily habits has surfaced. Just as there were two principal places to make wills—the home or the notary's workplace—there were two different groups of witnesses. Family members who were heirs could not serve as witnesses, so at home neighbors fulfilled that function. The relatives may have had an easier time finding witnesses in the early morning or evening, and probably neighbors were not able to shrug off such a request lightly.

Where people worked in Genoa is an open question. If they worked in or close to their homes, as seems likely, then witnesses would not have been hard to find, even during working hours. At the notary's work site a crowd of business people would have passed the time by striking up contracts or witnessing those of others. So if anyone turned up who needed to make a will quickly, finding witnesses would not have presented a problem. During the break in the early afternoon most people probably went home for a meal and some rest. The lull in notarial activity reflects the calm that pervaded the city.

Personal Time

So far I have located the making of testaments in public time, down to the very hour. There was also a personal time—age— that played a part in the decision to make a will. How old were the testators? Not a single one gave his age. How well did the Genoese keep count of the passing years? The *livello* contract, for renting land, ran for twenty-nine years, and the records indicate that people kept careful track of these contracts and knew how many years had passed or remained. Apprenticeship agreements had fixed terms of service which the master and pupil-servant disregarded at considerable financial sacrifice. Keeping track of time had its practical advantages, but did people measure their own span in years? Some did, but the known cases are very special. In 1160 the first historian of Genoa, Cafaro, noted in his chronicle that he was eighty years old and had begun this work when he was thirty.[49] He promised to continue to write for as long as he lived, though a promise to go on dictating would have been more accurate. A distinguished continuator of the city chronicle, Giacomo Doria, announced in 1293 that he was sixty years old and tired of the labor, so he was laying down his pen.[50] Even though these ages are suspiciously rounded, that historians knew how old they were is no surprise. The thirteenth-century city historians had a good grasp of chronology; their references to the city's past are usually accurate. These historians were mainly notaries, however, and one might expect them to be more familiar than most with chronology, and more aware of the need to be precise. The commune established the office of *podestà* in 1191, and the regular yearly elections to that office in the next century provided names for the years in a way similar to the consular *fasti* (lists) of ancient Rome.[51]

The existence of the *donatio causa mortis* proves that some people knew or were told how old they were. Persons under age, probably under twenty-five, were still subject to parental authority and hence not able to dispose of property by will. One can safely assume that all those who stated that they were making a *donatio causa mortis*, and those who made a will with the consent of their fathers, were under twenty-five. Marriage did not transfer parental authority to a husband; instead, married women who were still legally minors made wills with a father's consent. However, nearly everyone in the present sample was old enough to make a will.

Even though the testators found no good reason to give their age, it might be possible to derive this information from the wills. Robert Gottfried, in his study of fifteenth-century East Anglian wills, suggests a way to estimate age from a will.[52] He proposes three age groups. The first consists of people who mention living parents in their wills, and who may or may not have been married but in any case had no children. The author assumes that these individuals were under twenty-five years old. In the second age group are those without living parents who themselves had children under age. Relying heavily on the mention of children, Gottfried considers people in this age group to be from twenty-five to forty-five or fifty years old. The third group, people over fifty, includes testators with married children and grandchildren, and those who mention godchildren in addition to their own children. Even within the generous limits of these age groups, Gottfried was able to classify by age only 50 percent of his sample. His main problem was the difficulty of determining whether people were married or not. If a person mentioned no children, it was impossible to assign an age group.

In Genoa the situation allows for more clarity. Men with children under age appointed tutors in their wills to oversee the raising of the heirs and to administer the estate. If a man's wife was living, he would name her as a tutor, but most of the time he would also name a male relative or friend. If the eldest son was of age, he might be named a tutor for his younger brothers and sisters. Married women rarely named tutors for their children; they must have assumed, or been forced to concede, that the husband would fulfill this role. Widows usually appointed tutors for their children, so if they did not do so, one may assume that their heirs were of age. The authority of the tutors lasted until the heirs were twenty or twenty-five. Even if the children were no longer minors, the Genoese still mentioned them in their wills. Here the *lex falcidia* added more precision to the Genoese testament by instilling in people a legal fear of omitting offspring, however old, from the will. Adult sons, but rarely daughters, acted as tutors, and if none were needed, they might serve as executors of the estate. Sadly, testators also remembered deceased children, and often endowed masses for them. The mention of children and their status aids in fixing an approximate age for the testators. We cannot assume, however, that males and females were the same age at marriage. Two testaments specifically release daughters from tutorial authority at sixteen and eighteen, and daughters were often given in marriage at even younger ages. All this indicates that women married earlier than men, and thus conforms to other evidence about medieval marriage patterns.[53] The ages of unmarried people without children are very difficult and often impossible to determine. Most of the childless couples may have been young, but surely not all of them were.

The testators can be divided into four groups by marital status: unmarried persons with no children (88 men, including 11 members of the clergy, and 44 women); married persons with no children (57 men and 70 women); married persons with minor children (87 men and 64 women); and married persons with adult children (95 men and 127 women). Since the Genoese liked to believe that death did not end marriage unless the survivor married again, the category of unmarried persons does not include the widowed. Most of the women with children of age were in fact widows. There is no standard by which to measure the age of the unmarried. The mention of a godchild in a will tells us very little about the age of the testator, and anyone old enough to make a will was in a position to have nieces or nephews. In particular wills it is possible to determine from the details of a person's life that he had been an adult for some time. A few cases of obviously mature unmarried individuals do not warrant any general conclusions about the group as a whole. Likewise, there are no good reasons for believing that all the unmarried were young. Married men without children were perhaps mostly under thirty years old , but surely not all. Their wives were younger, though how much so is an open question. One might conclude that married men with children under age match Gottfried's second age group—people between twenty-five and forty-five or fifty years old—but the married women may have been as young as their late teens. The boundaries are generous and reveal little. Those married or widowed people with children of age were the mature members of Genoese society. The men may have been over fifty, the women perhaps ten years younger.

The categories of marital status summarized above reveal that marriage, the presence of children, and by inference age all influenced a person's decision to make a will. For married men there was a steady increase by age group in the number of wills. Older men and women with children were more likely than other people to make wills, but the rather large group of wills of unmarried adults reminds us that the absence of children prompted many people to think about the future disposition of their wealth. The age of these childless adults, predominantly men, remains uncertain, yet their family circumstances suggest that they represent a mix of young and mature individuals. Women predominate in the oldest group, which indicates that they outlived their husbands, not that they necessarily lived to a greater age than men. All the age groups exhibit a similar pattern in the sites of will making. At every age the great majority of people made their wills at home. Only the unmarried with no children tended to go to the notary's work site more frequently; the men of this group may have been making a will for travel reasons. Even for single men, the most common place to make a will was at home.

The Genoese made wills because they feared death, and in most cases this fear combined with present illness to create a need for a will. People of all ages shared this fear. Those whose children had safely reached adulthood anticipated their own end in only slightly greater numbers than their younger contemporaries. Whatever the leading cause of death was in Genoa, it was not old age. The unmarried people without children had fewer family ties and could choose among a wide range of potential beneficiaries. Intestacy would frustrate the intentions of single people, who were perhaps more likely to make wills in order to avoid uncertainty. The predominance of wills dictated at home argues in favor of the conclusion that illness was the principal motive, as does the time of day when most wills were made.

Men with children under age, and widows in the same situation, appointed tutors to protect and rear their heirs. Married women assumed that their husbands would take up this task. These women were able to bequeath freely their marriage gift and any other patrimony, so that they too had ample reasons for making a will.

Returning to the questions raised at the beginning of this chapter, we have seen that anyone, including some persons still under the legal authority of a parent or tutor, could make a testament. Wealthy people were more likely to need a will, but by 1250 even those of very modest means were expressing their last wishes in a notarial act. The Genoese made wills because they wished to provide for a future. However, many summoned a notary to their homes, frequently before or after the work day, because they were sick and afraid of dying without having settled their property and affairs. Some people made wills because they intended to travel for business or pious reasons; their anxiety, although less acute than that of the sickbed, was nevertheless palpable. Even the most sanguine were aware of the various and sudden perils of life. Another purpose of writing a will was to allow the individual to select a burial site. One wonders how many did so with equanimity? Perhaps the frankly distressing aspects of making a will explain why the testators concentrated on providing for their families and souls. In the next chapter I shall consider how the Genoese tried to secure the family's future.

3 / Family: The Principal Heirs

In 1 Timothy 6:8 we read, "But if any provide not for his own son, and specially for those of his own house, he hath denied the faith and is worse than an infidel." The purpose of a testament was to provide for one's own. For those testators with children, the next generation was the principal focus of the will. The wills do not provide a history of childhood or attitudes toward children; they give at best only a snapshot of a family at one particular moment. There were as many different family situations as there were parents, but some common themes emerge from the tangled stories of individual families. I shall consider three general issues: principal heirs, conditions, and tutors.

Parents did not always regard their children as equals with similar claims on the family patrimony. They devised rules of succession that pertained first to the order in which children inherited, and then to the sad prospect of the death of their own children, perhaps without legitimate heirs. Consequently, many testators established heirs of the second or third degree and even beyond. These choices reveal alternative strategies for family survival in the event that the direct line should fail. Parents often placed conditions on legacies to children. Some conditions reflect widespread customs or legal requirements, while others point to the individual problems of a family. If the children were minors, the testator had to select someone who would responsibly raise his youngsters and see that they received a decent start in life. Being a tutor was a heavy charge, and testators considered the choices very carefully. The testators, male and female, married, widowed, and occasionally single, provided differently for the futures of their boys and girls. The children themselves were treated unequally, and I shall try to suggest some reasons why this was so.

The church had its views on how parents and children ought

to behave, and it communicated these views to the laity through sermons. Jacopo da Voragine, the late thirteenth-century arch-bishop of Genoa, liked the story of Elijah and the widow, and he had several sermons on widows and children. These sermons are of interest because they suggest some contemporary opinions, albeit prescriptive ones, about the role of mothers and fathers. Jacopo told his congregation that women more than men mourned the death of a child because mothers had a softer spirit, and basically knew more about loving children.[1] Perhaps expecting some skepticism from his flock, he offered five reasons "among many" why mothers love their children more than fathers. Men are worn out in making children, and consequently love them less for it. Conversely, Jacopo contended that women labor more over children than men and so they love them more. Mothers work more when they carry the child, give birth, and educate their offspring. The certainty of parenthood provides another reason for more love, since the mother always knows that the child is hers. At best the husband only believes, and cannot know for sure, that he is the father. The mother contributes more of her sub-stance to the child, and derives rights from this that give her some reason for love. Lastly, Jacopo compared motherhood to friend-ship, and observed that since mothers spend more time with their children and talk to them more, their greater love results from this intimacy, which fathers do not share. Nature provides a bal-ance for this love: children tend to love their fathers more, mainly because they inherit their father's goods. For the same reasons, mothers mourn the death of children more than fathers, who in turn rejoice more over their children's prosperity. "A wise son brings joy to his father, a foolish son is his mother's bane."[2]

One may wonder whether Jacopo accurately observed the emo-tional value of family ties, but he was probably right that mothers know their children better because they spend more time with them. Given the preponderance of widows over widowers in Genoa, this difference did not result solely from personal preference. Whether age differences between husband and wife account for the major role mothers played in rearing children is an open question, since it is impossible to know exact ages in these cen-turies. Jacopo emphasized the importance of the tie between mother and child, which he saw as the foundation of life, overlooking any nuclear family or clan. The wills indicate that mothers and fathers had distinct senses of obligation, and intended different types of futures for the next generation. Jacopo did not distinguish between sons and daughters, but the Genoese certainly did. It is hard to know whether sermons truly reflect the realities of the family; for this the wills are a better source. Still, the sermons suggest a careful look at the sex of both testator and heir.

Since any discussion of heirs depends on, and helps to define, the idea of family, one must determine what definitions of the medieval family emerge from the wills. The Genoese family was a kinship group that varied in extent according to how it acted in any particular situation. A fine example of the different guises a family might adopt is the last will and testament of Guglielmo Embriaco, made on August 14, 1202.[3] The Embriaci were at the pinnacle of Genoese society in terms of prestige and wealth. Families such as the Embriaco were clans, vertical social groups which included all those with the cognomen Embriaco—their in-laws, clients, and subject peasantry. Such familial clans sprang from the rural feudal nobility and retained much of its ethos.[4] Only a small minority of Genoese belonged to these clans, which can hardly be said to represent the Genoese family. Even within these clans, individual members had a clear sense of where certain types of obligations and ties ended. For example, Guglielmo endowed an altar in the Church of Santa Maria de Castello, which lay in the shadow of the family tower. He wanted a canon to serve this altar and celebrate a daily mass for his soul, his brother's, and his ancestors'. Many Genoese, though most on a more modest scale, endowed masses for the dead. In every instance the masses benefited deceased parents, siblings, spouse, or children. The familial desire to intercede for souls extended no further than this small circle—the nuclear family as it existed in time with members departed and yet to be born. In this light Guglielmo belonged to two nuclear families, his father's and his own. His family had another definition when he wanted to make sure that the canon did a good job. If any problem developed, the elders of his house "Maiori de domo mea" were to select another priest. Guglielmo's children were still minors and not competent to do this, so he turned to his clan. The clan was in part devised to deal with the outside world, but no one left his worldly goods to a clan. Guglielmo Embriaco left most of his property to his sons and nephews. In his case these heirs formed the descent group—the available pool of principal heirs. Guglielmo's choice of heirs is somewhat unusual because the descent group and the nuclear family were most of the time coterminus. He appointed his mother and wife as the legal guardians of the minors, and four prominent men, including one blood relative and one affine, to counsel the guardians. One might as well call the other two counselors friends and note that friends often appeared with kin as persons worthy of trust, indeed occasionally more worthy.

In addition to the people named so far, Guglielmo had what is called a bilateral extended family, though in common with most Genoese he probably viewed his in-laws with a cold eye. Not all Genoese were fortunate enough to have as many relatives as he did. Bertolino de Leo named in his will only a sister, some nephews, and a woman he called his concubine, with whom he had had two sons.[5] Bertolino's family was small and in some legal jeopardy; no clan waited to help his kin. Yet his will, like his more powerful and wealthy contemporary's, displays concern about the same central issue—the heirs. This chapter is based on the premise that there is no better place to look at the medieval family than in wills, and no tie closer than the one between testator and heir. The largest category of heirs comprises children, and I shall consider these principal heirs first.

Children

In Chapter 2 I used marital status and the age of children to establish some age groups for testators, and these conclusions are again pertinent. Three hundred seventy-six Genoese (182 males and 194 females) acknowledged in their wills that they had children; the rest of the testators were either married or unmarried but childless, or were clerics or foreigners living apart from whatever family they may have had. The children named range in age from adults with families of their own to infants not yet baptized. There is no reliable way to estimate children's ages, although the use of diminutive names is one of the best, but still imperfect, guides. For example, Simone Buferio named eight sons—Ansaldo, Amico, Enrico, Guglielmino, Corradino, Buferetto, Ottolino, and Anselmino.[6] Since the father appointed the first three sons as tutors for the rest of the little ones, Ansaldo, Amico, and Enrico must have been at least eighteen years old, while the others were obviously still minors. The diminutive names themselves would reveal the age differences even if Simone Buferio had not explicitly stated that the first three were adults. A woman named Sopergia left everything to her sons Amigueto and Paganino— "who is not yet baptized nor a Christian"—more evidence that the diminutive accurately implies age.[7] Few adults in the Genoese notarial record would have called themselves "little." But conversely, this use of the diminutive, while indicating childhood, was not always applied to minors, so there were plenty of children who were known by "adult" names.

The appointing of tutors clearly signifies that the children were minors. As we shall see, however, although married men exercised this right of appointment, women, even widows, seem to have been severely restricted by their husbands on the one hand and by their late husbands' wills on the other.[8] Since most female testators did not appoint tutors, regardless of the childrens' ages, these ages remain ambiguous. Occasionally a will provides enough information about the children to give us some rough age limits. A married son, for instance, was at least eighteen, but a married daughter might be as young as twelve. If a testator had grandchildren, his own children were most likely adults. Unfortunately, the words *neptis* and *nepta* meant in different contexts "nephew" or "grandson," and "niece" or "granddaughter." The notaries recognized this problem, and usually appended a phrase such as "son of my son" to distinguish a grandchild from a nephew. When *neptis* or *nepta* was used without such a qualifier, we must assume that the testator meant nephew or niece. The great variety in usage precludes any effort to estimate children's ages; I shall consider as decisive only those cases in which the testators appointed tutors.

Several considerations bar us from assuming that the wills correctly name the total number of children. Some people left their goods to "my children" or "my sons and daughters." Such statements, which sixteen testators employed, imply two and four offspring, respectively, but these are minimum estimates. Deceased children, especially in this age of presumed high infant mortality, would appear in their parent's wills only in special circumstances.

A parent might leave some money for the soul of a deceased son or daughter, but in most cases we know about deceased children because grandchildren are mentioned. Some people outlived all their children, and often grandchildren shared in the direct succession. Thirty-four testators mention deceased offspring, almost all of whom had children of their own. As for all those children who did not survive to reproduce, their memories were dear to their parents, but the will did not usually record them. A case might be made that replacement ratios can be studied from wills, if one excludes from consideration what was probably a very high toll among the young. The will may be the best source for studying replacement ratios, but it is nonetheless a slender reed. Just because a will mentions a child does not guarantee that he survived to replace his parents in the population. We do not know what little Paganino's chances were of reaching adulthood, or whether his mother, perhaps ill as a result of giving birth, herself survived and had more children. The wills, at the risk of repetition, provide merely a view of a family at one hour of a particular day. Who can say whether the "various and sudden perils" of life, to use again the words of a Genoese mother, passed over the eight sons and four daughters of Simone Buferio?

Anyone attempting to determine the total number of children an individual had faces other difficulties. A parent owed no further responsibility to a married daughter who had received a dowry, and in exchange she usually relinquished subsequent claims to family property. A father or mother might note that he or she had dowered a daughter, and that she should be content with this and seek nothing else from the estate. A married daughter might receive a *falcidia* bequest, though the law did not require this, or a legacy of clothing or jewels—a spontaneous sign of enduring affection. The suspicion remains that married daughters are underrepresented in the wills. The inmates of religious houses, male and female, might also receive no notice in a will. In a way, illegitimacies and adoptions make up for some of the presumed undercounting of children. I shall discuss these children in more detail later, and observe here only that it was the fortunate "natural" (the favorite Genoese word) son or daughter who was acknowledged in a will. Less formal and public means were available to provide for this at least socially embarrassing admission. Finally, remarriage complicates the picture to some extent. Of the 377 known parents, twenty-one refer to previous spouses. We know that Giovanna Pevere's husband, Niccolò Embrone, had three sons by a previous marriage, but in her own will she mentions only the one child they had together.[9] Only those adults who produced two or more sets of children had any reason to provide for them all in a will. Stepchildren were therefore also partially undercounted.

All these likely omissions in the count of children indicate that the recorded numbers are too low. The 127 married people without children do not necessarily prove the low fertility of the urban population; the prospects of survival or remarriage made it possible that these people eventually had children. Those who had not yet married, or were widowed at the time of the will, did not necessarily remain permanently childless. Wills mention children mainly because they were the heirs, and it is this status that is the chapter's focus.

The list below provides figures on the number of children per family.

Number of families	Number of children per family
127	0
137	1
77	2
84	3
37	4
24	5
7	6
6	7
2	8
1	9
0	10
1	11
1	12

This gives a total of 943 children in 377 families (376 families with children plus one married person with only an adopted child). Among the 127 childless married couples there are four adopted children mentioned. Given the qualifications offered so far, the average number of children per couple is 1.87, which not surprisingly falls below replacement level. The number of children per couple with offspring, 2.5, is more significant for present purposes. Over one-third of all the testators mention only one child, and patterns of inheritance in these cases are very clear. Sixty-nine percent of Genoese children found themselves in families of three or more children, and from the point of view of inheritance and succession, these are the most interesting families.

Three hundred and seventy-seven testators—182 males and 195 females—name 943 children: 558 sons and 485 daughters (another clear sign that the wills undercount daughters). It is useful to distinguish six groups of parents: married men (142), widowed men (37), single men (3), married women (92), widowed women (102), single women (1). (The three single men had children but no legal wives.) The difference in marital status is striking: widowed males were not at all common, whereas 52 percent of all female testators with children were widows. The very small sample of twenty-one known instances of remarriage includes fifteen men and six women. Single-parent families made up over one-third of those with children, but in many, if not most of these cases, the children were no longer minors.

The children were named heirs to the "rest of the goods," or the bulk of the estate, in 325 cases, but not always equally so. In overwhelming numbers the Genoese passed on the greater part of their property to their children. Only twenty wills did not contain the conventional "rest of my goods" clause which named the principal heirs. Before considering the routine successions, let us look at the thirty-three wills in which the testator's children were not the main beneficiaries. Five men left the rest of their goods to their wives; significantly, none of them had sons. Four women similarly favored their husbands, but three of them had sons; three other women split the inheritance between their sons and husbands. Favoring a spouse in this way was a sign of esteem, and probably did not diminish the children's eventual inheritance. An interesting assortment of testators favored their own siblings. Four people, again having only daughters or stepchildren, named brothers or sisters as principal heirs, and six split the rest of their goods between one child and siblings or nephews. One widow left all her land to her son and the rest of her property went for her soul, as in the case of three other women who had only daughters. Apart from offering some ostensible slight to their daughters, these thirty-three people seem to have had personal and unfathomable motives for choosing other people over their own children.

Illegitimate children were on Jacopo da Voragine's mind when he preached about the certainty of parenthood. A will provided a last chance for a father to acknowledge an illegitimate child and settle some bequest on him. The mother, having given birth, had from that moment a public relationship to the child whom she raised. Ten men included natural children in their wills: four were married, three were widowed, and three were apparently single. All of these men were well-off, several were very wealthy. Guglielmo de Mari had five children—three sons (only one of whom was legitimate) and two daughters (one legitimate daughter, who had died, and one natural one).[10] He listed the illegitimate daughter and sons at the very beginning of his charitable bequests. He also left his natural daughter, Altilieta, L.100 for her marriage; with such a large dowry she was sure to find a husband and an honorable place in society. He left his natural sons, Giovannino and Lanfranco, perhaps a monk, L.100 and L.10, respectively. Guglielmo Sardena, who had five legitimate children, left his natural son Ansaldino L.25, and ordered that he should be fed and clothed by the estate until he was twenty-five years old.[11]

Alberto de Fontana, a widower, left his natural son Ansaldino L.25 and Aidela, the boy's mother, L.12 and all her clothes. If Ansaldino died without an heir, Alberto's daughter, Richelda, who was the principal heir, was to inherit, saving Aidela's rights. Aidela was probably living with Alberto at this time,[12] so Alberto had no real need to suppress the name or claims of his mistress. Giovanni Cafaraina, who evidently never married, left his natural daughter Zenoina L.100 and her mother, Rosa, L.15.[13] Here again the principal heir, in this case Giovanni's brother, would succeed if Zenoina died without an heir. Oberto de Rapallo left his bastard son Ansaldino L.3 and his natural daughter Giacomina L.7.[14] He left the bulk of the estate to the child his wife was carrying, "if it came to light." Oberto did not provide for the succession if no child was born, and no married person ever named an illegitimate child as a principal heir or successor.

Illegitimate children fared better when they had no brothers or sisters born in wedlock. Bertolino de Leo's will of June 15, 1212, was remarkably candid about his personal life.[15] He left everything to his two natural sons, Armaino and Leonardino, whom he had had with his "concubine," Lucentia Guercia, who lived in his home. It also appeared that Lucentia might be pregnant, and this child, male or female, was to share equally in the inheritance. If Lucentia aborted, or if no living child were born, the two sons would be heirs together. Bertolino's relationship with Lucentia closely resembles a marriage, since they had children and lived together. He even admitted that he had L.20 of her goods, in the kind of phrase usually associated with a husband's statement about his wife's dowry. Bertolino concluded his will, "I acknowledge these sons which I had from the said Lucentia, my only and sole concubine, and I am convinced in my mind without doubt that I had the only natural familiarity [with her]."[16] With these words he secured for these boys the right to be his heirs, and he displayed a faith in his mistress that Jacopo da Voragine thought wives did not merit. If his sons died without heirs, Bertolino wanted his sister's sons to inherit his goods. In a similar situation, Ansaldo Guercio left Alegrina, the mother of his natural child, L.120 and a completely furnished bed.[17] He also confirmed that Alegrina had purchased with her own money a chest which was in his house. Ansaldo wanted to make sure this was clear; he also wanted her to have all her clothes and personal possessions, "without contradiction by anyone" (presumably his relatives). As the notary Bartolomeo Fornari noted, Ansaldo even provided Alegrina a copy of the will, a sure sign that he was worried about her future after his death. These interesting Genoese households, existing for unknown reasons outside the bonds of matrimony, suggest that community standards were less strict than the clergy may have wished.

Other unusual wills include that of Simone Silvagio, who left L.25 to a woman with the unfortunate and perhaps revealing name Simona Bastarda so that she might marry after his death.[18] This bequest was contingent upon whether "she had been a good woman in her person," which presumably meant that she must refrain from producing any bastards.[19] Giulia, the widow of Guglienzone da Montoggio, had no children, and she bequeathed all her goods to her sisters.[20] She left the derisory sum of five solidi to her husband's natural son Giovanni. Baiamonte de Campo Rotondo left his natural son Simone twenty solidi. In comparison his daughter received a dowry of L.18, and his five legitimate sons were named his principal heirs.[21] These instances remind us that the future of an illegitimate child was problematical, and depended on the voluntary generosity of the father. No one can say how many illegitimate children were consigned to oblivion and a life of poverty. If the charitable bequests to orphans are any guide to contemporary sentiment, perhaps there was considerable pressure for fathers to do the "right thing." Other wills indicate that some Genoese were prepared to take in unwanted children; there are several instances of people raising children who were not their own. Anselmo Buxono left L.10 to Guglielmino, "who I raise for the love of God," and commended him to God and Lord Ogerio Vento, a powerful combination in Genoa.[22] Giulia di Bellocchio left Alda, whom she had raised, L.20 for marriage or to enter a convent.[23] Where these children came from is not always clear, but this generosity, which does not hint at kinship, indicates a degree of concern about these children and their fate.

The Children of Enrico Dietisalva

Enrico Dietisalva's will of September 30, 1220, is complex and revealing, and combines many diverse elements concerning children and succession.[24] As an example it raises and, I hope, clarifies several general points about the wills under study, as well as problems of interpretation and terminology. This example also illustrates the potential richness of the will as a historical source.

Enrico was married twice, to the late Maria, and to Aloisa. Altogether he had eleven children—seven daughters, six of them with Maria, and four sons, all with Maria. Enrico, after leaving L.25 for his soul, turned his attention to his daughters; but first he had to clear up some details which concerned Maria's will. Maria had left an estate worth L.800, and she had directed her husband to give three daughters, presumably the youngest, certain bequests. Giovannetta and Alda had received L.100 each for dowries, and Adalasia L.60, which Enrico had used to cover the expenses of making her a nun. (Enrico used the first person in his will, and he employed the verb *monachavi*—"I have made her a nun"—to describe how he had acted in regard to Adalasia.) It seems that Maria's will had not mentioned her other three daughters, probably because they were already married. Enrico confirmed that he had added L.100 of his own to Giovanna's dowry (note how the "Giovannetta" of Maria's will was now "Giovanna"), which gave her a total dowry of L.200. The other three daughters received, and were bequeathed as heirs, these dowries: Aidelina L.250, Ermigina L.300, Sibilina L.200. As the family tree in Figure 1 reveals, three of these daughters were already married by the time Enrico made his will. Audeta, the youngest daughter and only child of Enrico and Aloisa, did not fare as well. Enrico directed that she should become a nun, and he left L.10 for this purpose. Perhaps Enrico thought that if Aloisa wanted some other future for little Audeta, she could pay for her dowry, as Maria had done for her daughters.

Thus, of Enrico's seven daughters, five had married or intended to marry at a total cost of L.1050 (an enormous sum), and two had become nuns, at a cost of L.70. The case of Enrico offers a fine example of the problems facing a father with many daughters. Despite the size of his family, he managed to preserve his daughters' social status by providing dowries commensurate with his own rank in society. The dowries of his second wife and daughters-in-law (average L.312) confirm this, though by the time Alda (dowry of L.100) married, the wellspring of parental generosity seems to have dried up somewhat. He placed two daughters in convents; yet for L.60 Adalasia probably had a warmer welcome and more comfortable surroundings at San Andrea de Porta than Audeta could expect for L.10. A list of the sisters of San Andrea in 1246 reads like the social register of medieval Genoa, with representatives of the Cannavaria, Grillo, Rosso, Lercario, Tornello, Guercio, De Mari, Embriaco, and Malocello families.[25] There were some women, as we know from the many wills made by single women, who managed to escape both marriage and the convent. Enrico Dietisalva was a typical father in that he needed to envision specific futures for his daughters, and spinsterhood outside the church was not one of the options as far as he was concerned. He had to provide his daughters with something rather than leave the burden to his sons, who might have been reluctant to divide the patrimony further. Enrico married off as many of his daughters as he could afford; other parents were not as generous.

Enrico had four sons. Giovanni, probably the eldest, had died,

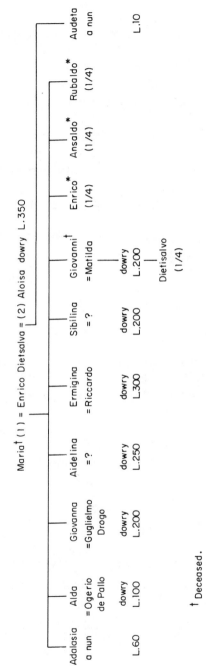

The Family of Enrico Dietisalva

Maria† (1) = Enrico Dietisalva = (2) Aloisa dowry L.350

Adalasia	Alda	Giovanna	Aidelina	Ermigina	Sibilina	Giovanni†	Enrico*	Ansaldo*	Rubaldo*	Audeta
a nun	=Ogerio de Pallo	=Guglielmo Drogo	=?	=Riccardo	=?	=Matilda	(1/4)	(1/4)	(1/4)	a nun
	dowry L.100	dowry L.200	dowry L.250	dowry L.300	dowry L.200	dowry L.200				L.10
L.60						Dietisalvo (1/4)				

† Deceased.

* Two of the three living sons were married, but which two is unclear. Enrico had two daughters-in-law besides Matilda: Mabilia, with a dowry of L.400, Adalasia, with a dowry of L.300.

leaving a son named Dietisalvo. Enrico left the rest of his goods equally to his three surviving sons, Enrico, Ansaldo, and Rubaldo, and his grandson. If Dietisalvo died without an heir, his uncles were to inherit, and the sons also were to substitute for each other if any of them should die without an heir. In wills in general, the great problem with the phrase "the rest of my goods" is that we seldom know just how much this was. The inheritance picture for Enrico's sons is nevertheless clear: they were the principal heirs. In a way, Dietisalvo substituted for his late father, and his right to one-quarter of the estate was unquestioned. The daughters were in a sense no longer part of the family; they had separate existences and had received all of the family wealth to which they had a claim.

A brief comparison of the Dietisalva and Buferio families is instructive. Simone Buferio had twelve children—eight sons and four daughters.[26] The strategies of large families depended to a great extent on the sex ratios of the children. Simone faced the challenge of providing for many sons, but first, as was usual, he had to take care of his daughters. He wanted Isabellina and Giacomina to become nuns, and he gave them L.50 each to do this. He wanted Aimelina and Carenzona to be dowered and married with L.150 apiece. Here again, the saving on dowries was considerable. As for his sons, Simone seems to have realized that dividing his goods eight ways would have resulted in insufficient legacies all around. His own wife had brought a dowry of L.270, and one of his sons had married a girl with a dowry of L.293 1/2, but his daughters seem to have slipped somewhat lower on the social ladder. He apparently tried to prevent his sons from suffering the same fate. Two of his sons, possibly the two youngest, were to become monks, Ottolino at Santo Stefano and Anselmino at Santa Maria d'Albaro, "if it pleases them." Each was to receive L.25 for this purpose; but if they declined to do this, they were to share equally with their six brothers, who were the principal heirs. The brothers were to succeed any of their number who died without an heir, but if Ottolino and Anselmino became monks, they were not to succeed to any inheritance. One of the advantages of placing surplus children with the church was that it eliminated permanently any claims they had on family wealth. This was also the case for the secular clergy. Too many sons presented a problem. Not every father gave his sons the choice Simone Buferio proffered, and only the exceptional father gave his daughters any choice at all.

A woman with a large family was confronted with a different set of issues. Giulietta, the wife of Fulcone Zaccaria, is a case in point, since she had three sons and six daughters.[27] In 1248 she left her husband L.100, and L.48 for her soul. Two daughters, both perhaps married, received L.10 and L.5, respectively. Giulietta named as her principal heirs her sons Benedetto (the famous admiral and alum merchant), Manuele, and Niccoloso. In a codicil made two weeks later she left her other four daughters for *falcidia* L.2 apiece. Since we know that she was still alive in 1280, the particular terms of this will were not executed. Still, her intentions are more important here than the eventual outcome. Giulietta, possibly thirty years old when she made her will, was a relatively young woman. The distinctive feature of this will is the extent to which she relied on her husband. No tutor was nominated to protect the minors, since Fulcone would naturally assume the responsibility. No dowries were provided for the daughters, since Fulcone would decide which of them would be married, and what dowry would be appropriate. Generally a married woman, having received a dowry from her father, had no other disposable wealth unless she had inherited something from another relative. As a rule, since fathers ignored married daughters when the time came to divide up the patrimony, married women had less to leave in their wills. But the situation was, as we shall see, different for widows.

Children as Heirs

The great majority of the testators followed the example set by these three parents: they left most of the property to their children. Whether all the children shared equally or not is the prime issue. Of the 325 Genoese who left the rest of their goods to their children, 224 named the children as heirs equally without distinguishing between sons and daughters. The complexities involved here contradict any superficial impression that the Genoese did not discriminate among their children. The high percentage of single-child families requires us to look closer at these 224 families.

One can consider the families to be of five types—families with sons and daughters, sons only, one son only, daughters only, and one daughter only. The composition of these 224 families is somewhat surprising: 45 of these families had both sons and daughters; 59 only sons; 13 only daughters; 60 but one son; and 47 but one daughter. Thus, 107 testators had only one child, and hence little choice to make, and 72 had children of one sex only. A mere 45, about 20 percent of the parents, had sons and daughters who shared equally in the inheritance.

If we turn to the wills that favor one heir over the others, the family situations look quite different. Of the 90 families in which the children did not share equally in the will, 78 included children of both sexes. Just four testators who had only sons and eight who had only daughters divided their goods unequally. (In addition, the wills of a few single-child families present a somewhat unclear situation, and in 11 more cases the will is indecipherable or totally ambiguous.) The personal motives for any bias within the family are very difficult to determine, though primogeniture was clearly not an issue for the sons: in 59 families they inherited equally and in only four they did not. Families with many daughters were more likely to favor some at the expense of others, as in the case of Enrico Dietisalva. Parents having only daughters usually favored unmarried or engaged daughters over the married ones. The number of families with only daughters is very low, and is a sign that some married daughters were not named in the wills as heirs. The families with sons and daughters remain the most important issue, however, because they enable us to contrast the future of children by sex. Combining the numbers, we find 123 families with sons and daughters, 45 sharing equally and 78 unequally. Seventy testators (47 men and 23 women) favored their sons over their daughters, while only eight (one man and seven women) gave the advantage to the daughters. How the testators regarded their children is of great interest, but the numbers are small and do not support any sweeping generalizations. Married women, as a group younger than widows, may have felt a greater responsibility to provide their daughters a start in life. Even for the sons and daughters to share equally was in a way a victory for the daughters in a society predisposed to slight them. Widows may not have had husbands, but they were still influenced by society and male relatives. Few women showed any signs of partiality to daughters. Table 6 demonstrates how the parent's marital status may have affected the choice of heirs between sons and daughters.

Two important conclusions emerge from this analysis of children as heirs. Many testators had no real decision to make; they had only one child to provide for, or children of the same sex. Often, the predisposition to favor sons was thwarted by cold fact, for many families had only daughters. When there were many sons or daughters, some had to enter the church, if the family's resources permitted such a choice. Judging just how far the family patrimony might stretch required some reflection. Any discussion of family strategies for survival must start with the fact that genetic circumstances, in the guise of an only child or children of the same sex, often left little room for maneuvering. Fifty-seven percent of the testators who had sons and daughters gave the sons the greater part of the inheritance. However, the real significance may lie in the fact that daughters received their equal share or more almost as often. The requirements of the blood tie were paramount; we have already seen that in overwhelming numbers the Genoese left their property to their children. In this society sons and daughters led very different lives, but both served as connections to the future. Sons may already have received their share of family land or property when their fathers emancipated them, and daughters had dowries. Many of the restrictions placed on women may have resulted from men's desires to make the transfer of property between males as smooth as possible. That is, daughters may have been only the mediators of family wealth from grandfather to grandson. Most Genoese found a daughter

Table 6. Relationship of parents' marital status to naming of children as heirs.

	Wills of—			
Status of heirs	Married men	Widowed men	Married women	Widowed women
Sons and daughters inherit equally	21	2	12	10
Sons favored	37	10	8	15
Daughters favored	1	0	5	2

Source: Archivio di Stato di Genova, Cartolari Notarili.

preferable to a son-in-law as a guardian of the family fortune. In this light the apparent equality among heirs makes more sense. And yet, even if women were only mediators under restraints, where they had means there was also opportunity. Both sons and daughters had to face the risk of a life of involuntary prayer in a convent or monastery, but daughters were more likely to encounter this prospect than their brothers were, if family size and wealth dictated such a decision. Let us continue to trace the children's contrasting paths by examining the way they inherited from one another.

Conditions

Parents often attached conditions to the bequests they left their heirs. By the beginning of the thirteenth century, husbands, no doubt in most cases at the notary's suggestion, began to provide routinely for the possibility that their wives might be pregnant at the time. Occasionally the wills indicate that this pregnancy was real rather than just a legal nicety. The problem of a posthumous child and the rights of such a child were known in Roman law. As the testament developed into a more sophisticated document, planning for a posthumous child became a wise foresight. In general the sex of the hypothetical child determined how it would fit into whatever inheritance pattern the will followed. Giovanni de San Ginesio's will of July 2, 1241, illustrates in amazing detail how providing for a possible child affected the status of the existing heirs.[28] In fact Giovanni had only one daughter, Giovannetta, to whom he left L.500 for marriage. Yet the details of his will suggest that his wife may have been pregnant at the time. In any event, if his wife gave birth to a daughter, the child was to receive L.600 for her dowry and nothing else. If a son were born, he would become the principal heir, and if more than one son, both were to share equally as heirs. If a son and a daughter were born, the son was to be the heir, and the daughter would receive a L.600 dowry. Finally, and logically, if girls were born, they were to inherit L.600 apiece. Giovanni had stated at the beginning of his will that he was gravely ill, so he was not contemplating future pregnancies so much as a present one which for some reason encouraged a hope for twins. If in fact no children "came to light" (a common contemporary expression), his brothers were to inherit the rest of his goods. Giovanni's will is a typical if in some ways extreme example of planning for future children, since no radical changes would result for Giovannetta from the arrival of another heir. The will also summarizes standard Genoese inheritance patterns and certainly conveys a bias in favor of sons. For a couple currently childless, the hope for a posthumous child and heir was a very serious one. Ottolino de Nigrone, who had no children, set out plans for posthumous heirs very similar to Giovanni's, even down to the possibility of twins.[29] However, if his wife were not pregnant, his brother would inherit everything.

The most significant condition concerned succession—that is, who would inherit from the principal heir or heirs. The testator had a right to name alternates to succeed if the principal heir should die without legitimate issue. For this reason if no other, wills were documents of enduring significance, since this question of heirs without heirs might arise years in the future. If Genoese society strictly observed these conditions, some people, lacking heirs of their own, may never even have made a will, since their parents' wills had already decided how the property would ultimately be disposed. Giovanni de San Ginesio's will offers a useful example of how succession operated. After all the above ruminations about possible births, he faced the fact that there might be no child. In this case, he made his own brothers the heirs, and stipulated that they should pay the L.600 dowry to Giovannetta. If she died without an heir, any male heirs would succeed; if there were none, then the brothers would inherit. If his direct heirs all died without issue, he wished his father-in-law to give L.1000 to aid the Holy Land, and the rest to his brothers or their heirs, by branch and not by head. Family affections may have prompted Giovanni to leave his property to his brothers if his own line defaulted, but his father's will probably required this course anyway. In the twelfth century testators often insisted that their heirs have legitimate male heirs of their own. In the thirteenth century this type of restriction largely disappeared, but the insistence on legitimacy remained strong.

Succession is also the most significant condition because it was the most common. I shall discuss next the sorts of succession plans formulated by 209 of the testators with children. (The rest of the testators with children did not explicitly provide for the possibility that their heirs would fail to reproduce. Single-child families account for most of these cases.) The first way a testator might approach the problem of succession was to require the children to inherit from one another. If a person had more than one child, this was the logical source to follow, and 126 of them did. For the single-child family, as well as some of the others, there were other possibilities, none of which were as common as succession among the children. Some testators passed on wealth to their own brothers, sisters, nephews, and nieces; others named spouses as secondary heirs. Only a handful of Genoese had their own parents or the church in mind as their ultimate beneficiaries. The most frequent alternative to any one of these options was some combination of them. This was especially true for heirs of the third degree, who had only a slight chance of eventually receiving anything. Perhaps the naming of an heir to inherit if two or more people failed to produce heirs of their own was mainly an honorific gesture. The major purpose of these succession clauses was to ensure that property remain in the branches of the family rather than in the hands of strangers. A son having no children was supposed to return his share to his more fruitful brothers, sisters, or nephews. In the same way, a daughter's dowry returned to her family if she died without children. While the law offered a framework of doing all this, the family needs that dictated these strategies were the main reason why Roman practice was retrieved in the twelfth and thirteenth centuries. The Genoese did not envisage that their children should have at some future date ultimate free disposition of family wealth unless they had children of their own.

Other types of conditions also stress the importance of family continuity. Some of the wills refer to previous divisions of land or money among the children. When mention of family land appears in a will, there are usually some standard conditions, for example forbidding the children (almost always the sons) to sell or alienate the land except to one another. Public estimators were to determine the fair market price (temporary hardship was not to be a factor), and usually the will stipulates that some fixed amount ought to be deducted from this impartial appraisal. The intent is obvious: to keep land in the family. The testators tried to prevent their landed wealth from being fragmented and diminished as the result of passing through too many hands. What desirable land there was in Liguria was often measured in very small plots; constant land sales and trades testify to the patient efforts of some people to obtain economically viable holdings. An untimely sale to a stranger might undo generations of methodical work. Perhaps for this reason land is not frequently mentioned in the wills, except, strangely enough, those of clerics. Most Genoese preferred to distribute land to their heirs while they were still alive, if this was possible, in order to guarantee a smooth and sensible transition. Ogerio Vento availed himself of another way of keeping his land in the family: he never divided the property. He wished his sons to live together and hold the family home (probably a tower) in common, down to his grandchildren and great-grandchildren.[30] The Genoese clans—extended families holding sizable fortunes together over generations—had their origins in this period.[31] The shares remained personal property in those early years, and when any heir married and wanted his wealth, the heirs were to pay a just price.

These general kinds of conditions apply to the broad spectrum of wills. Other conditions relate to specific family circumstances and to the desire of people to exert a posthumous influence on kin. One way for a testator to impose an individual condition was to instruct the tutors, again in broad or specific terms. These instructions will be considered when I take up the role played by tutors. For the time being, let us continue to examine conditions attached to legacies. In 1248 one Adalasia named as principal heirs her children Alberto and Aidelina for one-third each, and her nephews for one-third together.[32] However, she imposed a specific condition on Alberto's bequest. If Alberto married a woman from outside Genoa and left the city, he would inherit only L.10 as *falcidia,* and his sister was to receive his share. If he married a woman from outside but returned to live in the city, he would still be heir to one-third of the estate. Adalasia clearly had a specific woman from outside Genoa in mind, and she feared that this person would draw her son away from his home town and family. Evidently she did not object to the marriage per se as long as the couple resided in Genoa. Adalasia, by imposing this condition, used material incentive in order to influence her son's life after her own death. To what extent she succeeded we cannot know.

Some other special conditions pointed to even less harmonious family circumstances. Antulo della Croce left his wife, Altilia, L.50. But if she were not able to stay with his son Pietro, because he disturbed her and "she was not strong enough to endure it," she would still be allowed to use the money for food and clothing.[33] Antulo hoped that his wife would keep this L.50 together for some use, but if she had to move out, and he feared this, she could take the money with her in order to survive. Here we have another indication that life for an unprotected woman was probably very difficult. Superbo de Podenzolla wished his daughter, Paganella, to have L.15 for her marriage, but if his sons refused to pay, she was to become an heir equally with them.[34] Superbo used financial incentive to make sure that his sons would fulfill this promise to their sister; otherwise, the cost would surely be greater than L.15. Anita, the wife of the late Bartolomeo de Carmadino, made the most poignant condition. She wanted to leave the bulk of the estate to her sons Giovanni and Idone equally. However Idone was *stultus*—foolish—which probably meant that he was retarded. "If however my son Idone shall not have conducted himself wisely and well, and shall have remained foolish, I want him to have only the income of the part which may come to him of my goods, for however long he remains foolish, and the ownership goes to his other brother."[35] After Idone's death, Giovanni would receive the ownership as well as the income. If Idone remained foolish, he was not to be anyone's heir. The exact nature of his illness is unclear, since his mother seems to have insisted on the possibility that he might recover. Whatever the problem was, Idone was an adult, and mainly a burden to his brother. Individual family situations required special conditions and some very sophisticated solutions.

Tutors

During the early thirteenth century, as a knowledge of Roman law became more pervasive, the guardians appointed by Genoese parents came to be known by a variety of technical names: tutors, curators, administrators, and *domini*.[36] Often the distinctions between these functions were more verbal than actual, except for the *domini*. The guardian was known as a tutor or curator, although a few testators made the distinction that the curator was temporary, or was assigned to one specific task. When the term *administrator* was used, it only elaborated upon the business functions which the guardian had within his authority anyway. *Domina* was a title that acknowledged the special rights a mother had as the principal tutor. Armano de Cucurno made his wife, Maria, *domina* "as long as she remained with the children," and he named four people, including Maria, as tutors.[37] Baldoino de Caprili named his wife "domina, tutrix, curatrix, et administratrix," leaving no room for doubt about her authority.[38] While the terminology varied, the wills naming guardians did so very clearly.

Tutors exercised the full range of activity that any adult might undertake for a child. The tutors entered into various business arrangements "at the risk and fortune of the minors," and made marital and apprenticeship agreements on behalf of their charges. A few testators gave advice about what types of business the tutors should transact; for instance, Oberto de Marzano requested the tutors of his children to deposit all his money in the bank of the Pinelli. In most cases, though, the guardians were expected to rely on their own judgment.[39] The will carefully protected the tutors from any claims of mismanagement. Sometimes almost emancipated men made commercial contracts with the consent of their guardians, who were for all practical purposes foster parents. The guardians were responsible at law for the care of the minors. On January 10, 1203, the guardians of the daughters of the late Baldoino de Pavero and his late wife, Mabilia, went before the consuls of the parish of Mignanego, a village outside Genoa, in order to register the legitimate payments they had made.[40] This was done to ensure that the daughters would have no claim against the tutors. The tutors spent a total of L.26 s.1 d.4 in ways that reveal the kinds of duties they performed. They spent L.2 s.14 d.6 on notaries who wrote up various documents, and three solidi for a legal fee to a judge who gave them advice. Besides discharging numerous small debts and paying off the servants, the guardians buried Baldoino at a cost of L.1 s.12, and spent L.12 s.19 d.9 on caring for the minors. The guardians admitted that they had expended four solidi for food when they visited Genoa on the minors' business, and another s.9 d.6 for food for themselves and the consuls. Often the guardians were also the executors of the will; in this capacity they would conduct an inventory of the estate and, as in Baldoino's case, bury the testator. Sometimes the will provided for remunerating the tutors; the sums involved were never large.

Selecting the proper guardian was an important decision. In the present sample, 109 testators appointed guardians: 82 married men, 11 widowers, three married women, and 13 widows. Fathers had the right to name the guardian, but mothers had few opportunities to exercise any power of appointment; if the father survived her, he was the natural guardian, and if deceased, he had most likely already named a tutor in his own will. The three married women named as tutors husbands and a father-in-law. The widows had no greater scope of authority, though time may have overturned the plans of their late husbands and hence necessitated the naming of new tutors. Guardianship, although regulated by law, was largely a private matter. Only twice did the testators name the consuls of the *borgo* (neighborhood) as tutors, and only one member of the clergy served in this capacity. Caffara de Manica, who made her will while preparing to go on a pilgrimage, wished the prior of San Giovanni de Pavarano to safeguard her goods until she returned.[41] She left her son L.20, which the prior was to keep until the son was thirty years old. The prior was not, strictly speaking, a tutor; he was instead performing a service that the church offered to pilgrims.

Of the testators who nominated tutors, 58 named wives, 34 named friends, 30 named a brother, 15 a son, nine a mother, five a father-in-law, 34 named other relatives, and ten named other persons. Most named two or more guardians. Since married men dominated these selections, wives might be expected to lead this list. However, 26 married men did not chose their own wives to be tutors, and 25 named their wives to serve as tutors along with others. Only 25 times was a wife named the sole guardian. Some women had wide business experience, but Genoese fathers wanted their children to benefit at least from the counsel of men who were themselves accustomed to the marketplace. Having more than one tutor was a good idea for a number of reasons, such as death or travel, which might prevent one of the tutors from doing his job. A wife's remarriage usually meant that she would no longer be a tutor. Most of the men who named a wife as tutor insisted that she remain a "good wife, without a husband," and that she should stay in the family home with the children. As we shall see in the next chapter, a wife's inheritance also changed if she remarried.[42] A second husband, and the possibility of more children, might impair the heirs' rights and property; the mother would no longer be a free agent, raising the children as her principal task.

Within a family, different members continuously interact with each other, and society as a whole, over time. As a way to summarize some of the conclusions about children, and to introduce a discussion of other family relationships, I shall now examine one woman's life and her roles as wife, sister, mother, sometime nun, and pawn in the plans of two great families.

Giovanna Pevere

Occasionally it is possible to construct a "paper trail" and place a person's will within a continuing family history. Events that preceded and followed the making of a will enable us to interpret ambiguities and note what has been omitted. Giovanna Pevere's life can be pieced together and used to show how necessary it is to view the family as a dynamic unit and not just a collection of categories of husbands, wives, and children.

Giovanna, the daughter of the late Lanfranco Pevere, made her will on July 11, 1226.[43] Her very name, and the place where she made the will, hint at problems. Though married to Nicola Embrone, she chose not to be known as his wife but instead as her father's daughter. By itself this might not be significant, but Giovanna made her will in the house of her brother, Sorleone Pevere, where she lived. The Pevere and Embrone families were in the front rank of Genoese society; they wielded economic and political power and in fact lived right next door to each other, as is known from a later document, which I will consider shortly. A marriage alliance between these two families was natural and desirable, since they were influential in the same neighborhood. We do not know why Giovanna moved across the way to live with her brothers Sorleone and Sozo, but it seems likely that this marriage alliance had somehow fallen apart. For a rich and well-connected woman,

Giovanna wrote a will that was relatively simple. She left L.300 for her soul, of which the Franciscans and Dominicans were to distribute L.100, and she herself would see to the rest. Giovanna named as heirs her daughter Giacomina, and any other children she might have with her husband; they were to receive *falcidia* and nothing else. She left the rest of her goods to her brothers Sorleone, Sozo, and Giovanni. These circumstances seem to indicate that Giovanna had left her daughter with Nicola Embrone when she moved out. The will's subscription clearly states that Giovanna lived with her brothers, and had not merely gone to their house to make a will. The concluding formula contains two interesting variations. Giovanna vacated any previous testament; but more important, she swore that this one could not be altered and should remain in effect, except by the wish of her brothers. It was highly unusual for Giovanna to deny her right to add codicils or make another will, and especially to give her brothers complete control over what she might do. All this was aimed at Nicola Embrone and his own rights over his wife. The will itself raises some interesting questions, but it does not supply many hard answers.

The next piece of evidence appears in the city chronicle for the year 1227.[44] The author, or team of compilers, notes that a great feud was going on in the city because of the murder "last year" (1226) of Nicola Embrone. The sons and relatives of Embrone, as well as their allies and clients, were fighting in the city streets and roads outside the city against Sorleone, Sozo, and Giovanni Pevere and their supporters. No reason is supplied for why the Pevere killed Embrone, nor does the chronicle mention the surely well known fact that the principals were in-laws. In 1227 the *podestà* arranged for the parties publicly to exchange the kiss of peace and cease fighting, all of which accounts for the recording of these events in 1227. The next event noted in the chronicle occurred in March, so this peace was probably one of the first orders of business that the new *podestà* managed at the beginning of the year. Murder, even of prominent people, was common in Genoa. The city chronicle was an official record which preferred to mark the end of strife rather than the origins. Such impartiality was no doubt wise.

Since we know that Embrone was still alive on July 11, 1226, he must have been killed sometime between then and November 15, when we find Giovanna, now a widow, drawing up another notarial act. On that date, with her brothers Sorleone and Sozo as the only witnesses, Giovanna stated to the notary Maestro Salmone that she no longer wished to stay in the Hospital of San Giovanni or follow its "religion" (rule).[45] Giovanna claimed that if at one time she had said anything that indicated her consent to enter the hospital, she should not be held to those words because she did not have full freedom of mind. In any case she had always reserved the right to leave if the place was not pleasing. The real issue, she maintains, is that at the time she became a lady companion of the order, Giovanna was out of her mind and confused "because my husband had been lately and recently slain."[46] Evidently now recovered, Giovanna could no longer observe her vow and no longer wished to remain. This declaration took place in the Chapel of San Lionardo in the hospital at vespers. The merits of her case in canon law, although very interesting, are so artfully and legally constructed that they obscure Giovanna's authentic voice. This declaration highlights several family problems. Sorleone and Sozo, at least the instigators of Embrone's murder, again appear as loyal brothers trying to help their sister once more. Did grief drive Giovanna to enter a religious house, or was it guilt, or a desire for a temporary refuge from a raging feud? In any event her marriage seems to have been at the core of the difficulties between the Pevere and Embrone families. Ideally, a marriage like hers was supposed to prevent violence, and at least in this sense the marriage had failed months before Embrone's murder. We cannot know if somehow the marriage itself set off a chain of events which led to murder, or whether political or some other form of rivalry proved to be too strong for this traditional remedy. Giovanna's daughter Giacomina did not unify the families or consolidate the alliance, and Giovanna seems to have abandoned her once again, this time by entering religion.

Whatever conclusions emerge concerning the larger issues, the tantalizing personal question remains: what happened to Giovanna? For the answer we must turn to the last document that sheds any light on her life, and one that provides a view from the Embrone perspective. The notary Jacopo Taraburlo often drew up documents for the family, and by chance two contemporary notaries whose work survived wrote for different sides.[47] On June 28, 1227, after the end of the feud, the brothers Ansaldo, Simone, Ottone, and Bonovassallo Embrone, sons of the late Nicola Embrone, came to a long series of agreements about how to divide up the inheritance of their late parents.[48] The curator of the first three sons was Ansaldo Dietisalva, probably the Ansaldo who appears in the family tree in Figure 1, and who may have been married to their sister. Enrico Embrone was Bonovassallo's curator. When these four brothers spoke of their mother they did not mean Giovanna, whom we now know was Nicola Embrone's second wife. Since these sons were about to mature legally, Nicola was probably considerably older than Giovanna. With a large family already at hand (there is no information about any other daughters), the motives behind this ill-fated marriage alliance seem quite practical and not even related to a for more heirs.

The complicated arrangements made to divide up the extensive Embrone city property are interesting in themselves; for example one casual border reference reveals that the Pevere were neighbors. The brothers agreed to hold in common only the land in Voltri and any outstanding commercial contracts outside Genoa. The pertinent details here concern what the brothers had decided to do about their half-sister Giacomina. They each promised to give L.50 for her marriage within eight days after the event, and this donation was to be made known to the *podestà* and consuls of the commune. This was an unusual provision to say the least, and supports the conclusion that this division occurred after the peace. These dowry arrangements may very well have been part of the peace terms. Buried in the middle of the brothers' transactions is the last reference to Giovanna Pevere. Each brother acknowledged to the others that he had received L.100 of the L.400 dowry of his late stepmother (*noverca*), Giovanna. This money was to be held on deposit because of a pledge Giovanna had made to give the L.400 to Giacomina for her dowry. The brothers had therefore ensured that their sister would be able to marry with L.600, a respectable sum even for her social status. Giacomina thus survived to become an awkward detail. But by June 28, a little more than seven months after we last saw her trying to get out of the Hospital of San Giovanni, Giovanna Pevere was dead.

This L.400 pledge is at odds with the will Giovanna had made

eleven months earlier, before her husband's death, giving Giacomina only *falcidia*, and L.300 to charity. The will may have been
an effort to undo this pledge, but more likely the L.400 promise
was made when the Embrone "returned" Giovanna's dowry after
Nicola's death. Giovanna had a right to a settlement of her claim
against her husband's estate, but the circumstances surrounding
his death delayed payment. All this assumes that Giovanna lived
long enough to see peace between her two families, and perhaps
even to write a new will that was more generous to Giacomina.
Alternatively, the brothers may never have returned the dowry,
using an old pledge to justify their act. The former is the more
likely explanation, since if, as seems likely, the feud ended before
March 1227, Giovanna's death can be placed sometime between
then and June. Giovanna's death may have made peace easier to
achieve. It seems more likely, however, that her claims, and Giovanna herself, were still active at the time the Pevere and Embrone
came to terms. The pledge tips the scales in favor of Giovanna's
living to see the end of the feud.

The deaths of Nicola Embrone in 1226 and Giovanna Pevere
in 1227 were not quite the end of the story. These were noble
families, and a few subsequent developments found their way into
the city chronicle. With unusual precision, the chronicle notes that
on December 10, 1232, Enrigeto Embrone attacked and gravely
wounded Sorleone Pevere and his brother Sozo.[49] Enrigeto was
the son of the late Rubaldo Embrone, Nicola's brother, who had
been alive in 1227. The commune placed the assailant under ban.
We hear no more of this incident. Sozo Pevere recovered sufficiently to serve on a diplomatic mission to Venice in 1233; Sorleone served as legate of the commune at Ceuta in North Africa
in 1236. Enrigeto's attack is only additional proof of the durability
of feuds in medieval Italian urban politics.

In 1239 Genoa was racked with internal violence. The chronicle
of these events begins with the ominous statement, "In this year
many marriages or espousals had been secretly contracted in the
city of Genoa between such persons who were believed to be in
disagreement and were accustomed to hatred more than love."[50]
A well-phrased and perceptive comment; contemporaries knew
what to make of these marriages of the great. A son or grandson
of Sorleone Pevere accepted a daughter of Percivale Doria, a Vento

took a Grillo, a Spinola took a Vento, and there were other such marriages, all of which caused "wonder and fear in the greater part of the good men of the city."[51] In fact these marriages were a prelude to civil war and the election of captains of the people (heads of the city militia). The marriage of Nicola Embrone and Giovanna Pevere should be seen in this light. For them, though, something went tragically wrong. We have seen how much the will by itself reveals, and how much it does not.

For most people we have only a will, and it is not possible to construct even the barest family or individual history. Giovanna Pevere's will demonstrates that the testament has value as a historical source if its limitations are kept in mind.

Thus far I have concentrated on children as the principal heirs—the core of the descent group. Besides supplying a descent group, the kin had many other functions, as we have seen in the case of the Embrone and Pevere. The political family—a masculine game in which women participated only as peace offerings—extended beyond the nearest kin to include all those who claimed to belong to a particular clan or family. Most Genoese belonged to less powerful and more transitory families. If they sought security through pooling resources, they had to look beyond the family to a guild or even a confraternity. The religious family, as Guglielmo Embriaco's will demonstrates, provided worship for the dead, and formed a kind of timeless kinship group. Likewise the commercial family comprised more members than the descent group. In-laws were more suitable as business partners than heirs. Work, whether long-distance trade or weaving, created ties between people often as important and durable as ties of the blood. Urban business life lessened the need to rely exclusively on kin. Economic survival depended on a family's ability to reach out for good partners and wise investments; no longer, if ever it had been, was the family a self-contained and self-sufficient work unit. Finally, marriage was exogamous, always requiring a family to look beyond its boundaries for suitable matches.

How one defines the family depends on what particular role seems most important. To shuffle members in and out of the family as these roles change is a necessary but confusing task. The descent group represents a human desire to find a way for the family to endure, and offers a sure foundation for family history. The descent group was not limited to children as heirs. I shall now try to place children in the wider context of family and friends, and look as well at those families that had no children and those testators who had little or no family.

4 / A Good Wife without a Husband

When a testator had children, they were his natural heirs. But many Genoese did not have children, and their choices reveal how the descent group depended on the testator's marital status and the existence of children. A large contingent of the sample—254 men and women—did not have children at the time they made a will. Many of these people had not given up hope of producing heirs, as the provisions for posthumous children indicate. But their current situation forced childless testators to find heirs in the wider circle of relatives and even to make bequests beyond the family to charity and friends. These childless testators fall into six categories, again distinguished by marital status and sex: married men (57), married women (54), widowers (1), single men (81), single women (44), and widows (17). Once widowed, a man was likely to remarry quickly, and single men outnumbered single women. ("Single" is used here to refer to a person who shows no sign of ever having been married.) All of these people had, however, one common characteristic: they had not produced a legitimate heir, at least so far. Because they had not done so, to some extent such people did not have an absolute right to dispose freely of their property, for the previous generation may have placed conditions on any inheritance. As I have already noted, the most frequently mentioned condition concerned the possibility that an heir might die without a legitimate heir of his own. The intent of the condition was to ensure that the property would remain in the family's fruitful branches. For example, a parent naming his children as heirs often stipulated that if any of them died before twenty-five (the most common age of legal majority) without an heir, the surviving children would succeed to that share. A minor in this position had no need for a will, since his parent's will still covered him. It is clear from some wills that parents wanted this restriction to apply past majority, but enforcement was another matter. Trusts were known in Roman law, but the Genoese, except in the case of the woman with the "foolish" son, passed on ownership as well as usufruct to the heirs. Without the records of any legal cases concerning this particular issue, we cannot know just how much legal force testamentary conditions carried a generation or two later. Even if a parent had wanted a childless heir to pass wealth on to siblings or nephews and nieces, personal experience may have suggested other heirs. The wills of the 254 people without children provide a chance to test the durability of the conditions and, in a way, the family ties themselves.

Principal Heirs of Childless Testators

First let us consider the single men and women. Their kin consisted only of their parents, aunts, uncles, siblings, nephews, and nieces. This small kinship group includes all the relatives whom single people named as heirs. Table 7 categorizes the heirs by the testator's sex. Parents may have influenced these choices or insisted upon them as part of their own wills. Single men slightly preferred siblings and their children as heirs. Indeed ordinary family life and its emotional ties might suggest that bachelor uncles and maiden aunts would "naturally" select these relatives as heirs; probably the heirs had this point of view. Certainly some unmar-

Table 7. Heirs of single men and women.

Heirs	Number of wills of—	
	Men	Women
Siblings	25	6
Neps[a]	11	5
Other relatives[b]	11	7
Pro anima bequests	15	10
Unrelated persons	8	8
No main heirs	11	8

Source: Archivio di Stato di Genovo, Cartolari Notarili.
a. Nephews or nieces, or some combination of these.
b. Parents, aunts, uncles, cousins, or various combinations of these.

ried testators were only children and hence not able to make the preferred choice. Roughly one in three Genoese was an only child, though, and Table 7 shows that a considerably larger percentage than this of single people did not choose siblings and their children as heirs. As the two important alternatives indicate, there were no hard and fast rules. Single people without children were more inclined than any other category of testator to leave the bulk of the estate for their souls. A few members of the clergy belong to this group, but more often the clergy, like the laity, left their property to their relatives. Why were unmarried people without children the most charitable? Such individuals were not necessarily more concerned about the soul's fate, but they were not able to rely on descendants to pay for masses or other remembrances. Some single people seem to have realized that they themselves had to provide for any spiritual benefits they wanted to receive.

The statistics given in Table 7 on unrelated heirs are almost certainly accurate. The notaries took care to identify precisely the degrees of relationship, and in these cases they noted no kinship ties at all, and none is otherwise apparent. Medieval kinship terminology is a relatively unexplored topic, and wills would be an excellent source for such a study. The rich specificity of kinship labels supports the argument from silence that if an individual is not listed as a relative, it is because no tie existed. Friends were particularly important to single people. Sometimes a testator named a friend of the opposite sex as heir; there were informal liaisons in Genoa, and not all the partners had produced children, or cared to admit that they had.

Of course married men and women had the same set of close relatives that single people had, but they also had each other. Table 8 presents their heirs and includes one new category, the spouse. This table contrasts sharply with Table 7. Almost half the married men and women chose their spouses as heirs. To name a spouse as heir when there were no children meant that the testator was in effect transferring property outside his family. When the testator died, any connection between his family and the spouse's would be severed. Many parents placed conditions in their wills to avoid just this sort of occurrence, and the testator's blood relatives had a right to oppose if not thwart such a choice. Why then did so many men and women make the spouse the

Table 8.   Heirs of childless married men and women.

Heirs	Number of wills of—	
	Men	Women
Spouses	26	26
Siblings	4	6
Neps[a]	8	0
Other relatives[b]	7	10
Pro anima bequests	2	2
Unrelated persons	1	1
No main heirs	9	9

Source: Archivio di Stato di Genova, Cartolari Notarili.
a. Nephews or nieces, or some combination of these.
b. Parents, aunts uncles, or cousins, or various combinations of these.

principal heir? The fact that women did so as frequently as men runs counter to the legal notion that the dowry ought to return to a woman's family if she should die childless. (Married women often possessed only their dowry and a marriage portion, the *antefactum.*) To some extent trust may have been the point here. Many of these people may have retained hopes of having children sometime, and to name the spouse as heir was a provisional act which, after all, could always be changed later. In case any children arrived, the spouse was a good choice anyway, for the property would revert to the children eventually. Age may make the difference here. Young couples (particularly the wives) may have made the spouse the heir more frequently than older childless couples—but this is very speculative. Perhaps, more important, the spouse came to mind first. Even when children existed, men and women often left the usufruct of their goods to the spouse for life, while at the same time naming the children as the actual heirs.[1] A husband may have been concerned about how his wife would support herself after his death, though in this society the wives had less cause to worry about their husbands. While this was the age of the arranged marriage, there are few grounds for believing that the emotional tie was less strong for it. These dry statistics perhaps argue against assuming that these marriages were lived as coldly as they were contracted.

Whatever the motive, clearly the prominence of the spouse as heir meant less for the other categories, in comparison to the choices available to single people. Married people favored charity and friends very rarely, and in the case of siblings and their children, the testator's marriage adversely affected their chances of being heirs whether there were children or not.

Last, let us look at the wills of widows. Unfortunately, the only extant widower's will was partially damaged and is not usable for present purposes. However, the wills of seventeen childless widows do remain. Since death had removed the husband, the types of heirs resemble the choices made by single women. A past barren marriage had little effect on a woman's choice of heir, and the absence of any in-laws as heirs suggests that unmarried widows returned to the circle of their own kin. Two of the widows name siblings as heirs, five name nephews or nieces, three specify *pro anima* bequests, five name a person other than a relative, and two name no main heir.

The wills of childless widows who may have remarried are hard to distinguish from those of women who were never married. Siblings, nephews, and nieces again appear in significant numbers as heirs; so too do friends, mostly males. Widows without children represent less than 3 percent of the Genoese who made wills, so the sample is small. Urban life offered widows the possibility to exist independently and live apart from kin. When a widow had no children, such a life weakened ties to siblings and their children, and made charity and/or friends feasible heirs.

In Genoa the descent group, or the heirs, closely matched the kinship group, or the nuclear family. Marriage united two nuclear families; a spouse served as the focal point of this union. The wills of married people with children clearly demonstrate this matching of kin with heirs: children were the principal heirs in 91 percent of the cases (325 of 358). Childless married persons named some member or members of the kinship group as principal heir in 93 percent of the cases (77 of 83); but if the spouse is not counted as kin, the number falls to 30 percent (25 of 83). Single men and women chose an heir from the kinship group in 61 percent of the cases (65 of 106); the other 39 percent named charity and friends. Only single people diverged from the generally strong tendency to identify kin as the descent group, and even they named kin more often than not. If a Genoese wanted to separate from his kin, a hermitage was a much better option than marriage.

The principal heirs have all now been considered. Other legacies to family and friends are quite numerous and shed light on the Genoese family and its milieu of friends and servants. I will treat separately spouses, the rest of the family, friends, and servants.

Husbands and Wives

Wills provide much insight into the realities of married life. Thousands of dowry contracts appear in the notarial cartularies, but such contracts were very formulaic and usually provided only the actual sum. Some interesting details occasionally emerge about the method of payment. Laura Balletto has studied some cases of divorce, which occurs only rarely in the record, and this line of research is worth further inquiry.[2] No thirteenth-century Leon Battista Alberti wrote about marriage and the family; Jacopo da Voragine's sermons about marriage were particularly prescriptive rather than descriptive, even for sermons. Testaments somewhat paradoxically reveal that death did not end marital responsibilities. This is most apparent in the efforts husbands made to discourage their wives from remarrying. The legacies husbands left their wives and the conditions placed on them are rich in detail, and are quite personal.

Seventy-five men acknowledge in their wills that they had received a specific dowry sum and that their wives are to have or receive this dowry. Some men merely state that their wives are to have the dowry, without mentioning any specific sum. Almost all married men wanted their wives to have their rights (*raciones*), and this probably included dowry rights. A return of the dowry was the minimal legacy a wife had a right to expect. Roman law concerning marriage was quite explicit about dowry rights, and the notarial formularies prove that notaries knew about the legal aspects of marriage. For example, Salatiele's formulary includes sample marriage contracts and dowry agreements, and it refers inquisitive notaries to the law and jurisprudence of Justinian for more details.[3] The dowry formed most, if not all, of a wife's disposable wealth. As we saw in the last chapter, she usually passed the dowry on to her own children or used the money to dower her daughters. The dowry also provided security and a means of support if she were widowed, since children were customarily a man's principal heirs.

In addition to acknowledging that he had received the dowry, a husband would also state in his will that he had made the traditional marriage gift to his wife—the *antefactum*—the local term almost always used for the *donatio propter nuptias*.[4] Salatiele informed historically minded notaries that the term *antefactum* was related to the Lombard *morgencap* and was a gift made in exchange for the dowry.[5] When the specific amount of the dowry is mentioned, usually the *antefactum* also appears as a sum. Similarly, in cases where the dowry is unspecified or rights phrases are vague, the husband leaves the *antefactum* to his wife without stating the value of his gift. Usually the *antefactum* amounted to one-half of the dowry, but it varied from much less than one-half to a gift worth as much as the dowry itself.[6] The smaller the dowry, the more likely it was that the marriage gift was more than half; the reverse is true of the large (over L.200) dowry. Since the marriage contracts almost always state both the dowry and the *antefactum*, the families probably negotiated these variations in the value of the marriage portion. The *antefactum* was not deducted from the dowry legacy; the husband left his wife the dowry and the marriage gift. When a husband mentions the marriage gift as a legacy, it is clear that he had retained the gift in his own hands, even though the property was legally his wife's. So, the wife received more than the dowry, and she profited from the marriage at least in a financial way. Her husband had the use of the dowry for his lifetime. The custom of returning the dowry and the marriage gift may be a businesslike effort to share the profits which, it was hoped, would result fom the husband's wise use of the dowry. Since the size of the marriage gift varied somewhat according to the amount of the dowry, the return of the dowry along with the gift may reflect a shortage of marriageable women in the upper echelons of Genoese society. In this light the gift's return, if it had been withheld, represents a kind of premium. The large number of widows in the city and the age difference between spouses support the idea that women with large dowries were in relatively short supply. In demographic terms there may have been no real shortage of women in the city, but money made some, evidently too few, good catches.

Ansaldo Mallon concluded some marital arrangements in January 1233 that conveniently summarize typical dowry customs among the rich. His niece Giovanna, the daughter of his late brother Nicola, received a dowry of L.200, subject to the condition that if she died without an heir, the dowry would revert to Ansaldo or his heirs.[7] Ten days later Ansaldo found a wife for his own son Ugone. On his son's behalf Ansaldo accepted from Oberto Cavarunco a L.375 dowry for his sister Mabilia, and Ansaldo promised to make a L.100 marriage gift. Somewhat unusually, the next act supplies additional details about this contract. Oberto specifies that he would pay L.175 when the marriage took place, or before, as Ansaldo preferred, L.100 one year after the marriage, and the last L.100 two years later.[8] Many less wealthy families imitated this method of paying the dowry in installments. A lack of liquid assets may have accounted for this, but caution was also a factor. Two years was, after all, a long time; by then a child ought to have confirmed the marriage, or perhaps death ended it. Many families of all social levels did not pay dowries promptly; the groom's family seems to have had little choice but to accept the bride's conditions. If the husband was still a minor, his father had legal custody of the dowry. The father in this case would note in his will that the daughter-in-law had had a certain dowry, to be turned over to the son. Guerrixio de Matalana had allowed his son Moresco the use of his bride's dowry, and he generously allowed his son to keep the profit as well.[9] Dowries also helped to provide a son with a start in life, but in many ways the dowry only amounted to a loan.

The original dowry contract and the often complex payment schedule had some influence on when the husband returned the dowry to his wife. It seems that the original dowry agreement was often lost, or in the years before about 1220 not always recorded, because occasionally the dowry contract directly precedes the husband's will in the cartulary, even when the marriage obviously occurred years earlier. Normally the statement about the dowry and the legacy in the will sufficed for a missing marriage contract. Fulcone de Castello was very specific about his wife's dowry and how it should be returned.[10] He acknowledged that he had had a L.500 dowry from his wife, Aimelina, and he wanted her to have that sum in money or, if this was not possible, in goods. This was a vast sum; Fulcone thought his executors could raise it, but he was not sure. The way the dowry was returned may have depended on the manner in which it had originally been paid. Some husbands assigned land or a house to cover the value of the dowry. Often the dowry "sum" reflected only the agreed-upon value of some sort of payment in kind. Fulcone de Castello also admitted that he had received his wife's *strados*—a sum beyond the original L.500. Exactly where a *strados* came from is not always clear. The few times the word is used indicate that it may refer to inheritances which the wife received from her own family, or it may refer to an augmentation of the dowry made before marriage. Aimelina's *strados* consisted of two shares of a road toll (*cabella in pedagio*) which had been purchased from the Marchese di Monferrato. Fulcone had made a marriage gift worth L.100, and he wanted his wife to have some land and a house in Alexana to cover this sum and L.100 more, which was to be applied to the L.500 dowry. Probably this land formed part of the original dowry, since it would have been customary for Fulcone to give it back to his wife as a marriage gift. Here again, we see the fictitious nature of the marriage gift, for Fulcone admitted that he still owed his wife the gift. People of more modest means who had only to worry about a few lire often provided the same level of detail in the wills. Some husbands made a complete list of all the household goods which they had either purchased with the dowry or had received in kind.

A wife had a right to her dowry, but beyond this there was a hazy area of legacies, some to which the wife had a clear right, others that went beyond the minimum and represented the husband's voluntary bequest. Legally, a wife had a right to her *parapherna*—personal property brought along with her dowry.[11] For example, almost every husband left his wife her clothes. A wife brought clothes when she moved into her husband's house; no one would contest her right to this personal property. Then why did so many husbands bother to make this bequest? The clothes legacy may be only a legal formula; the frequency of its use implies as much. If the husband had spent money over the years clothing his wife, he may have thought that the clothes were his to leave. As we shall see, the Genoese thought about their clothes a great deal and valued them highly. Garments were often very expensive; even a shirt cost a lira, a cap ten or fifteen solidi. It seems that a wife had a right to her clothes, that they too were part of the minimal bequest. Michele da Mezzano indicated this when he insisted that his wife should have nothing *except* her clothes.[12]

Husbands also often left their wives the *massaricia,* a difficult word to translate. There are other similar words, most commonly *mobilia,* which mean movables or household possessions. Just what household items the *massaricia* included is not clear. Clothes and utensils were listed separately, and the furniture, except for the bed, usually went with the house. The wills rarely mention jewelry; perhaps it and other types of personal property made up the *massaricia.* Utensils were a less frequent but important legacy. Some husbands listed the utensils their wives were to have; others just left them all the utensils. (Tools were another matter.) The most important and valuable utensil was a copper or iron cooking pot. Pots were relatively expensive, hard to make properly, and vital to the kitchen. Whether upper-class women were personally familiar with their pots is another matter. These kitchen utensils formed a part of a husband's bequest to his wife, and hence were an additional way to tie the wife to the household, and the children. Husbands left the pots to their wives because they wanted them to stay put. Another common bequest, the bed, reveals this desire even more clearly.

In Chapter 5 the bed will figure as a charitable donation to hospitals. More often a husband left his bed, including mattress, sheets, covers, pillows, pillow cases, boards, and tripods, to his wife. The bed had a kind of metaphorical meaning; in this case it symbolized marriage. Giacomo da Lucca clearly articulated this when he left his wife, Lencia, usufruct of all his goods, subject to the condition that "she should have chastely kept my bed."[13] Male testators were preoccupied with the thought of a wife's remarriage. The most common condition attached to a wife's legacy was that she not remarry, that she be "a good wife without a husband," that she live well and chastely. This condition, set exclusively by men, provides a clear way to separate the mandatory bequests from those over which the husband had some control, unlike the dowry, which he had to return without any conditions.

Husbands tried to provide incentives for their wives to remain widows. Gandulfo the tailor offered his wife, Richelda, a stark choice. If she stayed without a man and did not remarry, she was to be his principal heir. If she married, she was to receive only her dowry, marriage gift, and a rabbit fur cloak lined with scarlet; someone else would be the main heir.[14] Few husbands were so blatant, but most obviously tried to forestall a remarriage. While quick to enter second marriages themselves, men did not want their wives to do so. Guglielmo Scarsaria dictated a condition like this to the notary Giovanni Scriba: "If my wife wants to fly off to a second marriage . . ."[15] The notary used the verb *convolare;* Guglielmo must have employed some dialect verb which also implied hasty flight and a departure from the nest. A variety of personal reasons may explain this implacable male attitude. The church permitted second marriages but did not encourage them. Even on a religious level, women bore the brunt of efforts to discourage remarriage. We cannot fathom the personal or religious motives that prompted individual men to think as they did. However, their main motive seems to have been a desire to protect their children.

A parent's remarriage complicated a child's life. Not all medieval children could hope to end up like Cinderella. Men tried to preserve the integrity of the household in order to provide a safe nest for the young. Most of the conditions placed upon women had this goal. Jacopo de Premontorio wanted his wife, Amanda, to be the lady *(domina)* of his goods and children, and have with their wives and families usufruct of his goods for life.[16] Amanda was not to go to a convent or any other place; if she dedicated herself to religion or married, she would inherit only her dowry, rights, and marriage gift. Thus far Jacopo's conditions are fairly standard, though not many husbands feared the convent as much as a second husband. Even a religious life deprived the household of its new leader, and this is what it had in common with remarriage. Jacopo added some more details to his will which clearly demonstrate the kind of role his wife was to play as *domina*. If the children caused any difficulties, he gave his wife the right to expel them from the house, provided she had not remarried. Evidently his sons, adults with wives of their own, still required an authoritative hand. Most stipulations were meant to influence wives not to remarry by offering this type of two-tier legacy. Material rewards encouraged a woman to remain a widow and head of the household. The number of widows in the city and their high percentage among all female testators suggest that the men were fairly successful.

There may have been plenty of good reasons for a Genoese woman to reject a second marriage, but without the material incentive some women may not have been able to survive without one. If she married, the only thing the wife of Gandulfo the tailor would inherit, beyond her rights, was a rabbit fur cloak. While this cloak may not have amounted to much, it was a voluntary bequest and not subject to any conditions. Some husbands willed their wives money or goods whether they remarried or not. Thus even the smallest legacy which the wife would inherit even if she remarried was often more than the legal minimum. How much more than the minimum depended on the private course individual marriages followed. Even a high-minded Genoese man, who justified his position on remarriage by pointing to the often sorry status of stepchildren, must have wondered whether his wife would share this view. Nevertheless, only one man, Oberto Malocello, specifically left his wife as lady of the household and administrator of his goods whether she remarried or not.[17] Significantly, she was his second wife. I shall look again at remarriage, but first the wife's legacy to her husband ought to be considered.

The great difference here is that wives were not obliged to leave their husbands anything at all. There may, however, be one exception to this general rule. The will of Alda, the daughter of the late Raimundo da Sori, contains a unique reference to a *capitula*, or law, which concerned a husband's right to a deceased wife's *antefactum (capitulus de uxoribus premortuis occasione antefacti)*.[18] Just as a dowry returned to her family when a wife died, the marriage gift returned to the husband if his wife predeceased him. The wife was obligated to return the marriage gift to her husband, not his family. Alda's own will confirms this interpretation; she waived any rights she had to her mother's *antefactum*, and we know that her mother was a widow. There are some reasons for not accepting this one mandatory legacy at face value. The contemporary Genoese legal code is lost, so we cannot know the law's date or for that matter exactly what it said. Only one other wife's will mentions the marriage gift as somehow belonging to the husband, but the details are contradictory. In 1197 a woman named Sora left her husband, Trencherio, L.100, and this legacy seems to have been a voluntary bequest.[19] Sora wished her husband to have use of another L.96 of her patrimony, which she said was her marriage gift. After his death L.50 would revert to Sora's sister, and L.46 was earmarked to benefit Trencherio's soul. The husband had some right, but perhaps not outright ownership, to the marriage gift. The law about marriage gifts may date from the twenty years between these two wills. Even so, none of the wills after 1217 mentions the husband's rights to the *antefactum*, and some wives left their husbands only a token bequest or nothing at all. These wills suggest that the law may have applied only in certain circumstances, or that it quickly fell into disuse. Apart from Alda's will, all the other wills of married women suggest not the slightest obligation to leave the husband anything. As I have already noted, married women with or without children frequently named the husband as principal heir or gave him usufruct for life, and they never appointed guardians for the children. If a married woman had children, the dowry did not return to her family; her own children inherited it. Even if the marriage gift returned to the husband, the wife's family could rest assured that their blood would eventually inherit it anyway. One might conclude that the law was designed to settle the issue of who inherited the marriage gift if there were no children. But Alda had chidren. To sum up this rather tortured argument, the husband had some right to his wife's marriage gift if he outlived her. In practice this right was largely irrelevant. Women's wills support this conclusion, and in fact point to no other.

There was no legal minimum bequest to a husband. His legacy might range from nothing to everything. Giacoma, the wife of Oberto the shoemaker, left her husband nothing but allowed that he might receive the necessities from her estate if he came to poverty.[20] Contessa granted her husband food and clothing, but she wanted him to inherit nothing else.[21] Both of these women had children. Simona, who identified herself as the daughter of

Martino da San Giorgio, was childless, and her will demonstrates the peripheral role her husband had in her life.[22] Simona left her sister Giovanna L.100 for her dowry. If she died without an heir, their brothers would inherit. Simona left these brothers L.50, and they were to succeed each other. The L.100 was to be in her father's custody until Giovanna married, and he was permitted to use the money in the meantime if he were in need. Finally, at the end of the will, Simona left her husband L.5. Given the range and size of her other bequests, her husband's legacy was derisory. Not all wives treated their husbands this way, but if they wanted to they could. Women left their husbands a wide variety of bequests, but unlike their mates they never imposed any conditions. Not one wife established the kind of two-tier inheritance so common in husbands' wills. No wife provided any incentive for a husband to remain a widower; no wife even mentioned the subject of remarriage. (No wife left the husband the bed either.) Women did not exercise any control over their husbands in this matter. Since remarriage affected children and family wealth, if a husband remarried again presumably the effect was less serious than when a widow remarried. Certainly society placed fewer obstacles in general in a man's path.

In the previous chapter I observed that many Genoese parents did not make married daughters their heirs. They knew that if their daughters produced legitimate heirs, the dowry would eventually find its way to blood relatives. A daughter's death was a sad event; the historian is in no position to calculate the true meaning of this loss. And yet in such a death there was also an element of bad luck. Any hopes that a daughter might live to administer a husband's estate were dashed. The grandchildren were now in the hands of a comparative stranger, whose probable remarriage would have unknown consequences for them. It is easy to see why his first wife's family would not favor his remarriage, though they could do little about it. In general, Genoese wives ignored the problem, and in this way they differed remarkably from their husbands.

Some of the wills of people who were married twice reveal the pressures and complexities that remarriage introduced. Oberto Lomellino, a prominent and wealthy Genoese, made his will on June 8, 1252.[23] He was married to Simona Grilla, who had herself been married to the late Daniele Doria. Simona had two children by her previous husband and none with Oberto. This will provides a means of testing how the second marriage affected Simona's standing, and to what extent the Doria and Grillo families had any role to play in protecting her position. As far as Oberto Lomellino was concerned, except for his two stepsons, the Doria family did not exist. No Doria received any legacy, witnessed the will, or administered the estate. Oberto willed the two stepsons L.50 each, to be invested in Sardinia in livestock, with the counsel of two Grillo in-laws. Simona had brought a L.500 dowry to the marriage; L.50 to her sons was not much. The Grillo family assumed the role of protecting Simona and her children. Simona's father, Federigo Grillo, was still alive, as were at least two of her brothers. Two members of her family witnessed the will, and, more important, the notary Bartolomeo Fornari noted that he had made three copies of the testament, for Amico Grillo, Federigo Grillo, and Simone Spinola, the husband of Oberto's sister Adalasia. The Grillo family managed to extract some interesting legacies from the childless Oberto. Oberto left his father-in-law his house for a price of L.300 (surely a bargain), but he wanted his wife to have an apartment there as long as she lived without a husband. Oberto named his wife as one of the distributors of his charitable bequests. He left most of his estate to Lomellini, but he was generous to his wife and in-laws. This remarriage benefited Simona and her children. Daniele Doria need not have feared for the safety of his wife and sons. Two important facts may have determined this marriage's apparently mutually satisfactory outcome. First, the Grillo family actively involved itself in Oberto's life and protected Simona's interests. And second, Oberto and Simona had no children. This may have disappointed the Grillo family too, yet they still profited from the marriage. There is a final perspective on Oberto's will—that of Simone Spinola. Simone's marriage placed him in the enviable position of having a childless, rich brother-in-law. Simone was an executor of Oberto's will, had a copy of it, and also served as one of the charity distributors. Oberto left his nephew Enrigeto, Simone's son, all rights to a joint business venture. Simone lived in one of Oberto's houses, which Oberto left to Adalasia. The Spinola and Grillo families derived benefits from their marriage connections to Oberto Lomellino. Any legacy to a spouse must be placed in this wider context, for the marriage might ultimately benefit a family in unanticipated if not unhoped-for ways.

In contrast to Oberto Lomellino's testament, Giovanni Marzoco's will created a tangled mess.[24] In all fairness, though, Giovanni died before a notary could be summoned, and the consuls of the parish of Molassana had to make some sense out of the testimony of witnesses who offered confused and contradictory accounts of what Giovanni had said on his deathbed. The witnesses agreed that Giovanni had two sets of children—two sons and some daughters by his first wife, and other children by his current wife, Diana. There was also general agreement on certain details. Giovanni had left the sons by his first marriage some land and a house, and the daughters another parcel of land. He had left other lands to his second set of children and granted his wife her rights, also naming her as guardian. All the rest of his goods were bequeathed to his children, presumably both sets. A second witness agreed with all this but said he did not know whether Diana ought to have her rights from the part of the estate her children inherited or from the first wife's patrimony. (As we shall see, this was the key issue.) The third witness agreed with the first, except he did not know who was to inherit the first wife's right, and he did not know who were the principal heirs. (What a useful witness!) The last three witnesses agreed with the first, and they mirrored his uncertainty about how the testator intended to satisfy the claims. This court case at least offers a favorable comment on notarial services, since no properly drawn will would have been so muddled. Giovanni's posthumous troubles resulted because in wishing all his children to be his heirs, he had forgotten about his first wife's patrimony. The second witness raised the issue of Diana's rights: was she to receive her rights from the part of the estate her children inherited or from the entire estate before any division? The first method of payment would have diminished her own children's share, but, as the second witness observed, the second implied that Diana would get some part, however small, of the neglected first wife's patrimony, and there was something troubling to contemporary sentiment about that. As a rule, the executors were supposed to return the dowry before the principal heirs divided up the rest of the goods. Most of the witnesses recognized this; hence the confusion. If Giovanni had mentioned his first wife's rights, he would have solved part of the problem. Usually a parent with two sets of children was careful to distinguish their rights; Giovanni's circumstances made this hard to do. The witnesses did not try to obscure these difficulties, and their own words illustrate a level of understanding of a wife's rights. The interesting questions the witnesses raised support this extended treatment of remarriage and its consequences.

A woman with two sets of children, and hence at least sequentially two husbands, was in a different position. Her first husband's will, presumably benefiting his children, would give the wife more leeway in her own bequests. In the same way that a wife had almost no obligation to leave her husband anything, her material responsibility to her first set of children was small if she produced another set. Giovanna, the wife of Martino da Recco, had been married to the late Bonafida.[25] She had a son named Jacobino by her first marriage, to whom she left L.7 *iure testamenti*, with which he was supposed to be content. She named as principal heirs her present husband and the children she had had by him. In this context *iure testamenti* meant *falcidia*—the minimal share (perhaps one-quarter) to which her son was legally entitled. Other women with two sets of heirs similarly left the first group only *falcidia* bequests. Given the widespread pattern of conditional bequests noted earlier, these remarried women had presumably forfeited a part, or perhaps all, of what they had inherited from the first husband. As their husbands had anticipated, the wife's remarriage was not advantageous for the children. In some respects this was a self-fulfilling prophecy since by penalizing the wife, the husband virtually guaranteed that his own children would get only minimal inheritances. He had diminished his wife's wealth, and her current husband could not be blamed for putting his own children first.

To conclude this analysis of husbands and wives, let us turn to a few rare marriages for which the wills of both spouses survive. There are some cases of wills made by a husband and wife on the same day. These are not very informative because they seem to represent some sort of tacit deal. These wills are brief and reciprocal: the husband makes his wife the heir and vice versa. Besides the conventional nature of these paired wills, the view of the family they offer is limited to one day. Of more importance are those

wills made by a husband and wife in different years. These surviving wills were discovered fortuitously, and they allow a rare
glimpse of family life over time. Ansaldo Conte, probably preparing for a commercial voyage, made a will on October 15, 1222,
written down by the notary Maestro Salmone. He was still alive
when his wife, Berta, had the notary Guido de San Ambrogio
draw up a will on August 21, 1233.[26] (This is yet another sign that
to draw up a will did not necessarily mark one for imminent
extinction.) In 1222 the couple had no children together, although
Berta had a daughter named Adalasia by a previous marriage. By
1233 the couple still had had no children, but Adalasia was still
alive. Like many other childless husbands, Ansaldo wished his
wife to distribute the rest of his goods for his soul. He gave her
usufruct of these goods for life but left his stepdaughter nothing.
Eleven years later Berta named her daughter as heir, and she
allowed her husband to retain her money for one year. There is
a kind of static quality to this family's bequests. In 1222 Ansaldo
left L.5 for his soul, and in 1233 Berta left the same. The fact
that Berta had a child and Ansaldo did not is the main difference.

The other such pair of wills demonstrates more change. Rogerio
de Bruscata made his will on May 25, 1231.[27] He was primarily
concerned with listing in his will all the people who owed him
money. He had no children, and he left the rest of the goods to
his wife, Adalasia. After her death he wanted his estate to be
distributed for his soul and his parents'. Also Jacoba, the daughter
of the late Nicola, was to receive 100 solidi; Rogerio's brother-in-
law Oberto de Resta was in charge of distributing all this charity.
Rogerio excluded his wife's dowry and marriage gift from this
charitable bequest, and hence she could do what she wanted with
her own property. When Adalasia made her will on August 1,
1236, with the notary Palodino de Sexto, she was a childless widow.[28]
Her husband had selected San Andrea de Sestri as his burial site,
and so did she. Adalasia left her brother Oberto L.8 and a mantle,
and she left two nieces a lira apiece. For her soul Adalasia left L.5
(100 solidi) to a Donna Jacopa Mallon, who was certainly the same
Jacopa to whom Rogerio had left the same sum. Lastly Adalasia
left the rest of her goods in the custody of Oberto and two others
so they would be able to pay her husband's legacies and give charity
for her soul as they saw best. Adalasia did exactly what Rogerio

wanted her to do. She scrupulously followed the conditions set forth in his will. With her death a family ceased to exist, but a responsibility was faithfully discharged.

Marriage, like the family itself, was not a timeless institution. A will suggests this perspective, but experience confirms it. As in the case of children, circumstances did not always neatly fit preconceived notions about the proper roles husbands and wives ought to assume. Husbands tried to use material incentives to persuade their wives not to remarry; they were not always successful, but the high number of widows in the city testifies to some measurable influence. There was a countervailing pressure at work here, since sometimes the wife's family might push her into a second marriage for reasons of their own. The husband was obligated to return a dowry to his wife, and he could not ignore her legitimate rights, including rights to such diverse items as clothes and pots.

The male perspective on marriage seems to have concentrated on the children. Their interest was best served by a mother and his own male relatives, not by a second husband. When there were no children, remarriage was not an issue, and male strictures on this subject vanished. Wives, by contrast, had virtually no obligations to their husbands. It was taken for granted that the husband might very well remarry, and that in any case the maternal relatives would look out for the children. There was not the same level of concern that a man's remarriage was not in the children's best interests. Remarriage complicated family life and inheritances, but it was in the nature of things for one spouse to outlive the other; women, although less likely to remarry, were more likely to outlive their spouses. Other considerations naturally affected a decision to remarry. A man might hope for more children—always a desirable hedge against mortality rates among the young—but he may also have needed a woman to take charge of his household. The widows with children do not seem as a group to have been eager to produce more children, nor do they seem to have been particularly willing to exchange their relative independence for a new husband.

All generalizations about remarriage must take into account the age difference between spouses, and the questions of whether there were children or not and which partner survived to be the heir of the other. These were the realities of married life—perhaps not the whole story, but the kind of facts on which documents shed some light. The wills indicate that there was a wide variety of families (big, small, scattered, concentrated), and the family situation helped determine, at least in part, the way in which individual couples had to leave their estates.

We have thus considered the nearest kin—husband, wife, children. Other family members have already appeared as principal heirs of childless adults. It is now time to place the nuclear family, from the testator's point of view, in the larger family context.

The Rest of the Family

In a city that had its share of immigrants, there were naturally some Genoese who appeared to be without any family at all, and also a few foreigners who had no relatives in the city. I will examine these people in the next section on patrons and friends. The rest of the Genoese, the great majority, had a family that varied in size according to the number of siblings and their children. These relatives were the *propinqui*, the *consanguini*, the blood relatives. The parents' siblings and their children, the uncles and aunts and cousins, were also blood relatives, but for a variety of reasons these people were not as important as the nearest kin. Younger testators were more likely to have aunts and uncles, but not many married individuals with children actually had living aunts and uncles, or for that matter living parents. Some people turned to the more extended familial group to serve as the nearest kin, though only as a last resort. In-laws were another set of relatives for those who needed them. The age of the testator also had something to do with the number of relatives he had. Marriage made a person somewhat less likely to rely on this more extended group of relatives, or even mention them. This last point raises difficult questions: what relatives do the wills list, and why? No one left something to every living relative, so no will provides a complete catalogue of living relatives. These bequests to the rest of the family were voluntary and therefore random. We can learn much about a particular individual by examining his bequests to family members. As a collectivity the testators merely provide thousands of random legacies which benefited some of their relatives. The few wills that survive cannot reconstruct family membership in any complete way. However, a few important conclusions emerge from this apparently intractable mass of random and incomplete data.

Family terminology itself supplies information about family life and the linguistic problems notaries faced. *Consanguinus,* or *consanguina,* was always used to refer to a blood relative, but the word practically became a synonym for cousin. The notaries did not know any special word for cousin, and other ways to identify cousins were too wordy. The classical word for blood relative, *cognatus,* had experienced an interesting change in meaning and in the Genoese cartularies almost always meant "related by marriage." *Affinatus,* the classical word for in-law, was never used, although the notaries correctly used other classical words for specific in-laws: *gener* (son-in-law), *nurus* (daughter-in-law), *socer* (father-in-law), *socrua* (mother-in-law). *Cognatus* was usually reserved for brothers- and sisters-in-law or even more tenuous relationships. There was a rich variety of Latin words to identify blood relatives, most of which had exact parallels in contemporary dialect, and in modern Italian. Two important exceptions are worth noting. One we have already seen—the confusing use of the same words *nepos* and *neptis* to describe a nephew or grandson and a niece or granddaughter, respectively. The notaries usually surmounted this difficulty by confining *nepos* to nephew unless otherwise stated, and qualifying the use of the term when it referred to a grandson. Modern Italian (*nipote*) perpetuates this ambiguity, although classical Latin used these words only to mean grandchildren. The will's context almost always clarifies the particular usage. The other exception has to do with uncles and aunts. The notaries preserved the classical distinction between paternal and maternal uncles and aunts: *amita* (paternal aunt), *matertera,* a rare usage (maternal aunt), *patruus* (paternal uncle), *avunculus* (maternal uncle). The Lombard word *barbanus,* properly latinized, almost completely replaced the classical word for paternal uncle in Genoa.[29]

In this case the different terms point to an important distinction. The paternal uncles and aunts were generally more involved in a testator's life as heirs or executors than their maternal counterparts. Genoese families were extended bilaterally, and a person recognized relatives on both his father's and mother's sides. But this was also a patrilineal society, and the testators tended to look to their father's relatives first, though as we have seen the maternal relatives stepped in when paternal relatives did not exist or re-marriage complicated family life. The terminology of uncles and aunts illustrates these different functions by making clear that contemporaries knew very well that there were two types of aunts and uncles. The paternal uncles were especially active in the lives of unmarried nephews and nieces. Alda, the daughter of the late Guglielmo Toxico, was a single woman, and she noted in her will that all her goods amounted to L.250.[30] The money had come to Alda when she inherited some of her father's goods and her moth-er's *antefactum,* and when her paternal uncles gave or bequeathed her something. Alda left L.50 to her mother and brothers, and the rest to her paternal uncles. She even agreed not to change her testament unless her uncles, or most of them, gave her per-mission to alter it.

Members of the clergy also found themselves involved in family life, principally as uncles. The original conditions in the parents' wills made this involvement inescapable, because a priest was ex-pected to make his siblings' children his own heirs. The priest Alberto of San Lorenzo left his lands to his nephews and nieces, children of his two brothers and one sister. He quite explicitly states that they should inherit *in stirpe,* by the three branches, and not by head.[31] His lands were divided into three portions, which the three sets of nephews and nieces had to share according to their numbers. Alberto, of course, acted as both a paternal and a maternal uncle. Many individuals found themselves in this posi-tion, so the distinction should not be overdrawn. The paternal aunts often served as distributors of charity and themselves re-ceived honorary bequests. Aunts and uncles may often have been godparents, a situation which would account for their increased responsibility.

Besides in-laws and blood relatives, there are two other kinds of family ties and hence terminologies. Remarriage, common enough in Genoa, created new relationships which required words to describe them. A stepson was not the same as a son. The classical word for a stepson or stepdaughter, *privignus* or *privigna,* was rarely employed. Instead a latinized form of the colloquial *filiastrus* was quite common. The notaries also used special words for step-parents. Lastly, godparenthood required a separate group of words to denote this spiritual relationship. One person could be at the same time a daughter, daughter-in-law, stepdaughter, and god-daughter. Natural children also existed in the background. Of course medieval society did not have a monopoly on these kinds of distinctions. Let us look at the types of relationships individual testators thought were the most important.

Since this analysis of heirs depends so much on individual pref-erences, a few particular wills should give some sense of how the family circle varied. At the risk of repetition, it should be em-phasized that the principal heirs have already been considered. The heirs under review here were the beneficiaries of specific voluntary bequests. Giovanni da Voltaggio left, in this order, these bequests to family members: to his mother, Sofia, L.250; to his sister Giovanna L.100 and his sister Aidela L.50; and to his brother Guglielmo L.50.[32] When the order followed this pattern of steadily decreasing legacies, the obvious inference is that these people were important to Giovanni and thus came to mind in direct relation to how much he left them. Giovanni had a father-in-law, but since he does not mention any wife or children, he may have been a widower. The order is typical in another way; if parents were alive they were usually mentioned first. Female relatives were more likely to benefit from these voluntary bequests and to receive the largest sums. Giovanni's brother Guglielmo came last and received a small bequest. Since sisters and mothers were rarely the principal heirs, male testators in particular tried to compensate for this by leaving the female relatives lump sums. Giovanni's brother Gug-lielmo was probably wealthy anyway, and the future of his female relatives might have appeared comparatively insecure.

An average woman's voluntary bequests to family members sup-port these conclusions. Adalasia, the sister of Tebaldo de Stacione, a widow with children, left these bequests: to her sister Marina L.50; to her brother Tebaldo L.40; to her niece Jacobina L.25 and her niece Adalasia L.10; to her brother Giovanni L.30; and to her nephew Niccoloso L.20.[33] Here the legacies do not diminish in order. If they are rearranged so that they do, these legacies also demonstrate that siblings generally inherited the most. (In this case the parents had evidently died.) Anything left to a sibling would eventually revert to nephews and nieces, but testators com-monly left this next generation individual bequests. Adalasia well represents female testators because she was not inclined to leave her female relatives more money. Her daughter was her principal heir; as we have seen, women did not discriminate against other women when it came to the major legacies. But for these smaller voluntary bequests, women did not so much ignore their other female relatives as place them on basically equal footing with male relatives. Men, however, were more disposed to take care of their female relations. Since men lived in a society where women endured material disadvantages, the fact that they attempted to compensate for inequities is worth noting. As I shall discuss shortly, men and women also differed in making legacies to friends and servants.

The two wills just cited fairly represent the kinds of choices men and women made. Some wills are more complex than these, and a few also provide some signs that the voluntary bequests, while still freely made, matched specific people with particular gifts, usually land. In other words, who the heir was determined what he received, as well as how much. Avegnata's will of 1244 shows this very clearly.[34]

Relationship to Avegnata	Bequest
My sister Rosa	all land of our mother
My cousin Cardiono	all land of my father, Enrico
My brothers Andriolo and Benvenuto	half of various lands
My brother-in-law Conte	the other half of these lands
My sister Rosa	a house
My brothers	a stole in Conte's house and the biggest chest
My sister	another chest, my bed, all my debts
My brother-in-law	half the rest of my lands, but he must pay debts to the commune and the cost of burial
My brothers	are to be my principal heirs

These legacies, listed as they appear in the will, are all in kind, except the debts. They do not differ substantially from cash legacies, many of which had to be settled in kind. Most of Avegnata's wealth was tied up in land. He left his sister Rosa those lands that came to him from their mother. This was a typical inheritance pattern, to pass on to sisters or daughters property inherited from other female relatives. Neither the law nor any conditions in his mother's will required Avegnata to act this way, so the bequest, however customary, was still voluntary. He identified Cardiono as a *consanguinus,* a cousin, probably a son of one of Enrico's brothers. The land left to Cardiono was itself a paternal inheritance, and Andriolo and Benvenuto already possessed shares of this land. The voluntary nature of these bequests is highlighted by the fact that Avegnata did not leave this property to his brothers, who might seem the logical choice, especially since he himself had no children. The Genoese drew no real distinction between wealth they inherited and wealth acquired during their lifetime. They were not obligated to keep the first sort within the family, unless they died without an heir. No one was able to attach any conditions to the second type, but as Avegnata's will indicates, it too was likely to remain within the family. He also exhibits a comparatively rare attachment to his brother-in-law by leaving him a fair amount of property, although Conte's inheritance was encumbered with the responsibility of paying Avegnata's debts and burying him.

There is not much more to say about these specific voluntary bequests to family members. Such legacies were commonplace and tell us something about individual families. In aggregate they reveal the significance of paternal uncles and aunts and the way in which men tried to take care of their female relatives. Otherwise these bequests were voluntary and, since many of them were made on the deathbed, spontaneous signs of affection. The wills were legal documents, and in the process of recreating the atmosphere of the original oral declaration one must not neglect the intense emotionalism of the event, even if it cannot be measured.

Friends

Thus far we have followed a continuum of legacies which were increasingly less obligatory. The kinds of legacies just discussed enabled the testator to put a personal stamp on his will. Friendship is the most voluntary and individualistic of all relationships—certainly more so than medieval marriage. A legacy to a friend was a sign of esteem; no law required it. These legacies diminished the total amount of wealth that went to the family or to help save the testator's soul. The capacity to put the family and the next world aside for even a moment, and do something not required and without any future profit for oneself, should not obscure the fact that friendship too has an element of self-interest. Above all, the will had to satisfy the testator. It probably reconciled few to death, but a completed will might at least content a person. Many Genoese were unwilling to leave their friends out of the will. Tradition may account for legacies to friends, in the sense that most people thought that they should leave something to their friends, as they themselves may have benefited from similar gifts. A legacy to a friend might also be the final act of friendship. But even if the spontaneity of friendship is seen as deliberate and traditional, no other relationship, certainly not the business ones, offered a person such a voluntary tie. Other ties were impossible or extremely difficult to sever, and had either been imposed or were unavoidable.

While legacies to friends appear to have been quite voluntary, friendship sprung up within the occupation or neighborhood. What a person did for a living often determined where he lived. Attending the local parish church or the guild, and participating in trade and politics, brought people into contact with each other and thus formed a pool of potential friends. A person might step out of these familiar confines to find a friend anywhere. (Marco Polo found a friend and collaborator in a Genoese prison.) The routine of daily living introduced persons who had similar backgrounds and interests. So the rhythm of a person's life largely determined his acquaintances and potential friends, and these facts, along with sheer emotional need, necessarily affected what I have called the voluntary nature of friendship. The wish to single out some acquaintances for special favor was, compared to all the other demands on a testator's time and purse, voluntary. In this way legacies to friends were much like friendship itself, and both were very important.

The terminology of friendship poses a few problems. The actual word for friend, *amicus,* was only rarely used in wills. Still, legacies to friends are not hard to isolate. Friends were not relatives, and thus most of the individuals mentioned in wills are eliminated. Where no apparent familial tie exists between two persons, and the legacy is a small one, one can assume that the tie was friendship. The Genoese also found their friends almost exclusively among members of their own sex. This section on friends is very conservative and probably leaves out more than it considers, but this approach is necessary for accuracy. Friends named as executors are treated in Chapter 7.

Small sums of money or articles of clothing were the most common kinds of legacies to friends. Berta de Manica left three solidi to her neighbor *(vicina)* Romana and named two others as recipients of small bequests.[35] These neighbors were her friends, and they were all women. Men followed the same pattern, though they were less likely to mention friends in a will. Single women, single men, married women, and married men were in this order most likely to leave a friend a bequest. (The presence of children created a need for tutors, which in turn often resulted in the naming of friends in the will, though not as heirs. Parenthood per se does not seem to have affected the likelihood of a person's naming friends as heirs). A married couple did not necessarily have friends in common; Baldoino de Caprili wanted his wife to marry off their daughters with the counsel of "my friends and hers."[36]

Why should women have been more inclined than men to leave their friends something? Single women, whether widowed or never married, had only a small scope for personal activity. All sorts of male relatives had claims or suggestions to make. Women who worked at a craft or were servants had friends of their own and also a chance to break through the net of compulsory associations. For these reasons friendship may have been more important to women, and the legacy to a friend was a clear sign of this importance. Alternatively, there may be a technical explanation. That is, tutors were not allowed to benefit from the estate. Since some men may have been unable to find reliable tutors except among their closest friends, these friends would have been ineligible to receive bequests. But even allowing for this factor, more women took note of their friends.

As an example of a single woman's reliance on friends, there is the case of Mabilia, who identified herself as living with Oberto the furrier.[37] She does not seem to have been a domestic servant; she probably worked in his shop. Mabilia was childless and unmarried, and her total wealth amounted to sixteen lire, of which she left ten lire for her burial, masses, and charity. Evidently

Mabilia had no living relatives she cared to name, and there is no sign that she was related to Oberto. The rest of her bequests all benefited women. She left twenty solidi and a bedspread to Gilia, the daughter of Adalasia, the wife of Oberto. This was an interesting way to identify her; it indicates either that Gilia's being Adalasia's daughter was more important to Mabilia than her being Oberto's, or that he was not the father. Oberto himself received nothing in the will. Adalasia was named one of the distributors of charity but was not an heir either. It is tempting to think of Gilia as Mabilia's contemporary and friend. The other five women who inherited small gifts seem to have been Mabilia's friends. A daughter and a female servant of Bernardo Bruno got twenty and ten solidi, respectively, and a woman who may have been a slave inherited another twenty solidi. Two other women, known only by their first names, round out Mabilia's legacies. Mabilia may have immigrated to Genoa some time earlier, or she may herself have been a former slave, which would account for the lack of relatives. A person in her circumstances would have relied on friends; evidently Mabilia found most of them among her fellow workers.

Married women with children also remembered their friends, and these legacies often took the form of clothing. Bellenda, the wife of Vassallo the dyer, left three friends cloaks, stoles, shifts, cloths, and even shoes.[38] Men, while very much aware of their wives' clothes, curiously neglected to speak of their own. A handful of men left their clothing for charity, yet inexplicably only one distributed his clothing among friends, as women so often did. The exception was the bachelor notary Giovanni Scriba, who gave relatives, servants, and friends various items of his clothing.[39] This is an odd difference between women and men regarding their clothing, especially since clothing was so expensive. What did men do with their clothes? Men left their friends cash when they left them anything at all. Women may have simply been short of cash, and so used clothing to compensate for this. Male relatives may have more readily parted with the deceased's clothing than her money.

One other aspect of these legacies to friends requires some explanation. Often these legacies were included in the general list of *pro anima* bequests. Here again women did this more often than men. Legacies of clothing to friends were sometimes mixed together with charitable donations. Clothing itself suggests another connection to charity, because usually women gave their clothing for spiritual purposes. Many people, and in particular a few notaries, included all sorts of bequests in the *pro anima* legacies. Some of these bequests had little if anything to do with charity. Friends seem to be the clearest example of this tendency to dilute the spiritual character of charity. Before concluding that some individuals abused the idea of charity by trying to kill two birds with one stone, one must consider the possibility that in fact friends may have been considered an acceptable charity, and that gifts to them would indeed benefit the soul. If friends were at the same time paupers, the connection is clear. This, however, is not a very plausible answer. Bequests to friends were freely given, and this may have been what such bequests had in common with either spiritual or social charity. To give away property when there was no obligation to do so may have passed for a kind of charity. How the church viewed all this is another matter. There is a final possible explanation. Legacies to friends, to the extent that they consumed money and goods, diminished the testator's patrimony and hence cost the heirs something. Charity had the same effect but was probably difficult to oppose or cheat. If a person included legacies to friends in the charitable list, the heirs may have been more easily reconciled to seeing wealth leave the family. Also, charity often had its own distributors, who were less significant than the executors of the estate. Women in particular tended to nominate other women to disburse the charity, and this kind of arrangement may have insured that friends would receive their legacies.[40] These explanations for why bequests to friends and actual charitable bequests were mixed together may make the Genoese seem too devious. However, one sees time and again that women had a keen sense for any loophole in Genoese society that would give them some scope for personal choice. However much the church encouraged people to make wills and leave something for their souls, it would not have viewed with equanimity the tendency to equate friends with charity. As we shall see, legacies to servants raise the same issues.

Servants

One hundred and three Genoese, roughly one in six testators (40 men and 63 women), left something to a servant. Some Genoese had more than one servant, so these people had together 146 servants—140 women and six men. An analysis of just what these servants did partially explains this incredible disparity. A variety of terms described servants. The words *serviciale, serviens,* and the classical *pediseca* refer to domestic servants, who evidently lived for the most part with their masters. Wet nurses went by a variety of names: the classical *nutrix,* the colloquial *mama,* and most commonly *bavila* or *baiula.* The third principal category of servants is more complex. Some people were classified as those "who stay" with the testator. Occasionally a noun was used—*manente*—meaning the same thing. Such persons were not lodgers, since the Genoese drew a sharp distinction between those who "stayed with" as opposed to "lived with" someone else. Still, the possibility exists that a few of this last group were not servants. The 140 women mentioned comprise 72 servants, 53 wetnurses, and 13 who "stay with" the master. The other two are identified as a bather and a water carrier. All six men are called servants. Even leaving aside the nurses, the women servants outnumbered the men 72 to six. While the figures for slaves are not so one-sided, female slaves were also more numerous than male ones. Servants were employed in households wealthy enough to afford help. This domestic service probably entailed cooking, cleaning, and other tasks, since some of the testators were very rich and not likely to do such work themselves. Few if any of these servants were apprentices learning a trade; the sex ratios and the testators' social position both suggest these were domestic servants.

The bequests to servants usually took the form of small cash gifts or occasionally items of clothing, but as we shall see, some servants received much more than this. Thirty-eight people who willed their servants something considered these legacies to be charitable, but about two-thirds of the testators did not think that such bequests were in fact charitable. Legacies to friends raise this same question: why did such legacies benefit the soul? A clearer case can be made for servants. The testators sometimes attached conditions to a servant's legacy, and these conditions are at least reminiscent of charity. For example, to leave money for a servant's dowry was a meritorious deed and worthy of the soul, as was pensioning off an old and decrepit servant, saving her from being thrust out into the cold. The amount most commonly given to a servant was about ten solidi, and the great majority of these bequests ranged from five to twenty solidi. A lira was close to a sufficient dowry, but by and large the amounts were more pittances than ample rewards for a lifetime of service. The poorest testators did not have servants, and the wealthy had many. Nothing required a person to leave a servant something, so the wills do not supply a complete record of all the servants even in any particular house. Even a person mentioning a few servants may not necessarily have listed them all. Bequests to servants were therefore voluntary, and it may be that here again some Genoese believed that anything voluntary was also charitable. Charity to friends or servants was personal. People knew their servants, and some evidently thought that they were as good a charity as anything else.

Wet nursing was an old and honorable profession. Not all the testators had children, but all of them had mothers and hence might have had a wetnurse. Suckling the young is one of the basic animal needs—older than society or humanity itself. Biology or the mother's health might make hiring a wet nurse necessary. Some people experienced an enduring relationship with their nurses, who might have been a kind of second mother; the use of the word *mama* to describe the nurse tells us much. Simona Doria left her *mama* Anna her bed for life and the tidy sum of L.10.[41] The testators distinguished between their own nurses and those of their children. Giuliana had employed two nurses for her two youngest sons, and she was careful to leave each of them a small bequest.[42] Altadonna had no children, but she remembered her *mama* Babilia and left her L.5, which was more than any individual relative received.[43] Adalasia left one lira for her nurse's daughter to use as a dowry.[44] These are only a few examples, all of which point to an enduring relationship between a man or woman and his or her own childhood nurse, as well as the nurse who fed his or her children. The Genoese included wet nurses with servants by grouping them together in the will. The *mamas* often appeared separately, as if to single them out for special notice. A wet nurse was a special kind of servant, but a servant nonetheless. The wills do not indicate whether the child was placed with the nurse or whether the nurse came to live with the family. The more wealthy families probably opted for the latter. The great majority of the servants were employed by the testator at the time the will was made; some of the nurses were, but some were not.

One woman making a will called herself Divicia, the nurse of Ugolino Mallon.[45] Being a nurse was one of the few professional opportunities open to women in medieval Genoa. To judge from her will, Divicia managed to support herself as a nurse; however, the long-term prospects for such a job were not good. Divicia named no husband, but she had a natural daughter and a son, perhaps also illegitimate, though there is a slight chance that she may have been a widow. Divicia relied on her employer, Donna Maria Mallon, to distribute L.1 in charitable bequests and also to be the executrix of the estate. Donna Maria was also named her son's tutor, and she was to invest his bequest—L.6, a mattress, and a cover—at his own risk. If he died without an heir, Donna Maria and her son Enrico would inherit. Divicia left her best mattress to Enrico, whom she had nursed. It is not clear what was supposed to happen to the natural daughter, Altilia, who received only L.1. Perhaps Donna Maria had already taken her in as a servant. Altogether Divicia left L.8, two mattresses, and her *massaricia,* which she left to her niece Imelda. She was a single woman who admitted to having a natural daughter, and who named only one relative other than her own children in her will. Divicia's life might appear to have been a hard one. Yet she could count on an important and wealthy woman to manage her estate and take care of her son. These two very different women were brought together by Donna Maria's need for a nurse. Even a potential outcast like Divicia could save herself by becoming a nurse, thus establishing a tie to one of Genoa's most prominent families. There was a kind of special intimacy created by being a nurse. The nurses received legacies, and if Divicia is at all typical, they could also count on this tie for other purposes.

The rest of the servants were overwhelmingly women. Some conditions attached to their bequests reveal the nature of the relationship between master and servant. Oliverio Bucadanello left

his servant Bruneta "for good service" L.10 beyond the L.10 that
had been placed for her in a joint investment.[46] The phrasing
implies that Oliverio had supplied her original capital. He also
wished her to have food and clothing and to live in his house
without having to perform any service, "and no one had the right
to disturb her." Bruneta's lot might compare favorably to the
average Genoese working person's status. She was worth at least
L.20 and was to have free room and board for the rest of her life.
Bruneta may have served the Bucadanello family for a long time,
receiving what was in effect a pension. Good service merited reward. Guglielmo de Predono similarly left his servant Agnesina
L.10, many household items, and the right to live rent free in his
house for three years, if she were a "good woman."[47] This condition is reminiscent of similar ones concerning wives, and Guglielmo was unmarried. Without prejudice to anyone, I should note
that some men were magnanimous to a female servant, though
in many instances duration of service may account for the bounty.
While women often left their servants small cash bequests, some
were also quite generous. Giulia, the wife of Ansalda d'Albaro,
left Adalasia "who stays with me" clothes, furs, and the right to
live in her house for five years without rent.[48] If Ansaldo did not
want her to stay, Adalasia was to have the value of this pension
from Giulia's goods. Although Ansaldo might reasonably have
objected to having this woman live in his house for so long a time,
he had no right to set aside the legacy.

For whatever reason, many Genoese who had servants recognized that they had a continuing obligation to them. While a few
of these servants were comparatively well off, many others had
no home or other place to go. A few lucky servants were, like
most nurses, in a real sense members of the household. But in
general few Genoese could afford to feed these extra mouths. For
those who could, running a substantial household required the
help of servants, primarily women. To judge from the wills—and
there appears to be no better source—more Genoese had servants
than slaves. Indeed some of the servants discussed here would
have been able to purchase three or four slaves of their own. Some
servants were probably former slaves themselves. Many societies
have faced the economic as well as the moral problem of employing servants or owning slaves. Genoa contained or was able

to attract a sizable population of women who were available to serve, perhaps at very little cost beyond food and lodging; and servants, unlike slaves, did not require an original capital investment. As we shall see the number of slaves in Genoa has been exaggerated, and the abundant supply of servants has not been given sufficient attention.[49] The servants named in Genoese wills generally inherited only small bequests. They were already free, they had been acquired at no cost, and were let go at almost none.

Patrons and Masters

This last category combines two parallel kinds of relationships—client-patron and apprentice-master. Wills shed some light on such arrangements. The Genoese borrowed much of their political vocabulary from the Romans, and they understood from experience the tie between a powerful person and his supporters. The century under review here roughly coincides with the gradual and ill-charted development of the guild system and apprenticeship. Patrons and masters had in common the fact that each exercised authority. From the apprentice's point of view his indenture to the master was not voluntary. Usually placed in the master's care as a child, the apprentice found himself bound to serve for anywhere from seven to twelve years, depending on his age and the particular craft. A journeyman was more independent, but he still needed to be employed. Patronage also had an economic component, but it was not closely tied to learning a particular trade. A person's need to rely on some powerful family for aid and protection was not exactly voluntary; neither was the patron's need for agents or supporters. Genoa existed in a feudal milieu and also apart from it. Especially in rural Liguria, feudal tenancy was still practiced, and labor services were still exacted. Over the course of the century from 1150 to 1250 mercenaries and communal mass levies largely replaced the need for a feudal host. The great city families still had vassals and feudal retainers in their rural strongholds. The ability to turn these people out in force contributed to a family's strength in the city. The wills tell us almost nothing about these feudal vestiges. Urban life brought about another kind of dependence. Common business ventures, neighborhood concerns, and city politics all gave the prominent families new areas of potential influence. Less exalted Genoese found personal success by serving these grand designs. By "patronage" I mean this tie of dependence without any apparent military connotation.

Two important families will suffice as examples. The Doria are already familiar to the reader; as far back as anyone cares to look this family was influential. The Fieschi family in the thirteenth century managed to enlarge their marginal influence as counts of the small coastal town of Lavagna. A move to Genoa, influence in the church, and some good marriages provided the keys to the family's rapid rise. The family in turn provided Europe with popes Innocent IV and Hadrian V.[50] The cathedral chapter of San Lorenzo in Genoa became the family's power base, augmented naturally by subsequent papal favor.

The wills provide another perspective on these families by showing us how humbler citizens depended on them. Ottone, a judge from Milan, made his will in July 1158.[51] He wished any daughter who might be born after his death to receive what his wife and Ansaldo Doria and his sons Enrico and Simone thought best. The three Doria were also named tutors for Ottone's sons. His wife was to have whatever the Doria decided. As a foreigner working for the commune, Ottone was certainly of use to the Doria, who were not his friends and themselves inherited nothing. Ottone's will demonstrates that he had some store of good will with this prominent family, and he used it to safeguard his own family. This was one way the Doria could reward service. The patronage ties might extend far down the social scale. Altilia, the daughter of the late Guglielmo, had some tie to the San Matteo neighborhood, which was the Doria seat of power.[52] She left money to that church and a priest there for masses. Modest bequests and a concern for her children dominate her testament. Surprisingly for a person of her station, she closes her will by naming Guglielmo Doria and Alda Doria to distribute her legacies. Here again neither friendship nor kinship explains the claim Altilia was able to make on their help. The great neighbor looked after the humble residents, who in turn might provide a lifetime of small yet useful services. The powerul did not expect to benefit from these people's wills; instead they were expected to repay loyalty.

The testators did, however, pay their debts to the powerful

families. Giovanni de Casali divided his time between Chiavari, very near Lavagna, and Genoa. When he made his will in 1239 he requested burial either at San Lorenzo de Chiavari or the Hospital of Santo Spirito in Genoa, depending on where he died.[53] He was rich enough to leave his wife L.80, a tidy sum. A list of his debts contained in the will reveals that he owed Ugone Fieschi L.25 and Lord Opizone Fieschi forty solidi. Ugone and Opizone were common names in the family. Just who these two were is not as important as the fact that someone from Chiavari in debt to the Fieschi was prospering in Genoa.

Occasionally the patron might benefit indirectly from a will. Zacaria de Mari, childless and unmarried, left his house and lands to the Hospital and Temple in the Holy Land.[54] If either wanted to sell the legacy or give it away, they were to do so to his nephews, paternal relatives (*parenti*), or the house of Fieschi. The De Mari family was important in the city; if Zacaria belonged to them, he seems to have been a comparatively poor relation. He gave virtually all his goods to charity. His mentioning the house of Fieschi again indicates a tie other than that a friend or relative would have. There are many more examples of ties to prominent families. A Genoese prosopography derived from the wills and other documents would enable us to see just how patronage functioned from the client's point of view.

The notarial cartularies contain many documents concerning guilds. Agreements between people practicing the same craft illustrate the very beginnings of guild activity. A parent or guardian would indenture a boy or girl to a craftsman. Records of many indentures survive. The master and apprentice had reciprocal duties: the young person was in effect a servant, the master a teacher. The Genoese guilds await their historian. Genoese artisans made many of the extant wills that enable us to see the wealth and status that particular kinds of labor produced. Here I am concerned with the master-apprentice tie and the manner in which this tie fit in with all the others. This business relationship could practically take the family's place, or at least forge alternate bonds. The master had quasiparental authority over the apprentice, who in turn had almost filial duties.

Oberto, the master shoemaker of Clavica, made a will that illustrates some aspects of the tie. He left Facio, "who stays with me," L.20, all the tools of the shoemaking shop (*apoteca calegaria*) and the manufacturing shop (*apoteca confizaria*), and usufruct of his house for life.[55] Facio and his wife lived with Oberto, who was himself rich enough to leave L.25 for his soul. Perhaps because he engaged in both the manufacturing and retail aspects of his trade, Oberto was very successful. Without a family of his own, Oberto treated Facio like a son and heir. Guglielmo, apprenticed to Maestro Giovanni the shield maker, left his master L.8 and his own brother L.9.[56] Even after the passage of time ended the formal ties, those years of close association still counted for something. Maestro Guglielmo de Frascario turned to his old master Giovanni to distribute his charitable bequests.[57] Though most of the masters and apprentices were men, not all were. Sofia, possibly a weaver, left her apprentice (*discipulus*) Guglielmino some household goods and tools.[58] Just what, if any, obligations remained if either the master or apprentice died is not clear. Apart from the need to settle debts, death dissolved the tie and ended all obligations. Though not voluntary in origin, this bond, unlike many others, was temporary. To mention a master or apprentice in a will was a purely voluntary act. To the extent that they did name each other as heirs, we know that yet another important relationship affected and in a sense imitated the family.

In this chapter we have looked at a great range of relationships between persons. If one type of relationship did not exist or failed, there was always another one on which to depend. The nuclear family was the centerpiece, the first place a person turned to for heirs. This is what unmarried people did. Marriage and daily life enlarged the scope of possibilities. A man might be an uncle, nephew, cousin, husband, brother, or son-in-law, a friend, servant, patron, or master. As the circle of ties widened, so too did the scope of voluntary activity. Beyond the nearest kin, a person had much more freedom to dispose of wealth; custom and the law were less restrictive as one moved away from the nuclear family. Each person was theoretically the focal point of a variety of social ties. Each will reveals how individual Genoese sorted all these relationships out. We have seen that gender, marital status, and wealth all affected these personal decisions. In a great many cases the network of social bonds failed to save people from poverty;

urban life offered a haven for loners, down-and-outers, and immigrants, but the going was never easy. This society, in common with the rest of Europe, devised so many kinds of ties that breaking them all was the exception rather than the rule. The wills as a whole bring out the great variety in human relations. The various ways people distributed their property tell us much about the strengths and weaknesses of these emotional, sometimes fragile bonds.

At the same time that the Genoese settled family matters, they also attempted to secure a place for themselves in the next world. Let us now examine these efforts at spiritual self-help.

5 / Charity: Gifts for the Soul, Funeral, and Burial

The Genoese responded to numinous locales—places that aroused warm religious feelings. From Santiago and Jerusalem to the neighborhood church, life seemed to offer a variety of opportunities to be in touch with the spiritual world. Their own city had many—but never enough—churches and monastaries. Although their own patron, San Lorenzo, had merely stopped in Genoa on his way from Spain to a Roman martyrdom, at least he had sensibly avoided Rapallo or Pisa.[1] Tales of Saint Peter's travels in Northern Italy nourished the sentiment that Genoa, though perhaps distant from the principal places of piety and devotion in Western Christianity, had merited and received its share of apostolic attention.[2] In A.D. 718 the body of Saint Augustine had passed through Genoa on its way to a final resting place in Pavia. When the Genoese representatives returned home from the Third Lateran Council of 1179, they brought with them the particularly prized bones of Saint John the Baptist. The contemporary city historian Ottobono Scriba recorded this coup as one of the year's few significant events.[3] In 1188 he described in uncharacteristic detail the rediscovery of the sarcophagus of Genoa's very own bishop and saint, Siro.[4] Genoa's close association with the Crusades earned the city the distinct honor of having a red cross as a heraldic emblem. Genoa was no capital of medieval spirituality, but it was a Christian town. This elemental fact, easily taken for granted, placed the city within a cultural ambience that molded Genoese attitudes toward charity and death. The church intertwined these subjects, creating a durable connection in the minds of all Christians.

From the beginning the church taught that charity was blessed. Alms giving had strong roots in the Old Testament, and the New Testament and the Church Fathers continued to emphasize this tradition.[5] Medieval theologians refined the doctrinal meaning of

136

charity, a central idea in Christian thought. Gifts to the church were encouraged, and an increasingly elaborate doctrine defined the benefits to the donor of these works. In this chapter I shall be concerned with one particular aspect of the church's attitude toward charity: gifts for the soul. How could a person help himself in the next world by charity in this one? That such help was even possible was a crucial idea. Philippe Ariès was correct when he focused attention on Gregory the Great's teaching on Purgatory, which implied a suspension of final divine judgment and left the door open to some kind of intercession.[6] The great Benedictine monastery of Cluny played a central role in the tenth century's main answer to the problem of interceding for souls—masses for the dead. All Souls' Day signifies the religious appeal of helping the dead to attain ultimate salvation through prayer. By the time the first wills appeared in the eleventh century, the laity had made providing for masses for the soul a routine aspect of the last will and testament. It was a small step from the mass to a belief that any pious deathbed bequest found favor with God. The poor were to inherit the Kingdom of Heaven; by aiding them sufficiently the rich could join their ranks. The donations for the soul demonstrate that the laity did indeed fear the judgment of God. Penitence and satisfaction for sins did some good, and for all this a will represented the last chance.

The testators, rich and poor alike, lived in this religious environment. As Robert Brentano remarks about medieval Roman wills, "It is hard to think of any evidence (except a penitentiary's) which could so quickly expose men's souls, so neatly define their final duties and affections."[7] Brentano is aware that the notary possibly influenced these last wishes, and points out that it is still worth knowing the notary's own sense of piety. However, he slights these problems in his analysis of thirteenth-century Roman wills. If a will is a window into men's souls, it is only partially open. The second will of Guirardo de Verzellato (see Chapter 1) reminds us that a person might give away his goods to charity while he was still alive. Perhaps many wills passed over a record of generous lifetime giving in modest silence. The sentiment of piety may have been nearly universal, but its scope varied significantly from person to person. From a will one can make some general estimate of the testator's wealth; it is clear that some gave all they had for their souls while others, occasionally quite wealthy, were content to leave very little or nothing for this purpose. As I noted in the basic outline of a testament in Chapter 1, the will usually contains a total sum left for the soul, followed by an itemized accounting of this bequest. There are exceptions to this pattern, however. Let us first consider those individuals who left nothing at all for their souls.

As usual there are exceptions to the exceptions. In some cases the absence of any pious bequest is at least comprehensible. When Ponzio made a will in 1229 while preparing to enter the Order of Preachers, he left all his goods to his mother, Pagesa, with the curious condition that she not leave home or give more than L.10 to his brothers. He also charged his mother to give small legacies to three other persons.[8] Since Ponzio intended to devote his time to religion, he wanted his evidently modest amount of property to support his mother. Four men making wills before a journey—two to Santiago, one to the Holy Land, and one to an unspecified destination—also left nothing for their souls. The three on pilgrimage may have thought that the expense and time involved in the trip represented a sufficient investment in the soul. Dying on pilgrimage was highly meritorious and offered a person the prospect of immediate salvation. Still, most people going on pilgrimage did leave money for the soul, including, as we shall see, the wife of one man who did not. Different cases suggest other explanations. Giacomo de Turcha's will, preserved by the monks of San Siro on parchment, contains no charitable bequests. However, the will of this prominent and wealthy man does include his request to be buried at the monastery, which suggests that he may have conveyed wealth to San Siro before his death.[9] Finally, a woman named Ingese, in one of the wills in the form of testimony of witnesses, left nothing for her soul. The witnesses noted that she lay ill at home while dictating her will. Ingese's only thoughts were about her three children; perhaps that is all the time she had.[10] (All other oral testaments and all but one of the wills explicitly referring to the testator's illness contain bequests for the soul.) These seven wills provide plausible internal explanations for a lapse in giving.

There remain twenty-five other persons who made no charitable bequests; the wills of eleven of them can only be described as terse.[11] Sibilia, the daughter of the late Ugone Mantello, named as sole heir her mother, Donna Giacoma. One Enrico left his sister Ursa all his goods, to do with as she wanted, without anyone to contradict her. On October 25, 1213, two brothers, Girardo and Giovanni, making each other the principal heir, combined their testament into a single act. The married couple Oraliono and Richelda made wills on the same day too. He left his wife all her clothes, household goods, their bed, and its furnishings; she left her husband usufruct of one-half of her lands, which would revert to her sons when he died. Guglielmo de Canali left his wife a totally furnished bed, her clothes, jewels, and rings. In these and five other cases the wills include the stated legacies and nothing else. Of all of them, only the will of Sibilia mentions a burial site, and the Mantello family may have been connected to the Church of San Donato anyway. These wills are simple and brief, betray signs of haste, and took only a few moments to finish. All of them contain a simple conveyance of property to a spouse or, for the four unmarried persons, a close relative. Only Sibilia made her will at home, and none of these people claimed to be ill. In these eleven testaments, specific family concerns dominate to the point of excluding any charitable impulses. They are for this reason very unusual, but they also suggest that one must be on guard for other testators whose pious donations, perhaps prompted by a notary or confessor, may have been only a veneer applied to the same basic fact: the family inherits.

The fourteen remaining wills that contain no pious bequests differ from the previous group in that they are more like normal wills: they are longer and contain a variety of legacies. The only remarkable thing about them is their failure to mention any charity or burial site. On March 17 and 18, 1200, three spinners, Ansaldo and the brothers Vassallo and Oberto, made wills with Oberto Scriba.[12] These wills concern only family matters and mention no burial sites or charities. The fact that all three were spinners suggests some sort of group decision to settle their affairs. Sometimes a single, driving purpose compelled a person to make a will. Occasionally charity was in fact the impetus, but usually the family, if any motive predominated, drove out all other considerations. However, 595 people did take the time to leave something for their souls. Of this number, thirty-one left such things as land, cloth, clothes, and wine for their souls, and it is difficult to assign a cash value to these items. The rest left a specified sum, although they might not actually have possessed the money at the time; rather, they expected the executor to raise the required amount. Table 9 presents the total amount left for the soul by men and by women.

A few words on the money categories are in order. People who were able to leave L.100 (the most common figure for that group) were the elite of Genoese society. The mean bequest is about L.5, and the largest single category of bequests is in the range of one to five lire with most at or close to one lira.[13] The dramatic drop off in numbers of those giving less than one lira indicates that this sum represented some sort of threshhold. Most of those with less than one lira to give for their souls may have been too poor to make a will in the first place. This table is no sure guide to economic status, as we have seen in the discussion of family wealth in Chapter 3. The charitable bequests stand by themselves, in the sense that they reflect personal, unfathomable motives. The division by sex of the pious bequests reveals a general uniformity of intention for gifts less than L.50. Men significantly outnumber women, thirty-three to eighteen, only for those bequests of L.50 and over. These figures do not suggest that wealthy men were more pious than their female counterparts but only that they may have had more disposable wealth. If they did, then the real question is whether men devoted a greater or lesser proportion of their riches to the soul than did women. We have seen, and will continue to see, evidence that men were in fact less generous in this respect than their wives and daughters.

Money to pay for the funeral and burial came from the total charitable bequest. Before determining just how much people spent on these items, it is necessary to consider any prior claims or obligations which might diminish the funds available to pay for mortuary expenses. There is one such claim to examine. After having stated the total amount for the soul, the testator would usually set aside a tithe for the works (building projects) of the Cathedral of San Lorenzo—"decenum operi sancti laurencii". The will of Guglielmo da Savona, dated August 23, 1179, was the first to mention this tithe.[14] The wills Giovanni Scriba wrote mention no tithe; his last will was redacted in 1164. Unfortunately, no

Table 9. Number of charitable bequests by sex of testator.

Sex of testator	Amount of bequest								
	Over L.100	L.50–L.100	L.25–L.50	L.10–L.25	L.5–L.10	L.1–L.5	Sl.–L.1	In kind[a]	Nothing
Male	17	16	27	44	38	131	13	17	25
Female	9	9	35	49	53	110	13	14	9
Total	26	25	62	93	91	241	26	31	34

Source: Archivio di Stato di Genoa, Cartolari Notarili.
a. Wine, bread, clothing, and other items with no assigned cash value.

testaments survive for the years between 1165 and 1179, so we cannot precisely date the inception of this tithe. Something must have prompted the city government, or perhaps the church, to institute this universal and obligatory tithe. The cathedral, begun in the early twelfth century, may have required additional funds for its completion. The tithe came off the top of the charitable bequests, in the sense that the testator set aside one-tenth of the sum for this purpose before dividing up the rest. Thus the other beneficiaries did not have to pay anything to the cathedral. This was a personal tithe, and it did not open the door to the inevitable disputes which would have resulted if the religious institutions had had to tithe from their own testamentary income to the cathedral. Catherine Boyd, in her study of tithes in medieval Italy, observed a "tithe of the dead" in Venice in this period. The Venetian tithe was evidently a general one on all the legacies in a will, and was not restricted, as in Genoa, to only the charitable bequests.[15] Richard Trexler has written about the short-lived and vigorously opposed efforts of the bishop of Florence in the fourteenth century to lay claim to fully one-third of the pious bequests left *indistincte*.[16] What resistance there was in Genoa to their own tithe was quiet and effective.

The first notary to include this tithe in wills was Oberto Scriba in the 1190s. Riccadonna Boterici left a total of L.60 for her soul, including L.10 for the works of San Lorenzo. She took care to note that this sum included her tithe.[17] Occasionally the statement of the tithe makes it possible to estimate the total amount of the charitable bequests when the will gives no total sum. For example, Matilda, the wife of Milo, whose testament jumbled together all types of legacies, included twenty-five solidi for the tithe. We can thus estimate her total giving at L.12 s.10—which is in fact the total of the scattered gifts which are clearly charitable in nature.[18]

By the 1230s this neat system of providing regular and substantial income for the cathedral began to show some strains. In some wills the total of charitable bequests no longer matches the stated total if the tithe is included. This either indicates that the burden of payment shifted to the beneficiaries, or that payment was no longer as regular as it had been. Ursa of Savona's will shows another way commonly used to avoid the full tithe. She states no total amount of pious donations, but her numerous gifts amount to L.40.[19] At the end of the list she notes that the tithe is to go to San Lorenzo, yet she sets aside no money for this purpose. In the main body of the will she leaves an additional L.60 to the order of the Humiliati of Murtedo, of which her brother was a member. Nothing prevented a person from leaving money to religion as a straight legacy unconnected to the portion of the will devoted to *pro anima* bequests. Gifts made in this way escaped the tithe. If the testator did not intend the cathedral to benefit proportionately from the total amount, he might easily shift the bequests to another part of the will. Maria, the daughter of the late Bonovassallo de Antiocha, left at least L.206 s.10 for her soul (the will is extensively damaged), yet she set aside only L.10 for the tithe, shortchanging the cathedral by at least L.10.[20] She did this, like Ursa, by moving some of the bequests out of the portion of the will pertaining to her soul. Both of these women, and others adopting similar strategies, clearly intended to give substantial sums for pious works. The obligation to tithe to the cathedral may have irked them. For some fifty years the cathedral had collected what must have been thousands of lire, and had, by the early thirteenth century, basically completed the present structure. The notaries did not assume the burden of zealously defending the cathedral's rights.

In 1227 the notary Urso recorded in his cartulary one of the few references to the manner in which the cathedral administered the works. Opizone Guercio, styled as "operarius et administrator operis sancti laurencii de ianue," for forty solidi ceded to the Hospital of San Giovanni in Capo d'Arena land and a house left to the works by one Alfarda.[21] Guercio was a very distinguished name in Genoa, and we know that there was an office, possibly lucrative to the holder, charged with the responsibility of running the cathedral's projects. Alfarda may have left the house and land as a gift intended for the cathedral, or more likely, she may have given it to pay the tithe of her charitable bequests. There is no way to be sure exactly why this property came to San Lorenzo. We can only wonder how Opizone Guercio viewed the wills of some of his contemporaries who seemed to go to great lengths to avoid paying their own tithes. Yet there he is, alienating a house and land to the hospital for the very low price of two lire. This may have been not a simple sale but a kind of gift from one church to another, or perhaps even some type of fraud.

The tithe affected funeral and burial arrangements by taking up a tenth of the available resources. Since the idea of death was inherent in a will, the tithe distracted testators while they attempted to calculate just how much money they needed to leave to pay for the mortuary costs. Most people, after having stated a total amount to be spent for their souls, went on to list item by item just how they wanted all or most of the money distributed. The testators usually mentioned first a burial site and the amount of money to be spent on the funeral. This planning for death prompted a very personal charity which betrayed a preoccupation with the self. The Genoese cared deeply about these matters, so much so that one can and should separate this kind of personal charity from all other forms. First let us consider the burial site and the factors influencing its selection.

The Burial Site

Those who intended to depart from Genoa and feared death on the trip did not name a burial site in the city, naturally enough. Guglielmo Mostarabo, lying sick in his house in Genoa, stated that if he died in the city he wanted to be buried at the Church of Santa Maria de Castello, or if in Sori at the Church of Santa Margarita de Sori.[22] Those visiting the city or having a dual residence often expressed preferences about burial sites that depended on where they would be when they died. These are relatively rare exceptions to the rule of one choice of place. What influenced this choice, which was, by every indication in the wills, very important? As a rule the parish church had the right to bury its parishioners. For example, a woman named Monaca simply stated that she wanted to be buried at the parish church of Lavagna.[23] The burial privileges granted by the popes to the principal city monasteries, the friars, and the cathedral complicated this picture. A church profited from having a cemetery, and these rights would have been stoutly defended against any encroachment.

The record lacks any trace of disputes over burial, except for a few instances when the testators themselves anticipated a potential difficulty. Romana, the wife of Guglielmo Grasso, wished to be buried at San Lorenzo, but "if this creates a scandal," as the notary Raimundo Medico put it, she was willing to be interred at the Monastery of San Andrea de Porta.[24] The scandal may have been expected to result from the fact that Romana was already committed to San Andrea either contractually or by canon law. In any case this was a problem she left for her executors to solve. In 1227 Oberto Bonizo, in a very early mark of favor to the new Dominican order, selected their Church of San Egidio "if possible," but otherwise San Andrea de Sestri Ponente. This may be a sign of the disputes between the mendicant orders and the older churches over parochial rights in the thirteenth century. In this particular case the problem may have been only that San Egidio, a recent foundation, was not yet prepared to accept burials.[25] One other testator, Rubaldo Galleta, chose San Lorenzo "if it is permitted," but otherwise he did not clarify the problem about the burial site.[26] The testators understood these potential conflicts. When they selected a burial site they were reasonably sure that the choice was lawful and would be honored. Eighty-five men and forty-six women did not make such a choice. We can assume that since men predominate in this group, they were mostly travelers, or perhaps for the group as a whole the choice of burial site was obvious or predetermined and required no explicit comment. The will of Anna, the wife of Enrico the furrier, may explain the failure of some people to select a site; she emphatically left the choice of burial place up to her husband.[27] Other people may simply have assumed that the family would lay them to rest as it seemed best.

The variety of burial sites did not remain constant. In the period 1150–1250 the principal new religious phenomenon in Genoa was the arrival of the Franciscans and Dominicans, though the Cistercians and Hospitalers also had some appeal in the city. Although there are early indications that the Franciscans were present in Genoa, they did not have a church for themselves until 1250, when the archbishop gave them one which they called San Francesco de Castelleto. So there were no Franciscan burials until that year. Upon the canonization of their founder in 1234, the Dominicans dedicated their church to San Domenico. The few known burials taking place there between 1227 and 1251 quickly placed the Church of the Dominicans in a tie for tenth place among popular burial sites. The new orders would figure even more prominently as burial sites after 1253.

The ten burial sites mentioned most often in the wills account for over one-half of all known burials for the period. They are the churches of San Lorenzo with 47 burials; San Stefano with 45; San Andrea de Porta and San Giovanni with 33 each; San Ambrogio, 26; Santa Maria de Castello, 24; San Donato, 21; Santa Maria delle Vigne, 20; San Andrea de Sestri, 19; and San Siro and the Church of the Dominicans with 12 each. No particular claims are made for the exact order, but these were the most popular places for burial in Genoa. Eighty-six other churches and monasteries account for the rest of the burials.

Why was any one particular place chosen over others? Family ties with a religious spot predetermined the burial site for future generations. The Doria family controlled the Church of San Matteo, which was located in the midst of their family towers, and they usually buried family members there. Later in the thirteenth century, when the family fell into political disfavor and suffered exile, the Doria buried relatives at San Fruttuoso de Capodimonte at Portofino. When they returned to the city the Doria continued this connection for a few years while they restored San Matteo. When the renovations were complete, they resumed burials there. The great Andrea Doria himself rests peacefully among his ancestors and descendents at San Matteo.[28] Other powerful families had similar ties, for example the Porcelli at San Bartolomeo de Fossato, and the Embriaci at Santa Maria de Castello. Enrico Dietisalva favored the Hospital of San Giovanni, and in his will he noted that his monument was already waiting for him there. This is another indication that people could choose a burial site at any time and even prepare it. Oberto Picteto left L.8 for anniversaries and commemorative masses at San Ambrogio for himself and his late wife.[29] Many others left money by will for the souls of their parents or spouse, who were buried at the same place they had selected for their own burial. This desire to join a parent or spouse may explain why the widowed tended to omit mention of a burial site a little more frequently than most other people. The family knew very well what the deceased wanted. These personal, human factors, by no means confined to the rich, influenced the choice. The reputations of the various institutions also played a part.

San Lorenzo was not the original seat of the bishop of Genoa. The bishops moved from San Siro, at the time in a western suburb outside the walls, to the comparative safety of San Lorenzo during the period when the Saracens routinely raided the area in the late ninth and tenth centuries.[30] After a time of dual episcopal seats— San Lorenzo in summer (the dangerous time) and San Siro in winter—in 1007 the bishop fixed the see at San Lorenzo. In 1133 Pope Innocent II raised the see to an archbishopric, an event which Cafaro, the contemporary city chronicler, linked closely with Genoese naval assistance to the pope against the Romans.[31] The cathedral, constructed during the twelfth century, was the largest church in town. The earliest burial there recorded in the wills dates from 1191, and all the rest are evenly spread from 1201 to 1253. Men and women are evenly divided (twenty-four to twenty-three) in their selection of San Lorenzo as a burial site.

The Benedictine Monastery of Santo Stefano, founded in 972, was the center of a suburb outside the 1155 city walls.[32] San Andrea de Porta, located next to the city walls at Porta Soprana, was a Benedictine convent of uncertain but probably eleventh-century foundation. When the bishop permanently moved his seat to San Lorenzo, he established a Benedictine monastery at the old and prestigious Church of San Siro. San Siro achieved prominence as the burial site of the Obertenghi, the feudal lords of the viscountcy of Genoa in the tenth and eleventh centuries. When Frederick Barbarossa frightened the city into building new walls in 1155, the enclosure included a new *compagne,* or city ward, called Borgo Novo, and San Siro acquired a measure of safety. These monasteries were familiar and established places, and the monks and nuns were local people who had an identity as family, neighbors, or friends in the community. A lay person might choose to enter a religious house as death approached and gain the spiritual value deriving from holy orders and burial in a monastic habit. Contessa de Porta, the wife of the late Rubaldo da Camogli, made her will on July 4, 1244, wishing to be buried at the Convent of San Andrea de Porta. She left the convent "if it will have made me a nun before I die L.3, otherwise nothing."[33] This type of opportunity partially explains the popularity of religious houses as burial sites and explains their advantage over the urban parish churches.

Geo Pistarino, in his study of Genoese urban monasteries, observed that these older houses were not able to pursue a traditional Benedictine economic policy.[34] Genoa and its vicinity had poor soil and hardly any flat land. The whole area was unsuited for vast estates or a heavy emphasis on agricultural production. Genoa also lacked a convenient pool of servile labor for a monastic signorial regime. Genoa's advantage was its position as a maritime center with a money economy. The economic development of Genoa provided the monastaries with a group of people who donated numerous scattered patches of land. This is the same period for which David Herlihy has shown a general resurgence in the amount of landed property that the church owned.[35] The monasteries in large measure replaced lay ownership of what agricultural land there was around Genoa. The older Benedictine monasteries united fragmentary holdings by trade, sales, donations, and by renting out land by *livello* (long-term lease) contracts with payment in kind and cash. All this helped to rationalize the economy and secure a more strongly based—but never sufficient—local food supply. As Pistarino notes, these trends were also good for the monks, who were even able to invest at sea the fruits of their landholding policies. This generally rosy picture for the older monasteries clouded over somewhat in the thirteenth century. However, the strong and durable economic base which the monasteries had endeavored to create in turn helped to assure the Genoese that the monasteries would be capable as well as worthy of taking care of souls and graves. In spite of the new orders and changed circumstances, the older monasteries continued to exert a religious appeal which in turn attracted a reasonable share of the city's burials.

With these three houses dominating the city and the surrounding countryside, the other city churches and monasteries seem to have concentrated on their potential as urban landlords. Santa Maria de Castello and San Donato were older urban churches in the heart of the city, as was San Ambrogio, which burned down and was quickly rebuilt in 1122. These churches, as well as others like San Matteo, were the centers of densely populated city parishes. Some of the other parochial churches were in the hands of the monasteries or the cathedral. The Church of Santa Maria delle Vigne, located in the center of the city, was refounded late in the tenth century. This church demonstrates that it was possible to succeed economically as both a city landowner and rural *signore*.[36] The roles these institutions played in electing the archbishops of the twelfth century clearly demonstrate their reputation and importance. In 1163, on the day of the funeral of Archbishop Siro, the clergy, religious men, consuls of the city, and the greater part of the senate chose as electors the abbots of San Benigno, San Siro, Santo Stefano de Porta, the prevosts of Santa Maria delle Vigne and San Donato, the priests of San Damiano, Santa Maria de Castello, and San Ambrogio, and some members of the cathedral chapter.[37] In 1188 the same abbots and prevosts participated in another election, as did priests from Santa Maria de Castello, San Damiano, San Giorgio, and San Giovanni de Porta, as well as some canons.[38] The list of electors never included the abbess of San Andrea de Porta. Even though one may wonder just how much choice the laity exercised in picking the electors, their preferences nevertheless bear a striking relationship to the most popular burial sites. The religious and social prestige of the institutions coincided wih their economic prosperity. The burials reflected this popular appeal, and also further strengthened the reputations and finances of the churches.

The Hospital and Church of San Giovanni, the Monastery of San Andrea de Sestri Ponente, and the Church of San Domenico represented the new wave of religious orders which reached Genoa and found ready acceptance in the twelfth and thirteenth centuries. The hospital and church associated with the international order of the Knights of Saint John in Jerusalem first appeared in Genoa sometime between 1160 and 1185, probably closer to the later date.[39] The commandary of Hospitalers found a home next to the cathedral in the heart of the city. The hospital served as a refuge for pilgrims, the poor, and the sick. In Genoa the order remained primarily a service to the community and not just a local branch of a far-flung military organization. In the thirteenth century the order acquired or established another hospital at Capo Fari, not far from the city. (The archrivals of the Hospitalers, the Templars, never had a foothold in Genoa.) The Genoese were deeply involved in the politics of the Latin Kingdom of Jerusalem, and this may account for the decided favor the Church and Hospital of San Giovanni received.[40] The crusading movement, an undoubted economic boon to the city, appealed to the Genoese, who never ceased to aid and join expeditions to the East. In the city the prestige of San Giovanni was high, and the hospital quickly became a favorite charity and burial site.[41]

An old Benedictine monastery dedicated to San Andrea occupied a tiny island off the Ligurian coast near Sestri Ponente, just to the west of Genoa.[42] Saint Bernard visited the cloister in 1129, and perhaps as early as 1131 San Andrea accepted the Cistercian rule. San Andrea was a daughter house of Citeaux, and the personal involvement of Saint Bernard added luster to the new arrangement. San Andrea offered men and women alike the opportunity for a religious life, but its status as a dual monastery is not very clear. The Cistercians may have accepted the presence of women at San Andrea as established by the older traditions of the house. In 1132 San Andrea moved from the island to the small town of Sestri Ponente. The move was necessary because the monks needed more space for themselves, and the new site could also accommodate the many lay people who wanted to be buried in the church or cloister. San Andrea remained the closest Cistercian monastery to Genoa; none of the city houses joined the new order. The traditional Cistercian economic plan required isolation from the laity and, preferably, a desolate rural setting. Genoa met neither requirement. However, San Andrea never had, or seemed to want, a total divorce from the secular world. While the known burials there come to only nineteen, doubtless a small fraction of the real total, the Genoese appreciated its reputed sanctity. Women outnumber men fourteen to five in selecting San Andrea as a burial site, perhaps a sign that women favored the Cistercian style of piety more than men did. Male and female burials at San Giovanni were equally divided; the connections with the Holy Land appealed to both sexes. The Dominicans had a similar broad appeal.

Cost of Funerals

In order to understand the attraction of the various burial sites and preferences of the testators, one must consider, as they always did, the cost. The notaries used several terms and phrases to describe the expenses of a funeral and burial. This variety of terms poses something of a problem. Raimundo Medico used the simplest expression—"pro sepultura"—to specify the purpose of a sum of money, and masses were always an additional cost. Other notaries differentiated between the expenses of a burial (*sepultura*) and the funeral itself (*exsequiae funeris*). Some notaries merely recorded a sum for the expenses of the funeral (*expensi funeris*), which presumably included a burial. A combined form giving the cost of the burial and funeral was also common. Clearly the two major expenses were the funeral ceremony and the burial, and these were two very different rites. As we have seen, Enrico Dietisalva had already prepared a tomb for himself at San Giovanni. Such a monument was more expensive than digging a hole in a churchyard or lifting a few floor slabs in a monastic cloister. Guglielmo Scarsaria left L.15 to the works of San Andrea de Porta, his burial site, out of which sum the monastery was to erect his monument.[43]

The works officials of the various churches must have closely supervised the creation of tombs or the development of a cemetery. The church's workers would carry out any necessary labor at a cost the churches themselves determined. The testators always left the cost of the burial directly to the burial site. It is impossible to imagine the executors seeking out a firm of contractors to do the work for an interment. The churches profited from the burials. The Genoese, when they planned for their burials, must either have known or inquired about the ost of burial so that they could cover the expense in their will. Burial alone did not account for the whole cost of the complete funeral, and in those wills that mention only *sepultura* (burial), one can assume that the term included a ceremony as well.

A final component of the total sum was the mass. Any ceremony—the *exsequiae funeris*—included at a minimum a mass which a member of the clergy would offer at the grave site or in the church. The variety of masses provided the churches with a lucrative income that exceeded the proceeds from burials. Masses for a week or a month were usually grouped together, and were the least costly form of continuing remembrance. A person might request a hundred masses for his soul, but a perpetual anniversary was the most highly prized and costly type of mass to endow for the soul. Frequently, the costs of funeral, burial, and masses were inextricably linked together as a lump sum in the wills. The notary Giovanni Scriba often included paupers in this combination too. As we shall see, this was not incongruous. Table 10 sets out the cost of funerals and burials provided for in the will. The wills that allot one total sum for the funeral, burial, and masses are included in both lines in order to illustrate how much difference the inability to exclude the cost of the masses makes. (The documents present two sets of figures: funeral, burial, and masses as one lump sum, or the funeral and burial as one sum with masses listed separately.) The table demonstrates that while masses increased the total cost, they did so across the board, pushing up everyone's expenses proportionally.

The mean expense for the table as a whole is about L.3. The most expensive funeral, burial, and masses cost about L.100, but wealthy members of society could purchase an elaborate send-off for about L.10. The sharp fall-off over L.25 marks the point of diminishing returns, in the sense that expenditures beyond that sum did not result in any tangible equivalent benefit. The table may underestimate the true costs, because nothing prevented a person from planning and paying for his funeral beforehand. Only 384 persons supplied any figure at all for these costs. Giacomo the shoemaker wanted his wife, Giulietta, to decide how much to spend on his funeral.[44] This is probably typical of those instances in which no fixed sum is mentioned in the will, but most testators preferred to settle this matter themselves. Many of the poorest testators named no specific sum to cover the burial cost, so Table 10 does not reflect the total picture. Probably the great majority of all Genoese funerals and burials cost one lira or less.

Masses

Masses added measurably to the total cost of dying. Oberto Picteto left L.1 s.16 for his burial at San Ambrogio in 1226. He willed the church L.8 for an anniversary and masses for a week and a month for himself and his late wife. By including his wife he clearly indicated that she was buried there as well. Each brother of San Ambrogio was to receive three denarii on the day of the

Table 10. Number of wills specifying burial and funeral expenses.

Purpose	Amount specified									
	Over L.25	L.15–L.25	L.10–L.15	L.6–L.10	L.5	L.4	L.3	L.2	L.1	Less than L.1
For burial and funeral without masses[a]	8	21	31	31	35	21	38	50	90	60
For burial and funeral with masses	10	28	38	39	27	20	31	51	85	55

Source: Archivio di Stato di Genova, Cartolari Notarili.
a. Where it is possible to make this distinction.

anniversary; and this pocket money must have been useful to men who had taken a vow of lifetime poverty.[45] The average cost of an anniversary was about L.2 to L.5; most Genoese could not afford that much. The anniversary's price represented an endowment that benefited the institution and its clergy. Guglielmo Embriaco left land to the altar of Santo Spirito in the Church of Santa Maria de Castello. He wished a canon to serve this altar and sing daily masses for his soul, as well as for his brother and their ancestors. If any problem developed, the elders of his house were to select another priest.[46] We may see here the beginning of an Embriaco family chapel centered around a particular altar. (Their family tower was virtually adjacent to the church.) The churches kept necrologies, which were basically calendars of the principal holidays and a record of the anniversary day for benefactors and donors by testament. The earliest surviving Genoese necrologies cover only the fourteenth century.[47] The absence of earlier records, which undoubtedly existed, makes the will the only comprehensive source for anniversaries and family connections to various churches. For example, a woman named Columba wanted to be buried at the Church of the Dominicans, and she left L.2 for her own anniversary and another L.2 for her mother's. Columba also left San Ambrogio L.2 for her late daughter Giacomina's anniversary, and twenty-five solidi for the parish and some masses for herself.[48] Giacomina was buried at San Ambrogio, which was probably also Columba's own parish. The Dominican church was a new factor, and in this case helped to sever a family tie to the local parish church. Other forms of commemorative masses are also useful in uncovering family connections to different churches. A person who could not afford an anniversary might have one hundred masses sung for his soul; this too was a very common type of bequest. One hundred masses cost L.1 s.5 at Santo Stefano and San Giacomo de Calignano to a high of L.3 s.12 at San Siro.[49] Nearly everyone who could pay for any sort of funeral was able to buy masses for a week or a month. The seriousness and piety with which the churches and monasteries prayed for the deceased, and the costs of these efforts, influenced the Genoese when they picked a place to be buried.

Beyond the question of masses, for what were the testators paying? There are three different situations to consider. First, most people evidently died at home, requiring some ceremony there. Second, the body had to be conveyed to the burial site. The ceremonies conducting a person from his home to his grave were the *exsequiae funeris*—the funeral. Finally there was the burial itself. This threefold scheme, which can be simplified with the labels home, street, and graveside, conforms well with anthropological models of rituals. The process might briefly be compared to Arnold Van Gennep's rites of passage, for two reasons. The funeral, or in a sense the death ritual as a whole, is after all a classic rite of passage, arguably the clearest example. More important, the medieval funeral remains a poorly documented and hence at least partly neglected field of inquiry. A useful theoretical model can greatly aid any effort to clarify the incomplete evidence we possess.

Van Gennep saw three principal components in all rites of passage—separation, transition, and incorporation.[50] For present purposes separation covers death at home, transition matches the funeral in the narrower sense of the term—that is, not including the burial—and incorporation quite literally refers to the actual burial. Incorporation has another equally significant aspect, however, a spiritual counterpart to the physical entombment. Concerning the funeral Van Gennep wrote, "On first considering funeral ceremonies, one expects rites of separation to be their most important component, in contrast to rites of transition and rites of incorporation, which should be only slightly elaborated."[51] In fact he found rites of separation to be "few and very simple." Transition rites were elaborate and important, and incorporation rites the most "extensively elaborated." The way he assessed the relative importance of these three components closely matches the evidence from medieval Genoa. Separation, or dying, was a brief and unceremonious act. Beliefs about the next world affected both transition and incorporation. When the body and the soul separated, God was supposed to preside over the soul's fate, while the corpse remained a human responsibility. The church monopolized whatever rituals attended the soul's transfer and union with the next world; this was the real meaning of the mass for the dead. (On this level of analysis one would find oneself pursuing theological explanations quite distant from the concrete thoughts the Genoese testators expressed about death.)

Richard Huntington and Peter Metcalf recently studied the

anthropology of mortuary ritual in part by reminding us that death is also a transition from life. They noted that a classic rite of passage—death—has three stages: alive . . . dying . . . dead.[52] All these stages occurred in the home. To extend the concept to mortuary ritual in Genoa, I have set up three stages: home (death) . . . procession in the streets (funeral) . . . grave site (burial). The concept of liminality, as originally proposed by Van Gennep, focuses attention on the transitional aspect of ritual. For Genoese culture in particular, the procession was the key element in the transfer of the body from the family to the church. If, as Huntington and Metcalf wrote in following Robert Hertz, "the fate of the body is a model for the fate of the soul," then the family handed the soul over to the Church at the same time.[53] The same transitional element, the procession, was the vehicle of transfer for both. Let us look first at the home, the most obscure stage of all.

Home

A person hoped to die at home in his own bed, surrounded by his family and friends. The will tells us little more than this, except for the hints about the emotional state of the testators, discussed in Chapter 2. Shortly before death, a priest would arrive at the home, administer the last rites, and give the *viaticum*. The priest Oberto, the principal witness to Ansaldo's oral will, began his testimony by stating, "I know that I gave him penance."[54] The priest's arrival symbolized the beginning of the church's role. Burial in the Mediterranean climate had to take place quickly, usually the next day. The body was washed, dressed, and prepared for the funeral. Materials for doing these things—clothes and some linen sheets to make a shroud—were readily at hand in the home. The cost of these preparations was minimal, and no testator gave them a thought. One Genoese, Imelda Macroanna, specifically stated, "I want to be placed in a box (*capsia*)."[55] She wished to be buried at Santa Croce, which was near Macroanna and some twenty kilometers from Genoa. This very rare reference to a coffin suggests that shrouds were the rule and coffins exceptional. Coffins were required only in cases where the body had to be transported over long distances. The word *capsia* usually meant a linen chest or other storage box. Perhaps the first coffins were already cheaply available in the home. Finally, dying at home seems to have prompted the Genoese to think about the deathbed itself. The Genoese often willed their own beds to hospitals. The idea of putting the deathbed to some future pious use became part of the ritual of death, at least for those who could afford and wanted to do so. A bed was the single most important and expensive item of domestic furniture. To die in it changed the bed somehow, and that the bed would serve the soul after death as well appealed to the Genoese.

Funeral Rites

The only evidence about funerals in this era comes from the wills, and the evidence is frankly meager. Some later information helps to identify funeral rituals that originated in the central Middle Ages. In 1384 the plague carried off the doge of Genoa, Leonardo Montaldo. One hundred notaries marched in his funeral procession, and they carried candles in order to honor their most illustrious fellow guildsman. Knights bearing banners rode on horses covered with shrouds—all this, as the contemporary chronicler Giorgio Stella noted, "according to the custom of magnates."[56] The rituals surrounding a funeral had old roots; just when the magnates' customs became fixed is not clear, but such pomp required funds. The doge, like the majority of his fellow citizens in the period under study here, died in his own home. The hospitals did not offer a higher standard of health care. An even later event helps to illuminate the question of funerals. The Florentine Lapo Niccolini died on December 24, 1430, at the tenth hour, at Vico Pisano, where he was governor. Three horses covered with the banners of Vico Pisano, the Niccolini family, and Pistoia led the funeral cortege. Files of men bore more family banners, as well as those of the three guilds to which Lapo had belonged. The clergy, canons, and all the orders of Florence also participated. His son Pagolo noted in his diary, "It was a great expense, and we four younger sons paid everything . . . I spent my fourth part with good-will, and so I hope did the other three."[57] The lesser ranks of Genoese society could not afford such elaborate displays of family pride. The variety of funerals seems largely to have determined the costs of the funeral and burial, at least before the family chapel fully developed.

Religion became involved in the transfer of a person from his family to the church at the deathbed. Most of the rituals beginning after the moment of death concerned the family, and are the ones for which people provided in their wills. Having participated in funerals as mourners or interested spectators, the Genoese could envisage what they wanted. Not one of them described the ceremony in any detail. The conservative and familiar structure of funerals explains this omission. The most important stage for present purposes is the procession. Once the body reached the grave site, the church took over and performed the established ritual. The church played a role in the procession as well, but a subordinate one. As we have seen, by 1384 there was a way of organizing this procession for magnates. The presence of the notaries at Montaldo's funeral indicates that the less exalted might also count on some visible sign of their standing in the community.

The funeral procession had symbolic meaning, but the fundamental purpose of this trip was to conduct the body to the burial site. Occasionally the burial site was quite distant from where the testator had expected to die. Avegnata, the son of the late Enrico de Begino of Monterosso, making his will in Genoa, wished to be buried at Santa Maria de Monterosso, "if I [it?] can be carried that far."[58] A more detailed example of this problem comes from Bonifacio, a Genoese colony on the southern tip of Corsica. The Genoese notary Tealdo da Sestri drew up a will for Orenga, the wife of the late Armano the furrier, on November 12, 1238. Orenga wanted to be buried at Santa Maria Lebetis, "and if there should not be enough time for me to be carried there, I want to be buried in a certain box [capsia] until that time when I might be able to be taken or carried there."[59] Santa Maria Lebetis was on a small island about five kilometers from Bonifacio. Orenga appreciated the difficulties of a winter sea trip of even so short a distance. In Genoa the logistics of the funeral procession posed no great problem, since the overwhelming majority of Genoese selected local burial sites which were either in the city itself or in the adjacent suburbs. Unlike those of some other cultures, Genoese burials did not take place at home. The procession originated in the practical desire to take the body someplace else. Funeral ceremonies represented elaborations on this basic need.

We know some additional facts about the customs which preceded the actual interment. Elena, the wife of Turco, left L.3 in 1214 to pay for her burial, masses, and "other things which need to be done."[60] Giovanni the key maker left thirty solidi "for performing my funeral office and celebrating masses and doing all things which shall be necessary to do for my burial."[61] Everyone knew what these "things" were, so no one explicitly stated all of them. These affairs cost money, and the great majority of Genoese gave thought to this expense and arrived at a specific sum to pay for what they wanted. The Genoese made clear, in the earliest surviving wills, that they wanted paupers at the funeral. For example Druda, the wife of Merlone Guaraco, left L.10 for her funeral and paupers.[62] She left no doubt that the paupers had an important function to fulfill. Philippe Ariès wrote, "The gathering of the poor at funerals is the last work of charity of the deceased."[63] He associated the presence of the poor with the influence of the mendicants, and to some sort of desire to replace both the family and the hired mourners banned by the church. I find no sign that the Genoese wanted the paupers to replace the family, either as mourners or companions in the procession to the grave site, and the Genoese were feeding the poor at funerals long before the arrival of the mendicants. It seems likely that the family made gifts to the poor at the church rather than at their own doorstep. Paupers tended to congregate at churches for this reason, among others.

The principal point is that this gathering of the poor was not in fact the last act of charity of the deceased. The family and executors had to disburse the expenses of the funeral, and presumably the paupers as well, at once. Druda's own will supplies evidence for this view. She left a total of L.38 for her soul and L.14 for the funeral and annual masses, to be paid at once. The executors were to pay the rest of the legacies within a year. Tommaso da Sestri the caulker wanted his executors to give paupers five solidi in bread on the day of his funeral.[64] The testators themselves distinguished between what needed to be spent immediately and what could be put off until the executors inventoried the estate and raised sufficient cash. So the funeral ritual, which included the paupers, was an act of immediate charity.

As we shall see in the next chapter, concern for the poor was widespread. Whether the poor marched with the family and friends to the burial site or were conveniently gathered there already, the church had taught for a long time that charity to the poor is a good thing. Such generosity at funerals fostered social prestige and drew attention to the fact that the deceased was not a pauper. The sheer numbers of poor aided on the day of the funeral reflected the family's dignity and position, and attracted the same sort of attention today received by the number of limousines.

The poor were not the only people adding to the dignity of a funeral. Giovanna, the wife of Ingone Tornello, made her will on December 23, 1231, in the sacristy of San Lorenzo. She wished the archbishop and cathedral chapter to attend her funeral, which was to take place at the Monastery of San Andrea de Sestri.[65] Giovanna did not set aside any money for the archbishop or chapter, but she did leave L.5 to the altar of San Lorenzo and an additional L.5 for masses for a year. The Tornello family was prominent and politically active; such a request anticipates acceptance. Ansaldo left only twenty solidi for his soul, and no sum specifically for his funeral, which was to be at San Andrea de Porta. He wanted three crosses at his funeral ceremony (presumably, that is, he wanted three priests to carry their churches' crosses in the procession).[66] Portella left two solidi to the Church and Hospital of Santa Croce, and for this gift the churchmen were to attend "at her death" with a cross and sing a mass. She left the same sum to San Vincenzo for this purpose.[67] Where the priests would actually sing the mass is not clear. Portella wanted to be buried at the Church of San Giovanni de Pavarano, some distance from Genoa, so perhaps the masses were celebrated in Bisagno, where she was staying when she made the will. Oberto the shoemaker left L.7 for his burial at San Donato, and so that the school might attend ("scola adsit").[68] He probably had the cathedral school in mind, but scola might refer to his guild. These five people were not the only ones to specify details of their funerals. The common theme was a desire to ensure some special appearance at the funeral, usually by the clergy.

Ariès saw the funerals of this period as not particularly individualistic, and mainly the business of the laity. Apart from the *viaticum* and prayers at the grave site, the funeral was not an ecclesiastical matter but mainly concerned family and friends. Why this should detract from the funeral's individuality is not clear. Beginning sometime in the thirteenth century, he says, death was "clericalized," and the laity began to adopt the mentality of the cloister toward death.[69] This new mentality resulted in some changes in funerary ritual—more inscriptions in churches, masses for the dead, and a developed sense of purgatory. Before this change in funerary customs, Ariès saw an attitude toward death characterized by natural acceptance. This attitude did not change so much as the rituals did. In other words, the laity wanted their funerals to be like the clergy's, but almost as a matter of taste, and not because deep-seated convictions had changed.

Does the general silence of the pre-1250 wills support Ariès's conclusions? The cases described above may mark the first glimmerings of clerical influence on lay funerals. The general silence of the rest of the testators may support the idea that most people knew very well what a typical Genoese funeral was like and were content to leave the details to family and friends. The influence of the clerical funerals is uncertain, especially since almost nothing is known about them. So many people were related to members of the clergy that it is easy to see how such influence might have been transmitted. There seems to have been a kind of Gresham's Law of funerals—the triumph of pomp over simplicity. The presence of the clergy at lay funerals also influenced their evolution. There is ample evidence of the role of the clergy at funerals, and yet they were not the only official presence. As in the case of Leonardo Montaldo, the family and fellow guildsmen also attended the body. Confraternities (lay religious societies) developed in Genoa during the course of the thirteenth century, and by 1260 there were at least twelve active ones in the city, centered around the prominent churches.[70] One of their principal activities was the series of processions through the city at the high points of the religious year. Many testators left money to confraternities, and it seems likely that the members would appear in the funerary procession to honor another member or a donor. The growth of the confraternity may be another sign of the manner in which lay spirituality emulated clerical habits. In keeping with its transitional symbolism, the funeral was a mixed ceremony, composed of religious and secular components that emphasized the departure of a soul and the acknowledgment of a recent, permanent change in social and family relations.[71]

Burials

Finally, let us consider burial itself. According to Ariès, the burial did not much concern the laity. "Thus the body was entrusted to the Church. It made little difference what the Church saw fit to do with these bodies so long as they remained within its holy precincts."[72] The evidence from the wills, however, does not support this impression. Not any holy precincts would do; most people had a specific church or monastery in mind. They also knew roughly how much a burial would cost. The great disparity in these costs demonstrates a similar diversity among burials, which ranged from the lavish through the modest to the pauper's grave. Presumably all the testators were at least able to avoid burial in the anonymous trench that churches reserved for paupers. Some patterns emerge from analyzing burial places and their respective costs. For example San Andrea de Sestri buried the well-to-do. No one wanting to be buried there left less than L.3 for that purpose, and more than half of them left over L.10. Distance from Genoa may have accounted for some of this expense, yet the prestige of this house must also have figured into the cost. The equally prestigious Hospital of San Giovanni, however, accepted burial for as little as ten solidi, and more than half of its burials cost less than L.3. A few wealthy people selected the hospital for their interment, but modest burials were the rule. Perhaps the hospital filled a void in the thirteenth century by providing this service for those having only a few lire at most to spend. The hospital was not alone in this service. The urban churches such as San Donato and San Ambrogio also provided burials for as little as sixteen or seventeen solidi, and no one spent more than L.10 at either place. The most popular burial sites, San Lorenzo and Santo Stefano, displayed the widest range of cost, in both cases from ten solidi to L.20. We can conclude that, perhaps with the exception of San Andrea de Sestri, cost alone did not determine the burial site. Other factors, like reputation and parochial obligations, must explain the choices. This inclusive nature of Genoese burials is amply demonstrated by San Matteo, which served as the resting place for both the wealthy Doria and a woman named Imeia, who left only nineteen solidi for her funeral and burial there.[73] Whether the burial of different social classes at the same site somehow ratified the existing social order is doubtful. The burial customs reflect the diversity of wealth within the parish, the universal appeal of the different sites, and even a measure of competition for business.

I agree with Ariès that the testators did not really care where the church placed the body, except for the stigma of the pauper's grave. As discussed above, burial was a matter that concerned the fabric of the church, and not the laity. The only Genoese who seemed to express a desire to be buried at a specific location was Giovanna, the wife of the late Vassallo da Sori. She wanted to be buried at San Ambrogio "in the ground before the main door."[74] In fact she was identifying the whole churchyard or cemetery, and not a specific spot. Only those rare individuals who prepared a monument for themselves, or who came from prominent families with strong ties to a local church, such as the Doria or Embriaci, knew precisely where they would be buried. Only the notary Oberto Scriba regularly used the word *cimiterium* to denote the burial site. This word refers to the church's courtyard, the most common place for burial. Those whom Oberto Scriba notes as having specified burial in the cemetery did not set aside less money for this purpose than the majority of people, who supplied only the site's name. This range of burial expenses in the cemeteries indicates that the burial itself probably does not account for the diverse costs. If the Genoese believed that one part of a church was a better site for a tomb than another, the church would have charged more for these favorite spots. However, theologians would have been hesitant to admit that some parts of the church were holier than others. There was no stigma attached to the church cemetery, and many wealthy people joined their fellow citizens there. The location of these courtyards is not always clear. The premium placed on city land, in the period under review and ever since, has obliterated all surface traces of them. In at least one case, that of San Matteo, a monastic cloister of the fourteenth century still exists, and funerary plaques from later centuries can be seen there.

It is significant that the notaries did not use the word *cemetery* by itself, and most notaries omitted the term altogether. Instead they referred to the burial site by naming the saint to whom the church or monastery was dedicated, and employed a preposition—*apud* (at) or *iuxta* (next to). The notaries never used the preposition *in* when they noted the burial site.[75] Peter Brown has carefully traced the relation of Christian burial to the rise of the cult of the saints. The Genoese wanted to be buried with a particular saint, who exerted an unknown but perhaps very personal appeal. San Siro was a local saint of great antiquity, Saint John the Baptist a recent but renowned arrival. Burial *apud sanctos* was clearly desirable and in fact by this time required by law, but as Brown notes, "once obtained, it mapped out in a peculiarly blatant manner, in terms of proximity to the saint, the balance of social power in the community."[76] There was, again, in Brown's words, "a play of family influence around the holy graves," though in subsequent centuries the church took over from powerful families the control of these holy bodies and extended the aura of holiness from the relic or tomb to the entire grounds of the church. The laity did not expect to be buried inside the church walls proper, even though some wealthy people had always secured this distinction. Time and changes in decorative taste have eliminated any funerary inscriptions from this period. Money may have purchased such a remembrance; an inscription may have accompanied a well-endowed anniversary. Most people were content with the cemetery, and I do not know of any monuments in the cemeteries of this period.

While money kept a person from a pauper's grave, it could buy only so much in a cemetery. It is hard to see any distinction between a pauper's grave and what the average Genoese seemed to want. A pauper's funeral was another matter, and no one wanted that. Types of burial, particularly the few that actually took place inside the church, explain some of the differences in the cost of a funeral and burial. One must count more heavily the cost of the funeral ceremony and masses. In later centuries this would all change, and the tomb itself would become an object of great expense and a fitting subject for artistic endeavor. In this period, however, the ephemeral funeral ceremony and perpetual prayer marked the transition of a soul to the next world.

The three expenses associated with death were the funeral, burial, and masses. Most Genoese planned for these expenses in their wills. The first of the three stages of the ritual of death took place in the home and required little or no expenditure. The procession in the street—the funeral—transferred the body to the church, which conducted the burial. Masses were an integral part of the burial, and continued on into the future for as long as the deceased was able to afford. Masses and the funeral were highly variable expenses; the burial, usually in the churchyard, was less so. The funeral, burial, and masses were customarily the first legacies the testators listed in the portion of the will reserved for the benefit of the soul. The Genoese meant to be taken quite literally. They were conscious of a process of transfer, mediated by the church, to the next world. The first step was to depart properly from this one. The amount of money expended enhanced the style of this departure. Money might buy a rare tomb inside the church walls, but it was most often put toward the expenses of the funeral and masses, where a small increment made a noticeable difference. The Genoese left bequests to a wide range of charities, but not one of them left money for burying paupers; the church assumed this responsibility. People were willing to pay for the burial of relatives who had neglected to provide for this themselves. In his own will of 1209 Oddone the cooper acknowledged that he owed one-third of the burial price of a relation, which he had agreed to share with two of his relatives.[77] The Genoese were willing to feed, clothe, and provide dowries for paupers, but the thought of a pauper's funeral seems to have been too horrible to contemplate. Ariès might be correct in saying that most burials (except for those of the rich) were not individualistic, but the funerals, so far as one can tell, certainly were. Lack of evidence should not be taken for lack of individuality. The wills suggest that one should distinguish, as the Genoese did, the funeral from the burial. One needs to know more about the burial before concluding that they all necessarily resulted in the same anonymous graves.

Whether these concerns about death reflect any increase in the individuality of the Genoese is an open question. I will have more to say about this as I consider the other bequests for the soul.

6 / Social Charity

In their wills the Genoese distributed money across a wide range of charities. Pious giving was considered the obligation of the wealthy, and indeed of every Christian, apart from paupers. I have already discussed the theological basis of charity. The church communicated these ideas to the laity by means of the sermon. Especially in the thirteenth century preaching to the laity became one of the church's principal activities. Genoa contributed one of the most prolific and popular preachers of the Middle Ages, Jacopo da Voragine. He distinguished himself in many fields: he was archbishop of Genoa (1291–1298), a city historian, and the author of a work of enduring popularity, *The Golden Legend*. Jacopo entered the Dominican order in Genoa in 1244, and for many years he practiced the art which eventually brought him prominence and papal favor—preaching. His sermons have survived in many collections and cast much light on what the church wanted the laity to hear and believe.[1] Jacopo knew his audience very well. His language is rich in the metaphors of business and the sea. His sermons addressed the great theological issues, but he also took time to guide the laity on questions of marriage, children, and wealth. Rich and neglected historical sources, the sermons are nevertheless not a sure guide to the beliefs and motives of the laity. Sermons are by nature highly prescriptive, and at best they only suggest what the Genoese had in mind when they made their bequests.

In one Lenten sermon Jacopo da Voragine chose as his text a verse from Luke, "There was a rich man, who was clothed in purple and fine linen."[2] His theme was of course the rich man and the pauper. The verse evokes the only Gospel parable with a named character—Lazarus. A poor man covered with sores, Lazarus would sit at the gate of a rich man, who gave him nothing. After his death Lazarus, welcomed to Abraham's bosom, eventually saw the rich man burn in hell; he had become, in Jacopo's words, "a parishioner of the Devil." By the central Middle Ages Lazarus was a recognized saint, the patron of paupers and lepers. The story of Lazarus and the rich man provided powerful scriptual support for church doctrine on avarice and charity. Jacopo describes the three ways in which the rich man sinned. "First, by avariciously retaining wealth, because he wanted to give nothing to the poor. For this is the nature of avarice, that he would keep all his goods for himself and give nothing to anyone."[3] Thus far Jacopo has explicated the text in a conventional manner, but the rich man's second offense is more striking. The archbishop condemned as vanity the habits of the wealthy, who spent money on clothes and feasts.

Indeed we ought to spend our temporal goods in a useful way since they are not ours, but are committed by God to us to distribute to the poor. For that these goods are not our own is made clear in death, because we are not able to take them with us. For once a dog followed two men, one of whom he did not know. But when the men separated from each other, then the dog followed his own master. Thus the two persons are man and the world, and to which in life the riches belong, man or the world, is not apparent, but in death it is. The riches remain in the world and man leaves the world naked. Therefore it is said in Job, "Naked came I out of my mother's womb and naked I shall return there."[4]

Riches tested Christian morality, and as I have noted, the will was the last chance to pass the test. In fact this passage was a reminder of death, and seemed all but to name the testament. The third failing of the wealthy was the excessive love of riches. His basic message was that the people to whom riches were imparted were not damned by wealth but rather by their misuse of it.

The poor endured three corresponding ills—poverty, sickness, and grave temptation—a list which Jacopo attributed to Gregory the Great. Poverty and sickness we may easily understand. Such was the case for Lazarus, whom God tested as gold in a furnace. As Jacopo said, "For he endures great temptations when he sees himself to have neither bread nor health."[5] The rich could imagine what these temptations were, as well as the dangers to themselves which might result. The benefits of charity could be practical and spiritual. The social order depended on keeping the poor from revolt. When some people feast, those who, as Jacopo put it, "long for crumbs" can be dangerous. If feasting leads to voluptuousness, starving could lead to rebellion. Jacopo might have limited himself to premonitions of hell, but it is to his credit as a preacher that he consistently tried to relate his spiritual message to the laity's daily life. The stark contrast between rich and poor makes sense only if all those above the level of the pauper were in some sense rich. The primary task of this chapter is to investigate those having something to give, and to see whether the beneficiaries were the same for all those who gave to charity.

Curiously, Jacopo did not mention the church in his sermons on wealth and poverty, nor was the church named in connection with charity. The omission reflects the church's pervasive charitable role. There was not much charity outside the church. The Genoese commune had an extremely broad view of its obligations to the citizens. The commune supervised the construction of city walls, helped to build the navy, sent embassies to foreign capitals, fought wars, administered justice, and collected customs duties and forced loans to pay for these endeavors. The city government's only apparent social goal, besides fostering trade and defending the republic, was to support the church in administering and financing charity. The poor and the sick, the widows and the orphans, were Christ's poor, and were entrusted to the church. There certainly was a sense of public responsibility to these people, in the sense that the destitute and defenseless had legitimate claims on Genoese purses and hearts. These demands help to explain the significance of the *pro anima* bequests. W. K. Jordan in his classic study of philanthropy in England pointed out that the charitable donors were instrumental in fashioning what he termed an "ethic of social responsibility."[6] For sixteenth-century England the real test of charity became the need to replace the church as the primary agent of social service. The period under study here witnessed the reverse process, as the church undertook the first great elaboration of a system of philanthropy in the first society (Italy) since the fall of Rome with substantial moneys to devote to charitable causes. Secular government, just beginning to develop, had enough tasks to perform. The church was equipped, in terms of a ready bureaucracy and sustaining ideology, to oversee and direct social goals in the thirteenth century. This bureaucracy consisted mainly of local people who knew very well what the city needed in order to maintain social peace, and what the laity was prepared to support.

One must differentiate between the church's social and spiritual goals. While all pious donations were charitable, some donations aided the churches as institutions while others enabled them to dispense charity. After all, the church was primarily concerned with fostering the Christian religion, and much income answered to its institutional needs. A large proportion of charitable donations went to endow masses, to construct or maintain the fabric of churches and monasteries, and to support the clergy. These were in a sense social goals too, but from the laity's point of view such causes were primarily spiritual. All charity benefited the soul, so the ultimate purpose was always the same.

Donations made to the church, or entrusted to clergymen, family members, or friends so that they might distribute them to fulfill what I have distinguished as social goals, are the main focus of this chapter. I shall look at a few specific social charities: hospitals, lepers, the poor, bridges, ransom for captives, the Crusades, emancipation of slaves, and the Franciscans and Dominicans. I shall consider the numerical relationship of this sort of giving to all pious bequests, and shall investigate whether the various levels of society had different social goals. It should be clear that the spiritual as well as social motives were never absent from charity. Most forms of charity had an impact on this world's social fabric, but they were intended to secure a place for the donor in the next one.

A word of caution is in order here. There is no necessary, neat fit between social goals and personal motives. The decision to be charitable was made at a moment of approaching death. Social responsibility and guilt may have played a major part in the decision, but so too did a variety of other considerations, such as family ties, personal habit, the advice of others, or sheer caprice. We do not know why someone was more concerned about lepers than orphans. Concerning this question of motive Jordan sensibly concluded that "this most essential datum remains buried deep in the recesses of our nature, immune, perhaps happily, from the fumbling probing of the historian and, certainly happily, from the arrogantly pitched enquiry of the psychoanalyst."[7] Why different social groups favored one type of charity over another is a question with which the historian can come to grips.

The wealthy are a good subject with which to start the survey. The people who left over one hundred lire or more for their souls constitute a discrete group of individuals. In the same way that the custom of making a testament spread throughout the population between 1150 and 1250, so too did the charitable habits of the rich find some imitators in the less wealthy social ranks. Table 9 in Chapter 5 has shown that seventeen men and nine women gave this amount or more. Four of the men did what Fulcone de Castello ordered: they left one-tenth to San Lorenzo and the rest to be distributed as others saw fit. One woman, Giovanna Pevere, left L.200 in the same way, but as we have seen, some difficult experiences with the church may explain this lack of specificity.[8] The complete *pro anima* bequests of four people, two men and two women, are listed here in order to demonstrate the wide scope of Genoese charity, and to highlight the individualistic nature of these bequests.[9] The right-hand column shows what percentage of the total each individual bequest represents.

Rubaldo Galleta
June 7, 1210
Raimundo Medico, notary

L.500 (approximately) *pro anima:*

L.50	tithe to San Lorenzo	10%
L.40	funeral and masses	8
L.20	works of the servants of San Lorenzo	4
L.50	works of the harbor mole	10
L.50	widows, paupers, and dowries for orphans	10
L.50	clothes for paupers	10
L.50	his brother Oberto	10
L.15	works of Santa Maria d'Alsenorio	3
L.10	works of San Andrea de Sestri Ponente	2
L.20	the sick of Fari, in land	4
L.10	works of San Tommaso de Canoni	2
L.20	four hospitals	4
L.5	works of the city gates	1
L.13	the new hospital in Rapallo	2.6
L.5	Hospital of Pozolo	1
L.50	ransom for captives	10
L.21	six bridges	4.4

Oberto Bonizo
September 19, 1227
Jacopo Taraburlo, notary

L.25	*pro anima* bequests:	
L.10	burial	40%
L.2 s.10	works of San Lorenzo	10
L.5	masses for a year	20
L.7 s.10	rest for his soul	30
L.148 s.10	additional bequests:	
L.10	his relative Villeta for her marriage	6.7
L.8	Giovanna, daughter of his late nurse, for marriage	5.4
L.10	his relative Roseta for her marriage	6.7
L.30	Dominicans for anniversaries	20.2
L.25	Church of Santo Spirito	16.8
L.12	Hospital of San Giovanni	8
L.10	Church of San Lazaro	6.7
L.5	works of the Franciscans	3.4
L.20	aid for the Holy Land	13.5
L.7	L.1 to each of seven hospitals in Genoa	4.7
s.10	works of the port of Camogli	.4
L.1	bridge of Polcifera	.7
L.5	works of Santa Maria delle Vigne, provided he can be buried at San Egidio	3.4

Aimelina Galleta
January 26, 1235
Lantelmo, notary

L.100	*pro anima* bequests:	
L.10	tithe to San Lorenzo	10%
L.15	funeral, burial, and masses	15
L.75	San Lorenzo for anniversaries	75
L.156 s.10	additional bequests:	
L.10	Alasina de Bombello for her marriage	6.4
L.18	her servant Anneta	11.5
L.5	Margarita	3.2
L.20	works of the harbor mole	12.8
L.10	the sick of Capo Fari	6.4
L.10	the Hospital of San Giovanni	6.4
L.20	aid for the Holy Land	12.8
s.10	the Hospital of Pozolo	.3
L.2	bridges at Lavagna and Polcifera	1.3
L.1	Monastery of Mesema	.6
L.10	her daughter Alasina for *falcidia*	6.4
L.40	orphans, widows, and dowries for paupers	25.6

| L.5 | Guidetta, servant of priest Rollando | 3.2 |
| L.5 | San Andrea de Porta for masses | 3.2 |

Contessa Braxili
December 27, 1241
Bonovassallo de Casino, notary

L.10	*pro anima* bequests:	
L.1	tithe to San Lorenzo	10%
L.9	for my soul and burial	90
L.90 s.10	additional bequests:	
L.10	the sick of San Giovanni	11
L.5	the sick of Capo Fari	5.5
L.10	San Ambrogio for anniversary and masses	11
L.1 s.10	three hospitals	1.6
s.10	Santa Savina for masses	.5
L.6	Dominicans and Franciscans	6.6
L.3	Santa Sarafia	3.3
L.5	three hospitals	5.5
L.2	recluses of Bisagno	2.2
L.1	Monastery of Rapallo	1.1
s.10	bridge of Lavagna	.5
L.10	her servant Audonia	11
L.10	Alasina	11
L.10	the widow Caracosa, for her marriage	11
L.3	Viride, servant of Oberto Castaldo	3.3
s.10	works of the cross of the Castello of Sori	.5
L.12 s.10	clothes for paupers	13.8

These four are representative of the wealthiest class; the six wills from before 1200, all in print, are basically similar. The only difference is that some wills contain long lists of friends who were for some reason included in the charitable bequests. Some of the items included as pious bequests, such as legacies to friends and relatives, may have been construed as charitable because they were voluntary.[10] Most people stayed on the broad path of recognizable charity. It is possible that some people did not want to leave any money to charity, and they preferred their friends or relatives to unknown paupers or lepers. Some testators found a happy compromise by leaving money for the dowry of a friend's daughter. Providing dowries was an acceptable act of charity, and here again some preferred to dower girls they knew rather than some unknown orphan. The main point is that almost any gift might be construed as charitable, but most people stayed on the broad path of recognizable charity.

The charitable donations of the rich confirm the idea that the social charities should receive the most attention. The cathedral, except for the obligatory tithe, the great local monasteries, and the parish churches do not figure prominently among their beneficiaries. For a comparison to the wealthy, let us look at the modest pious bequests of Sibona, the wife of Giovanni de Mondaruco.[11]

Sibona
September 21, 1226
Urso, notary

L.2	*pro anima:*	
s.20	funeral	50%
d.6	the confraternity of the hospital	1.2
s.2	works of the Church of Saints Cosmo and Damiano	5
s.8	priest Ottone for masses in remission of her sins	20
s.3	San Siro de Molassana	7.5
s.2	Hospital of San Giovanni	5
d.6	her goddaughter, the daughter of G. Rufino	1.2
d.6	her godson Ansaldo	1.2
d.6	her godson Pausatoro	1.2
d.6	her goddaughter Floria	1.2
d.6	the sick of Fari	1.2
d.6	Hospital of the Crociferi	1.2
d.6	Hospital of Santo Stefano	1.2

These small bequests imitate the scope of the charities of the rich, at an appropriately diminished scale. "Imitate" may be the wrong word to describe what may have been just a similarity of intention which had nothing to do with wealth or social position. Though the rich may have dominated charity, they did not monopolize it. Sibona's bequest represents an exceptional case, however; most people having about L.2 for their soul chose to spend a little more on their funeral and restrict the number of beneficiaries, with an increase in the donations to a favored few. There is an interesting tension at work here between the desire to give to many charities and the wish to give effectively. The rich could hope to do both. Most wealthy people followed the pattern set in the first four lists;

they gave substantial sums to a wide variety of charities. The average testator donated smaller amounts to fewer charities. Two strategies were open to the beneficiaries: to pursue the small number of large donations or to attract the average Genoese testator. Charities seemed to try to follow both courses. After considering the specific social charities, I shall return to the question of who supported different charities. In all wills, the single most popular charity was the Hospital of San Giovanni, and not far behind was the leper colony of Capo Fari. In order to understand the Genoese philanthrophic impulse, let us consider these social charities in detail.

San Giovanni and Other Hospitals

The Hospital of San Giovanni has already been mentioned as a popular burial site. From its foundation sometime between 1163 and 1186, the hospital benefited from one hundred ninety-four wills, and was the most popular Genoese charity. From 1186 to 1253 the hospital remained a yearly favorite, secure in first place among beneficiaries. The local reputation of the Hospitalers was high. The best and most recent historian of the order, Jonathan Riley-Smith, notes that one of the first saints of the new order was Ugone, a brother in the commandary of Genoa.[12] Having a saint added to the reputation of the hospital, especially when he was one of their own. Archbishop Ottone Fieschi wrote a book (now apparently lost) about Saint Ugone's miracles.[13] Saint Ugone led an austere life at the hospital, where he served the sick and poor with great charity and love. He performed various menial tasks, and helped to bury the dead. Once, lacking enough water to wash the clothes of the sick, he made the sign of the Cross and caused a fountain to spring up. Several other miracles involved water, always a precious commodity in Genoa. Another time he saved through prayer a ship beset by a storm in the harbor. The seamen attributed their rescue to Saint Ugone's merits. Anyone who could prevent shipwrecks would find favor in Genoa. Saint Ugone died on October 8, 1233, and his tomb in the Church of San Giovanni was the site of many miraculous cures. His life illustrated the important point that the hospital served both patients and paupers. Famous as a military order, the Hospitalers in Genoa produced a charitable saint, who actively ministered to the "miserable persons." This man was not a distant historical or mythic figure; he was a contemporary sign that the Hospital of San Giovanni was a spiritual place.

People from all social levels donated to the hospital. The gifts of the least well-to-do are notable, because those who gave to only two or three charities, in small amounts, almost always selected the hospital. Apart from a few big bequests, most gifts to the hospital were small, and represented a small portion, 10 percent or less, of the total charitable giving. This pattern holds for almost all testators. Some of the donations were for specific purposes, or in kind. Vassallo de San Donato, a draper, left the hospital a barrel of must, a cheap wine; five other communities received the same salubrious gift.[14] The most common targeted gift was money to feed the sick, or at least to buy them bread. I have already mentioned the most common gift in kind—beds and furnishing such as mattresses, sheets, covers, and pillows. A sign of Sant' Ugone's asceticism was that he slept on a bare table without a mattress. The sick needed to be more comfortable than that.

The widespread pattern of gifts to the hospital and the generally small value of these donations require an explanation. Tradition alone may have been at work here. The Genoese respected the hospital and its services. Small bequests, almost pittances, were a local custom, which, in the absence of any reason for stopping, became a fixture of the wills. The wills Raimundo Medico wrote from 1213 to 1216 can be used as a test case. The lepers of Capo Fari have been included in this test because the Genoese themselves so often linked the leper colony with the Hospital of San Giovanni. The issue at hand is whether these bequests were merely routine and random, or whether they reflect deep-seated preferences and conscious decisions within the Genoese charitable impulse. Some people had obvious reasons for not giving to the Hospital of San Giovanni. Ugone Vacario of Rapallo gave L.5 for his soul, and all his charities were located in his home town.[15] A woman named Virdilia had the same attachment to her native Fontaneggio.[16] Neither of them betrays an inclination to contribute to Genoese charities. Other individuals, after having left some of their *pro anima* bequests for their funerals, commissioned their trustees to determine what charities should be remembered.

Trusting relatives and friends to do what was best does not imply an indifference to charity, since the testator might have left nothing at all. One man, going to Santiago, left nothing, though his wife did. After putting the cases of no specific bequests aside, we are left with eighteen wills, eleven from 1213 and seven from late 1215 to early 1216, presented in Table 11.[17]

These wills reveal some patterns. Eleven of the eighteen left the same amount (including nothing) to both charities. Of the five people favoring one over the other, four chose the hospital, one the lepers—but in all five cases the proportions were roughly the same—two to one (a bed and a pot were worth at least L.1). Only two people left money to one and not the other; in both cases the hospital was the choice. The total number of charitable bequests in the last two wills listed is rather small. The whole set of char-

Table 11. Partial breakdown of charitable bequests in eighteen wills, 1213–1216

Total amount left to charity per will	Number of charitable bequests per will	Amount left to Hospital of San Giovanni	Amount left to lepers of Capo Fari	
L.3	2	s.2	0	
L.5	9	s.3	s.3	
L.3	10	s.10	s.10	
L.4	2	0	0	
L.14	9	s.1	s.1	
	12	L.1	L.1	L.30
L.1 s.10	4	0	0	
L.60	approx. 23	L.1	L.1	
L.100	17	L.10	L.5	
L.4	5	0	0	
L.30	14	L.2	L.1	
L.8	5	s.5	s.5	
L.15	7	0	0	
L.20	11	L.1	L.1	
L.22	11	L.2	L.1	
L.10	10	a bed, a pot	s.10	
L.1 s.7	3	d.12	0	
L.7 s.10	3	0	0	

Source: Archivio di Stato di Genova, Cartolari Notarili, N. 5, notary Raimundo Medico.

itable bequests demonstrates a rough correlation between the total amount of money given and the number of bequests. The Hospital of San Giovanni and the lepers of Capo Fari attracted an equal amount of attention. The work of other notaries supports this conclusion. Though the value of the donations is in most instances small, in aggregate the sums provided a large and reliable income. Raimundo Medico's clients displayed a slight preference for the hospital, as did the Genoese as a whole. The bequests outlined in Table 11 support the conclusion that these gifts were not pro forma tokens.

One of Raimundo's clients, Lavorabene of Messina, while leaving no money to San Giovanni, wished Maestro Guglielmo of the hospital to take charge of the expenses of his funeral, which was to be at the hospital.[18] Since the order was international, this stranger from Sicily facing the prospect of death in Genoa would at least find at San Giovanni a familiar religious name and purpose. Enrico Pelato left most of his goods for his soul, to be distributed by Maestro Guglielmo of the hospital, and his paternal uncle Ansaldo.[19] There are cogent reasons for believing that in both cases the testastors called on Maestro Guglielmo for their own reasons, but their notary, Raimundo Medico, may have brought them together. The regular amounts given to these two charities, and even the proportions when the sums differed, may indicate that either the notary suggested the sums or the prominence of the institutions in some sense demanded equal attention. The latter is the more probable explanation, for reasons I shall consider shortly when I examine the other hospitals.

Unfortunately, very little is known about how the Hospital of San Giovanni, or any hospital, supplied medical care or dispensed relief to the poor. The commandary of the hospital in Genoa was a branch of a far-flung health service provider, almshouse, and military order. The commandary was supposed to provide a portion of its revenues to the headquarters in Jerusalem, or after 1187 in Acre. The local hospital services dominated Genoese concerns; only three people specifically left money to the Hospital of San Giovanni in Acre to aid the Holy Land overseas.[20] While some hospitals may have served principally as inns for traveling pilgrims, in Genoa the hospital mainly served the sick and the poor. A lay confraternity is known to have been associated with the hospital as early as 1191.[21] Giordano Richerio's will of 1198 demonstrates the process of founding a hospital.[22] He left to Richerio and Pietro Richerio all he possessed in Nizza (Nice)—a considerable property which was worth at least L.1000. But he attached a condition to their legacy: they were to build a hospital on this land in Nizza next to the sea and sufficiently endow it so that twelve paupers could live there. Giordano named his brother Lanfranco as the legal representative of this new hospital. Lanfranco was to hand the new foundation over to the Hospital of San Giovanni at Capo d'Arena, itself a dependency of the main house in Genoa. Here is an example of how the medieval hospital served as an almshouse. The paupers in turn would nurse as best they could the inmates—the sick. Whether the paupers or the sick benefited the most is not our concern, since either aim sufficed for social charity.

Hospitals of all types became important features of the Genoese social scene. Nearly all testaments containing charitable bequests set aside some money for them. Frequently the legacy took the form of five solidi or some such amount for every hospital in Genoa. Ansaldo de Narbona in 1186 left five solidi for each hospital from Capo Fari, just west of the city walls, to San Fruttuoso de Via, east of the city at the mouth of the Bisagno. He left a total of L.40 for his soul, and all the other legacies amounted to L.38 s.10, which left L.1 s.10 for the hospitals—enough for six.[23] Besides the two named above the other four were the hospitals of San Giovanni, Santo Stefano, San Lorenzo, and Castello. Just past the Bisagno was the Hospital of the Crociferi of Bisagno, a local branch of the new Italian hospital order which Pope Alexander III had recognized and ordered to follow the Augustinian rule. The 1225 will of Giulia, the wife of Ansaldo d'Albaro, enables us to determine in the same way that there were ten hospitals from San Lazaro de Capo Fari to the Hospital of the Crociferi.[24] The three additions, if they are that, since 1186 were the hospitals of Santa Croce, San Antonio, and San Giovanni de Capo d'Arena. There were more hospitals in other coastal towns and up in the mountains, and new ones continued to appear during the thirteenth century. All these hospitals received the same types of gifts as San Giovanni—small and numerous. The growing number of hospitals suggests that these new institutions were responding to

real social needs. Everyone who recognized some obligation to
these institutions seemed prepared to bear only a small part of
the social cost. After San Giovanni, none was as important as the
community of lepers who dwelled at Capo Fari.

The Lepers

Leprosy evoked a real sense of horror in the medieval mind.[25]
Coupled with this loathing, however, was the knowledge that Christ
himself had displayed special concern for lepers, and for a few
people who knew victims of the disease, horror was tempered with
compassion. William of Tyre describes how he discovered the
incipient leprosy in his young student, the future King Baldwin
IV of Jerusalem, by noticing a numbness in the extremities; the
author vividly conveys his own deep emotions.[26] Leprosy caused
a struggle in the healthy between feelings of charity and revulsion,
and it was a serious social problem as well. The disease was not
well understood, and in fact was often confused with a variety of
other skin ailments. Communities enforced a strict quarantine
against lepers, and at least in France the church cooperated in
this venture by devising a new rite—the separation of lepers. In
the most graphic form, the community would conduct the leper
to the local cemetery and make him stand in a grave, while a priest
told him that as far as the world was concerned, he was dead.[27]
Whether this interesting social custom was practiced in Italy or
not is unknown. The usually compassionate Jacopo da Voragine
conjured various unhappy images with the disease. The archbishop helped to spread the strange story, originally found in the
Donation of Constantine, in his sermons on Pope Sylvester that the
pope had cured the emperor of his leprosy by baptism.[28] This line
of reasoning implied that the disease had something to do with
the state of the soul. He further developed this idea in a sermon
on the Gospel, of all things. After listing some of the more noxious
manifestations of the illness, he pointed out that "just as leprosy
corrupts all the physical senses, so too does sin corrupt all the
spiritual virtues of the soul."[29] The suggestion that the soul of a
sinner appeared to God as a leper's body did to men must have
given his Genoese audience a few queasy moments.

And yet the city acquired something of a reputation for taking decent care of lepers. Guirardo de Verzellato left L.30 in his will "to clothe lepers who come to Genoa from divers parts to seek alms."[30] A community of lepers lived on the small peninsula of Capo Fari, just west of the city, which separated Genoa from Sampierdarena. The first document that sheds any light on this community is an agreement reached in 1153 by the Church of San Teodoro and the "infirm of Capo Fari."[31] The lepers, who had evidently only recently settled there, wanted a church of their own. The archbishop of Genoa had to sort out the conflicting parochial claims, but the document gives the clear impression that everyone was eager to see the lepers have their own church. Though there were lepers at Capo Fari as early as the mid-twelfth century, they began to attract significant attention only at the end of the century. Testators usually referred to these people as the sick, the infirm, the recluses, or the lepers of Capo Fari. In 1210 a will identified the community by a new name—that of their church, San Lazaro.[32] The lepers had evidently had a church there for some time, but we do not know the name of that church. The name San Lazaro suggests a link with the international religious order of lepers which had been organized in the twelfth century in the East. Such a connection is suggested at a later date by an act in the cartulary of Bartolomeo Fornari.[33] On June 23, 1248, Brother Gandulfo, styled as "syndic of the house and community of the sick of San Lazaro of Fari," and originally appointed to this position in 1246, acknowledged to Ugone Navaro that he had received L.18 in the name of the lepers. This sum represented one-sixth of the goods of the late Ugone di Baldizone (Navaro's father-in-law), which he had left to San Lazaro for his soul. The lepers needed a legal representative who could handle such business in Genoa. That the community was organized enough to have a syndic indicates that the lepers lived according to a rule of some sort, perhaps that of the order of San Lazaro. Brother Gandulfo was himself probably a Franciscan.

    In the period under review here, 166 Genoese left the lepers something in their wills. The legacies were often small amounts of cash, or gifts in kind like beds, clothes, food, and wine. There were a few sizable donations for the lepers to buy land; Giordano Richerio gave them L.300 for this purpose.[34] Probably sometime around 1248 a second colony, or *lazaretto*, was founded to the east of the city near the Bisagno. The city thus possessed these two rather substantial communities of lepers to its east and west, each with a church, hospital, refectory, and other buildings. Genoa served more than the needs of its own inhabitants who succumbed to this unfortunate illness. The church directed the life of the communities, but the laity remembered the lepers in their wills and tried to solve their problem with charity instead of savagery.

The Poor

The historical record of medieval Genoa is very unlikely to have included any reference to the poor. The hundred thousand or so notarial acts had nothing to do with the poor, since they did not figure in the commercial life of the city. Genoese chroniclers confined themselves to warfare and diplomacy, and when they described the affairs of their fellow citizens, it was usually the wealthy and the rancorous who achieved notice. Sermons sympathetically mentioned the poor, but they never gave a sense of local conditions, and tended to view poverty as a constant of life. In short, only the Genoese wills give us any information about the poor, and they are sources of questionable value. However, comments about Genoese poverty must rely on the wills if they are to have any basis in fact. It is possible to study those who gave to the poor, and from this giving we can learn indirectly about the nature of Genoese poverty. First, though, it is necessary to define carefully who the poor were. As Lester Little notes, "The term 'poor' is relative, referring to such conditions as weakness in relation to power, illness in relation to good health, or lack of money."[35] Some people of very modest means have appeared in these pages, and the "relatively poor"—those not needing a will—might have had goods worth a lira, or in fact virtually nothing at all. Poverty need not have been a lifelong condition; one may hope that some escaped it through their own labors or the charity of their fellow Genoese. The relationship between disease and poverty must also be kept in mind; the medieval hospital, as I have already noted, served both needs. Disease, in the vivid case of Lazarus, resulted in poverty, and in turn one of the principal attributes of poverty was physical debilitation. For the Genoese testator, paupers, widows, and orphans made up the poor population. One must carefully examine this apparent tautology. The general class of paupers included men and women, but there are signs that the plight of poor men aroused less sympathy. Not all widows and orphans were in fact poor, yet those who were seem to have had special claims on the Genoese conscience. The concern for destitute women and children placed them in a special category.

The wills allow us to assume that poverty existed in medieval Genoa, and to judge from the wills, a sensitivity to this problem was increasing in the thirteenth century. As Genoa became a wealthy town, resources to devote to charitable purposes also grew, and this alone may account for the more extensive donations in the post-1200 wills. Besides increased social awareness and available cash, a third possible explanation for a rise in giving is that there may simply have been more poor people in Genoa as the thirteenth century progressed. Shipping dominated the economic life of the port, and it was a seasonal business, employing crews and dock workers in great numbers during a relatively short time of the year. Periodic warfare disrupted trade and often interfered with the importation of foodstuffs, which may itself have depressed local peasant agriculture in the mountains. We know that immigration was increasing, both from rural areas and the other Ligurian towns. We see here the makings, at least, of a class of seasonally unemployed and unskilled laborers, and a flood of rural folk with no particular skills for earning a living in the Genoese economy. This century was a boom time for Genoa, but the ranks of the poor seem to have swelled as well. Seventy-three testators left something for the poor; these legacies were generally larger than those to the hospitals, and included many quite significant bequests. The poor were the special concern of the affluent. While some people of moderate means set aside a few solidi for the poor, it was the rich who gave most consistently and in large amounts. While only about 35 percent of all testators gave L.10 or more for their souls (see Table 9), 60 percent of those who gave to the poor donated that much or more. After about 1225 people of modest means—those with L.5 or less to give for their souls—increased their giving to the poor. The rich maintained their position as the real force behind this charity, especially in terms of total giving.

Not much attention was paid to the poor before 1200; only

eight of the testators mention them at all, and in some of these cases only as participants in the funeral procession. Donations made to the poor carry the largest number of conditions; that is, the testators usually supplied some details as to how the money was to be spent. The most common condition is that the money be spent to clothe paupers. A few people left their own clothes to the poor. One person, himself a wool merchant, wished his clothing to be sold and the proceeds used to clothe orphans and widows around the feast of Saint Michael.[36] Perhaps he wanted to help the trade and honor his guild's patron saint as well. Most Genoese left cash to clothe the poor. Rubaldo Galleta left L.50 for this purpose, and Guirardo de Verzellato left L.25 to buy clothes for poor people who wanted to enter religion.[37] On a smaller scale, one Benvegnuta left L.1 to buy a shirt for a pauper.[38] Shirts, which were made of a light fabric, usually linen or cotton, were expensive in this period, as in fact was all clothing, despite the fact that Genoa had a wool weaving industry. At least to the Genoese, a lack of clothing seemed to be a very distinctive attribute of poverty. Guglielmo de Mari left money to protect "the miserable people" from a most basic threat—the natural elements.[39]

Another pressing need of the poor was food, but hunger received less attention, perhaps because food was not as hard to come by as clothing. The testators usually left food to the poor in kind, such as bread. Aidela, the wife of Bernardo the shoemaker, left thirty solidi for masses and for one quarter of farina to be distributed to the poor, all to benefit the soul of her late sister Adalasia.[40] The daily begging of the poor may have kept them from starvation; the wills do not indicate that starving was a serious problem. Hunger is always another matter. Guglielmo de Mari left L.60 for paupers, orphans, widows, and miserable persons. By charging his sister Giovanna and his friend Zacaria de Castro to disburse this money in such a way that no one received more than ten solidi, Guglielmo ensured that 120 people would benefit from his largess.[41] The money was enough to buy some food, but not enough for any clothing or much else. Most testators who simply stated that some amount was to be given to the poor probably intended their money to buy food—that is, to be distributed like alms to help feed the poor.

Sheltering the poor did not figure prominently as a charitable concern, perhaps for two reasons. As we have seen, the hospitals played a role in providing housing for paupers. And a house was a very expensive item in medieval Genoa, one that few Genoese could afford to give away. One interesting document sheds some light on the problem of shelter. On April 24, 1248, Brother Jacopo, prior of the Dominicans in Genoa, went before a notary to record an act of charity. He was the ordinator and provisor, basically the executor, of the well-known Genoese notary Maestro Salmone. Unfortunately, the notary's will does not survive, so we do not know the range of his charitable bequests. Brother Jacopo had considered how best to aid Maestro Salmone's soul. He decided to permit Giovanni, "useless in his hands and a pauper," his wife, and family (*familia*) to live in an apartment on the bottom floor of Maestro Salmone's house.[42] Brother Jacopo stated that the notary had been living in this house when he died. Giovanni and his family were to be allowed to live there for ten years rent free. Giovanni was evidently not an old associate of Salmone but a homeless, disabled man who had a family to support. It is appropriate that a Dominican conceived this unusual act of piety. The friars were instrumental in forming the social conscience of Italy, so it is interesting to see the prior of Genoa arranging to shelter a pauper. He might easily have sold the house instead or rented the apartment. But the sort of private poor relief that the Dominican devised in this case represents an important stage in the development of the charitable impulse.

A final specific purpose contained in the charitable bequests was that of providing dowries for poor women. This kind of legacy is perhaps the most revealing one from the point of view of social charity. The notarial cartularies preserve dowry contracts involving as little as one lira. The wills indicate that there were women who possessed virtually nothing, and consequently were not able to marry or remarry without charity. The most magnanimous Genoese philanthropist, Giordano Richerio, left L.50 for orphans to marry; his brother Ogerio and Guglielmo de Pallo were to select worthy recipients. Guirardo de Verzellato left L.30 for dowries for virgin paupers, and in this case at least two of the four people charged with executing this portion of his testament were clerics.[43] Only seven people mentioned providing dowries for paupers, but together they contributed L.215 for this goal, enough for perhaps one hundred women to marry. (One woman left all her clothes to a poor orphan for her marriage.) Since only about 2 percent of the original notarial record survives, this L.215 suggests a very substantial social investment in the institution of marriage. The church played a role in this particular charity as advisers and advocates of marriage, and the clergy might claim some credit for conveying the idea to the laity that it was meritorious to help poor women marry. Women were the sole recipients of this type of gift; no one gave men money so that they might marry. The Genoese recognized that the plight of unmarried, poor women in their society was not a happy one. Poor men would eventually receive these dowries anyway. Marriage without a dowry was unthinkable, and by providing dowries for poor women, the rich enabled a group of people to take an honorable place in community life, and evidently also enabled their own souls to rest more easily.

Bridges

At first glance donations to bridges may appear to be of dubious spiritual value. Yet ninety-eight Genoese—forty-eight men and fifty women—included bequests to bridges in the charitable section of their wills. Frederico da Soziglia left L.45 to "churches, bridges, hospitals, and pauper," and to him as well as others this combination was not incongruous.[44] In a few cases bridges were associated with religion. Four wills—one each in 1186 and 1192 and two in 1197—mention a bridge of the priest Berardo. Another person left ten solidi to "the Church of Santa Margarita de Murvallo and the bridge," implying some sort of connection between the two.[45] This was the first will to mention any bridge at Murvallo; later it was simply known as that. Nothing indicates that the Genoese commune assumed any responsibility for these bridges. Genoa was bounded by two rivers, the Bisagno to the east and the Polcifera to the west. For most of the year these rivers were merely dusty valleys with perhaps a few wet stones in the middle. During the spring run-off from the mountains to the north, or sudden storms, torrents quickly filled these valleys. Bridges were necessary just to make crossing these deep and wide ditches possible, either by pack animal or cart, or on foot. By around 1200 there were two principal bridges crossing the rivers, and the bridges received numerous small bequests, in a manner analogous to the hospitals. Bridges which were at some distance from the city—at Lavagna, Gavi, Pomaro, Celasco, and Recco—also received a steady stream of gifts. The mountainous area of Liguria made travel by road impossible without bridges, and the rivers were simply impassable and definitely not navigable. The bridges over the Bisagno and Polcifera rivers received the highest number of donations, and the most valuable ones. It should be pointed out that no one gave a great deal of money to bridges. Finally, the church played a role in administering the bridges. A church at one end of the bridge might serve as a convenient toll station, and a religious community could supply or pay for necessary routine maintenance. Bridges acquired a regular income from wills, but they may have been endowed as well. Since the city was always beset by warring factions, the church provided the most organized way to take care of these crucial links of commerce. To allow prominent families to control these potential strategic weapons would have invited the disruption of local trade, something no true Genoese could serenely contemplate. Up to the 1250s at least, people of all income levels continued to support these unusual social charities in their wills.[46]

Ransoming Captives and the Crusades

Two types of social charity involved matters of foreign policy—ransoming captives and the Crusades. Ransoming captives, either from the infidels or the Pisans, benefited the soul. Pietro de Silo left L.45 for captives, bridges, hospitals, orphans, and widows, in that order.[47] There was only one such bequest after 1228, which probably reflects the growing strength of Genoese power, and the fact that the church itself was becoming more active in this area. Nine of the eleven people leaving money to ransom captives were men, who must have been more aware than women of the possibility and consequences of capture. All of the people whose wills contained this bequest were rich; ransoming captives was the expensive business of merchants and warriors.

The crusading movement had extensive support in Genoa. I consider the Crusades a social charity because they were, particularly in the Italian ports, a war effort and a kind of commercial investment. Religious fervor and indulgences may have motivated the Genoese to give, but of great concern here is the effect of this giving, which was to promote warfare and Genoa's prosperity. Since the series of extant wills dates only from the 1150s, it is not possible to measure the degree of popular support behind the first two Crusades. But to judge from the narrative sources, this support was enthusiastic. Timber from Genoese ships helped to make the siege equipment for the capture of Jerusalem in 1099. The city actively aided Conrad of Montferrat during the Third Crusade, and supplied Philip Augustus of France with much of his shipping. Only one contemporary testament, from 1191, contains a bequest of L.7 s.10 to God and Oltremare—the land overseas.[48] In 1214 Aidela, the wife of Rubaldo Busso, left ten solidi "to fight Saracens in Spain and Galicia"; perhaps she was reacting to news of the recent great victories in Spain.[49] Genoa had close commercial ties with Barcelona and in general was well-informed about events in the Iberian peninsula.

The twenty-three men and fourteen women who left money to support the Crusades usually specified that they wanted their funds to go "for service Oltremare" or "to aid the Holy Land." Twelve of the wills originated in the period from December 1215 to February 1217, when preparations in Italy for the Crusade to Damietta were at their height. The rest of the donations occurred regularly over the next three decades. In the 1230s, a slow period for the Crusades, a few testators began to doubt whether any serious effort to recover the Holy Land would be made. Giovanna Tornello left money in 1231 to aid a general passage to the East if one took place within three years; otherwise the money was to be used for ransoming captives.[50] In 1236 a woman named Maria made a similar bequest, though she stipulated a period of five years.[51] This loss of popular confidence may be one of the principal reasons why the movement itself waned. Usually the legate of Oltremare or the archbishop collected these donations in order to ensure that the cause would benefit. People of all social levels left money for the Holy Land. Some of the wills indicated that the testator was going on crusade himself. This phenomenon was particularly noticeable in 1248, when agents of King Louis of France were recruiting in the city. Sometimes these donations took very practical cast. In 1228 one Sibilia left L.5 for service Oltremare, in order to buy iron munitions for a pilgrm.[52] Even in such a case the church, whether locally or through a representative of the Latin Kingdom's hierarchy, would again have served as the principal organizing force. The church never relinquished its authority in the effort to implement the goal of recovering the Holy Land. This goal had both social and religious overtones, since there were almost as many motives as there were donors. Even though the commune was active militarily in the Crusades, no one left his money to the city government; instead the Genoese trusted the church to see that the money was properly spent.

Slavery

Slavery presents several problems with regard to social history. Manumission of slaves by testament occurs only twenty-two times in the existing record, which contains many more *inter vivos* manumissions. There was no need for a person to wait until death to free his slaves, and many people did not. Freeing slaves, especially if this led to their conversion, was an act of undoubted spiritual merit with serious social implications.

Before looking at the wills, let us inquire how extensive slavery was in medieval Genoa. The great historian of slavery in the Middle Ages, Charles Verlinden, has recently given support to Alfred Haverkamp's older estimate that 10 percent of the urban population of Genoa were slaves in the early thirteenth century.[53] Finding ninety references to slaves in the surviving notarial record (again, about 2 percent of the hypothetical total record), Haverkamp deduced that 4,500 slaves were in the city over the period 1150–1200. If roughly two thousand were present per generation, this meant that slaves constituted 10 percent of an estimated total population of twenty thousand, a figure contributed by Josiah Cox Russell on the basis of very little evidence.[54] If the population of Genoa is estimated solely on the basis of the number of people the notarial acts recorded, one is left with the unlikely conclusion that the city contained at least two hundred thousand inhabitants. This type of statistical method is its own worst critic. Verlinden himself wondered how many of Haverkamp's ninety recorded slaves were counted more than once or were simply pasing through the city. Slaves, being a commodity, were more likely to enter the record than many free Genoese. Unfortunately, the view of Genoa as a town teeming with slaves is widespread. The evidence will not support any valid estimate of the number of slaves in Genoa, but 10 percent is surely too high. Michel Balard, carefully studying the extant notarial record from 1239 to 1300, found 418 references to slaves—155 men (37.1 percent) and 263 women (62.9 percent). While offering no general estimate of the number of slaves in the city, he concluded that slavery was not yet widespread in Genoese society.[55] Domenico Gioffrè, using extensive sources, has found that slaves made up between 2.4 and 4.1 percent of the total population of fifteenth-century Genoa.[56] Genoese slavery has attracted scholarly attention because the city was one of the principal slave entrepots of Western Europe, a dubious distinction it would carry well into the sixteenth century. Genoa's prominence in the slave trade has led to inflated estimates of the number of slaves resident in the city. While I accept Balard's conclusion about the extent of slavery in the thirteenth century, it remains remarkable that slavery was in the process of being reestablished in Western Europe at the same time that some of the most oppressive features of serfdom were withering away. This coincidence had more to do with Southern European urbanization than with agriculture, since slaves were not employed in agriculture, and northern cities were apparently able to thrive without them.

Usually wills mention a slave only when the testator was freeing him or her; only three people left a slave to someone as property. It is possible, but not likely, that the slaves were included in the general "rest of my goods" clause. Balard's work has shown that slaves in this period came to Genoa from a variety of places— principally Spain and North Africa, and to a lesser extent Sardinia and Corsica. Depending on the economic and political situation in any given year, one place would dominate the market. Slavery was a small-time business; the price of slaves never rose much above five to seven lire on average, and occasionally it was lower, as when a large influx of slaves from Valencia in 1248 depressed the market somewhat.[57] Female slaves, usually in good supply, were often more expensive than males, and were put to work as domestic servants. Some males may have been similarly employed, but this is less certain. Balard has shown that artisans tended to own, in contrast to wealthy merchants and professionals, a larger proportion of the male slaves, and presumably put them to work at heavy tasks in cloth manufacturing and other craft endeavors.[58] The need for male slaves is not at all clear, since they did not man the galley crews in this period.

Slave owners usually included some conditions in manumissions of slaves by will. The testators sometimes freed their slaves only if they continued to serve for a specified time. For example, Simone Buferio manumitted his slave Obertino, who had to continue to serve Simone's wife for ten years.[59] This future service might last anywhere from seven to fifteen years. Some testators about to travel proposed to free their slaves, but only if they should die on the trip; in this type of situation eventual freedom was by no means certain. Several owners, acknowledging that their slaves were not Christians, made their liberty contingent upon conversion. Simona Doria freed her slave Gionata, provided Simona died on her pilgrimage to Rome, and left her L.15 for her marriage or to become a nun, whichever she preferred.[60] This was a very generous settlement, if it ever came to pass. Some slave owners were concerned enough about their female slaves to provide them with dowries, but none of them went as far as Safran de Clavica, who freed his slave Vera provided she found a husband.[61] A few owners left small sums of money or clothes to slaves, but most made no such provision. However, Genoese law recognized a slave's right to a *peculim,* so presumably no slave was thrust out into the cold with nothing. Balard, who looked carefully at emancipations, found that many freed slaves found an enviable place in Genoese society, while others, "prematurely old," remained in basically their former position, tied to the service of their former masters.[62]

Because the price of slaves was comparatively low, people with as little as four or five lire to leave for their souls might nevertheless own slaves. The church discouraged ownership of Christian slaves and preached the conversion of infidels, so slavery in Genoa was hemmed in by some religious scruples. The act of manumission was a financial sacrifice, but so was every sort of charity. The fact that people believed that to free slaves aided their souls indicates some lingering doubts about the morality of slavery. The church, offering the prospects of conversion and salvation, provided a motive for manumission and an official way for former slaves to join the community.

The Friars

The last major category of social charities I shall consider here are the Dominicans and Franciscans. The first donation to the Dominicans by will occurred in 1225, and the Franciscans were not far behind in 1226.[63] Frequently the *fratres predicatores* and the *fratres minores* were linked together; of the forty-two people who left money to the friars, thirty-three left money to both. Sometimes a single bequest went to the two orders. A woman named Sibilia left twenty solidi to both, presumably to be divided evenly.[64] Twelve people left the Dominicans more; twenty-six left equal donations; and only four left the Franciscans the larger share. The bequests ranged from one solidus to several hundred lire, and most of the donors were wealthy. Many of the smaller donations were for bread—and some were actually made in kind. This may have been a tribute to the emphasis both orders originally placed on begging for their food. Some testators—twenty-four women and eighteen men—also gave money to clothe the friars, but the small sample does not allow us to assume that the friars appealed more to the religious sensibilities of women than of men.

Both orders combined spiritual and social goals. Preaching and charity formed the new orders' principal message. In 1229, after some confusion had arisen over the way in which the new *podestà* had been selected, the electors asked the archbishop, the papal legate, and the Franciscans and Dominicans whether the oath they had taken not to reelect a *podestà* were valid.[65] Even at this early date the new orders were trusted to give a judgment of great political importance. In 1230 both orders, together with the wives of Genoa, appealed to the *podestà* to release some men accused by foreigners of piracy.[66] This curious episode, which resulted in a riot by the women and an assault on the *podesà*, again demonstrates the active role the orders played in city life.

When a man named Ponzio, probably from southern France, made a will in 1229 to prepare for entering the Dominican order, seven brothers witnessed the will. At least four of them were foreigners—from Rome, Bologna, Piacenza, and possibly England.[67] The historian Salimbene, himself from Parma and at least for a time resident in Genoa, described in his famous *Chronica* a similarly diverse Franciscan community in Genoa.[68] The fact that both orders of friars had a strong foreign presence and also managed quickly to attract donations and influence may reflect a similar paradox encountered in politics. The commune found it necessary to import an outsider to serve as *podestà* because internal dissension made it impossible to trust any Genoese with that much authority. The Franciscans and Dominicans may have provided a similar kind of detached objectivity about the spiritual needs of the community.

The friars, as well as other members of the clergy, either advised about, or themselves served as the distributors of, the *pro anima* bequests. As the legal format of the testament developed, several people were named to distribute the charitable donations; often, these were different from the executors of the estate. Almost anyone might be a distributor—relatives, friends, clerics, even women. Guglielmo de Mari nominated Zacaria de Castro, Oberto Pulpo de Mari, and Jacopo de Mari to distribute his charitable bequests, with the counsel of his sister Giovanna, his wife, Alda, Brother Marco of the Franciscans, and Maestro Giordano of the Dominicans.[69] All the good intentions of the testator might come to naught if the distributors failed in their job. Around 1400 a friar, Giovanni Domenici, gave this advice to a lady testator:

If devotion should incline you to use these possessions for God's glory and Christ's poor, bethink you well as to who shall be the executor of these bequests—since well we know that money is much loved by both great and small, clerks and laymen, rich and poor, monks and prelates . . . With such bequests the rich feed themselves, please their friends, clothe their servants, and marry off their maids and bastards.[70]

All this was certainly a frightening prospect for anyone hoping to save his soul.

The will made by the priest Marchisio, canon of Santa Maria de Castello, confirms that such warnings as Fra Giovanni's were not exaggerations.[71] While he was not anyone's distributor, Marchisio acknowledged that Guglielmo Lacagnono had left the church L.15, which the church should now take from his own goods.

Marchisio also left his own house to Guglielmo's heirs (perhaps to keep them quiet?) and L.10 to aid the Holy Land (possibly to make up for another suppressed legacy?). Since the priest Andrea had left L.8 to the church, which Marchisio had also evidently kept, and one Guglielmo had left forty solidi, Marchisio wanted the church to have another L.10 from his own goods. The obvious implication is that Marchisio had defrauded these people, at least temporarily. Certainly he was a wealthy man, with L.25 to leave for his soul, and houses, lands, and expensive garments to leave to his relatives. The laity were not immune from temptation either, as Fra Giovanni pointed out in his warning. The Genoese may have concluded that the Franciscans and Dominicans, whom they so often nominated as overseers of charity, were, along with close relatives, the most trustworthy individuals available.

This is an appropriate place to observe that the clergy's own *pro anima* legacies differed from those of the laity. Maestro Giovanni de Cucurno, whose fortune consisted mainly of ninety "new and select" North African bezants (coins), left, with typically erroneous addition, a total of forty-nine for his soul and forty-two to his family.[72] Most of the clergy who had passed their lives within the church left more for their souls than the laity did. The kind of social charity emphasized in this chapter is conspicuously absent from clerical wills. The clergy understood perhaps better than the laity the financial needs of the institutional church. They were more likely to leave money to individual priests, friars, or monks, who in a sense constituted another family to remember in a will. Still, if the clergy urged the laity to donate to charities that had a social impact, it is ironic that they themselves did not take their own advice.

These social charities—the Hospital of San Giovanni, lepers, paupers, bridges, captives, Crusades, and friars—reveal some important trends when we look at them as a whole. Table 12 offers a complete profile of these charities by taking the number and value of the donations into account.

The number of donors bears no relation to the aggregate value of the bequests. The donations to the hospital and the lepers, though quite numerous, amount to only a small percentage of social charity. Bequests for bridges follow the same pattern. The

Table 12. Breakdown of bequests to social charities.

Charity	Number of donors	Total value of bequests	Average bequest	Value as % of all charitable bequests
Hospital of San Giovanni	194	L.213.3	L.1.1	9.3
Lepers	166	L.198.5	L.1.2	8.6
Paupers	73	L.606.6	L.8.3	26.3
Bridges	98	L.103.9	L.1.1	4.5
Captives	11	L.457.5	L.41.6	19.9
Crusades	37	L.197.6	L.5.3	8.6
Friars (all)	42	L.527.0	L.12.5	22.9
Dominicans	38	L.344.6	L.9.	15
Franciscans	38	L.182.4	L.4.8	7.9

Source: Archivio di Stato di Genova, Cartolari Notarili.

average bequests to these charities hover around one lira, and many are much smaller. At the other extreme, the eleven people who left money to ransom captives gave more than twice as much as the 194 people who donated to the Hospital of San Giovanni. The wealthy members of Genoese society, if they chose to do so, were able to have a decisive impact on charity. Where an average bequest exceeds one lira, it was the rich who made that difference.[73] Gifts in support of the Crusades illustrate the power of big bequests, but the donations to the poor show even more clearly just how the rich were able to set the pace of giving. The biggest charity, in terms of valuable donations, was the poor. The average bequest, over L.8, indicates that the well-off members of society at least recognized that poverty was a problem and tried to do something about it; we cannot know to what extent they succeeded in alleviating the problem. This emphasis on the poor, which amounted to about one-quarter of charitable giving, also demonstrates that the Genoese found social and spiritual goals compatible. Even in this century, when Genoa's economy was growing at an unprecedented rate, poverty remained a serious concern. The friars, who were present for only half the period, quickly became an important charity. Real differences become apparent when the two orders are considered separately. By chance, the number of donations to both is exactly the same. However, the Dominicans received almost twice as much money as the Franciscans.[74] The wealthy subsidized the Dominicans; the Franciscans, while benefiting from some big bequests, found more support among the middle class. (One would have to know more about the way these new orders involved themselves in city life before explaining their different appeal.) Finally, the total amount of giving to these charities represents a large social investment. Giving by testament was not the only form of charity, but most other ways of giving left no trace in the written records. If the extant wills do represent, as I have suggested, about 2 percent of all wills made in this century, then these social charities together received more than L.115,000—by any reckoning a huge sum. This may have been only a part of their actual income, yet these charitable donations by will testify to Genoese concerns and social attitudes.

Other Charities

There are some miscellaneous charities, more personal then social or spiritual, that shed some light on the broader questions about charity. Many of the testators had godchildren, often as many as four or five, and in one case twelve. In the *pro anima* bequests the godchildren often received a token bequest—a few pennies or solidi. Women left these bequests more frequently to godchildren than men did, and the richest members of the communty were the least likely to remember godchildren in their wills. The wills also show that occasionally these ties lasted a lifetime; adults mention their own godparents as beneficiaries or business partners. We know very little about how this social institution actually functioned, particularly in the absence of parents, when presumably the godparents assumed some particular responsibility. Some people may not have remembered the names of their godchildren; at least they identify the child only by its parents' names—for example, my godson, son of Giovanni. The only notarial references to godparenthood are in the testaments, though some of the tutors who were not relatives may have been chosen because they were the minor's godparents. By encouraging people to stand as godparents, the church was in effect trying to do something about the plight of orphans. Even among the poor, this additional social tie potentially saved some children from isolation and oblivion. Jacques Toussaert has pointed out that the church in Flanders tried to control godparenthood by legislation. The statutes imposed a limit of three godparents—two men and one woman—for boys and the reverse for girls.[75] There seems to have been no limit to the number of godchildren an adult might have. Godchildren and godparents are subjects that seem to have been neglected, and they await their historian.[76] The church fostered a spiritual family that was a pale substitute for the ties of flesh and blood; it was intended only to step into the breech when ordinary family ties proved insufficient.

Hermits and recluses were another class of people in need of protection, and a few Genoese remembered them in their wills. With rugged mountains and stretches of uninhabited territory, Liguria had its share of hermits, and city life provided reason enough for some to abandon the world. A woman named Sofia left five solidi to two hermits living in a hermitage near San Lazaro—perhaps they were lepers who were not official members of the community.[77] Guglielmo, the provost of Santa Maria de Castello, and Sofia's friend Maria Mallon were supposed to make sure that the hermits received the money. (One of them had an interesting trip to make.) Aiding hermits was good for the soul, and was one of the very few charities that the church did not directly control.

A last miscellaneous charity is the problem of the pilgrimage not taken. A few people admitted in their wills that they had made pilgrimage vows but not fulfilled them. One Giacomo left all his goods to his sons Anselmo and Ottone, but he insisted that one of them go to Santa Maria de Bezeto, "for me in my name for a vow I made to go there," or failing that, send someone else.[78] A variant of this legacy was a request by some testators to have a pilgrimage made in their name, without any indication of a broken vow. Guglielmo Sardena placed a heavy burden on his son Oberto, who was to go to Santiago de Compostella for his father's soul. Guglielmo said only that he "wanted" his son to go, and he provided spending money of up to L.25.[79] The laity believed that pilgrimages could be made for them, and would even confer ben-

efits after death. The church did not discourage this view, yet
more people made wills while preparing for pilgrimage than left
money to have others go for them.

The amount of charitable bequests depended on the wealth
and intentions of the testator. Can additional insight be gained
by examining the order in which the charities themselves appear in the wills? It is again necessary to recall the act of dictation.
After the introductory formulas, almost all the wills proceed directly to the burial arrangements, followed by the *pro anima* bequests. If the order of these bequests reflects the actual spoken
words of the testators, we can develop some ideas about what
charities came to mind first, and some other way to measure their
relative importance. Let us examine one more time the question
of whether the notaries intervened in these decisions. The notarial
formularies do not suggest any specific structure or order for the
charitable bequests, and since most charities were local ones, the
formularies were probably intentionally vague about them.[80] If,
however, the notaries suggested the appropriate charities, the idea
of social charity might require some rethinking. As a test, let us
look at the wills written by the notary Maestro Salmone. Two
cartularies, with some substantial gaps, contain fifty-nine wills written by this notary from January 16, 1222, to May 9, 1242.[81] Thirty-
five of these wills contain no specific pious bequests beyond the
burial and masses; that is, in these cases the distributors gave away
the remainder as they saw fit. Four of the wills contain no *pro
anima* bequests at all. These thirty-nine wills show that the testators
had two options if they had no specific charities in mind: they
might leave the choice up to someone else, or they could leave
nothing. If Maestro Salmone tried to influence the charitable bequests, he did not try very hard. Twenty wills make one or more
charitable bequests, and the order of these bequests is entirely
random. If the notary had been in the habit of prompting his
clients to give to specific charities, one would expect to see some
sign of this in the order of bequests in that notary's wills. There
is no evidence to support the hypothesis that Maestro Salmone
suggested any charities to his clients; evidently he wrote down
what he heard.

Some charities cluster together in the lists. Hospitals, for example, are often grouped together, as if mentioning one hospital triggered a recollection of the others. In Maestro Salmone's wills the Hospital of San Giovanni and the leper colony of San Lazaro are often coupled together—more proof that the Genoese knew these institutions well and often thought of them at the same time. The reader may consult again the five sample *pro anima* lists at the beginning of this chapter to see how random the bequests are. Simona Doria, one of the richest women in Genoa, left a total of at least forty-seven charitable bequests (a few lines of her will are missing).[82] Fourteen of these bequests were to servants; as for the rest, perhaps her confessor helped her to compile the long list of her favorite charities. Simona composed her will at leisure (she was going on pilgrimage) and not in the throes of illness. Only a few people outside Simona Doria's station were attended by confessors, even on their deathbeds. The *pro anima* bequests written by any one notary have no common thread that reveals any notarial intervention, although other people, such as relatives or friends, may have made some suggestions.

The notary's experience with wills may have played a part in one aspect of the charitable bequests. Since the total amount left for the soul was usually listed first, perhaps in response to a question from the notary, the notary may have kept track of the sums to ensure that the testator did not go over the self-imposed limit. Some of the changes in figures discussed in Chapter 1 support this hypothesis. We are left with the conclusion that testators gave to charity in a largely spontaneous and self-willed fashion. Even if they were susceptible to suggestion, the notary was the least likely person in the room to have wielded influence.

The random order of the bequests indicates that the relative importance of the different charities may be judged, collectively and individually, in monetary terms. The order in which any single charity appears, and the amount it receives, reveals something about the testator's intentions. Beyond this lies the question of individual motive, which is, as W. K. Jordan noted, not a profitable path. Instead, let us conclude by observing some collective trends. The century 1150–1250 witnessed the rise of what I have termed social charity. Wills tell only part of this story, but we are not likely ever to learn any more. The wills reveal an increased effort by Genoese society to take care of the sick and poor. The church served as the conduit for funds intended for these social goals, and had some role to play in determining priorities and administering operations. This effort to some extent diverted charity from its traditional path—the great local monasteries. The cartularies of San Siro and Santa Maria delle Vigne indicate that the pace of donations slackened in this century. The testaments are the best evidence for this change in direction. The reasons for this increase in social charity are many, and relate to intellectual and religious developments in which Genoa was basically a follower, not a leader. However, the urban setting imparted a special urgency to the problems which social charity tried to address, and in this regard Genoa was an important place. Poverty and disease were potential menaces to the social order. Government had enough trouble coping with political disorder; in any event, nothing in the experience of medieval government argued in favor of the idea of public charity. The Genoese knew that charity was good for the soul, and when they made their wills they gave to pious causes having a significant social component. The social charities helped to preserve the stability of the family and community in a society that faced many external threats. All these good intentions required some wealth and responsible executors to carry them out. To be sure, if the intentions of the testators were to be realized, reliable trustees had to be found. Let us now turn to the subject of executors and inventories, in order to see what happened to these intentions.

7 / Inventories and Executors

Inventories in their various forms present a more complete picture of how a person gained his wealth than do wills. The selection of executors—the persons charged with seeing that the will took effect—poses several complex legal and social questions. A close look at inventories and executors will enable us to consider two important questions. First, just how much did "the rest of the goods"—the residual part of the estate that the principal heirs inherited—amount to? Another look at the estate from the vantage point of a different document will permit a second estimate of the amount that the principal heirs received, and perhaps some indication of the origin of this wealth. Second, how were the testator's intentions implemented, and, perhaps more important, what sorts of people did the Genoese trust to carry out these intentions? Discovering who the executors were and how they were related to the testator will help answer this question.

Inventories

As we saw at the end of Chapter 1, the inventory as a historical source has several problems.[1] The number of extant inventories is small, and the number of inventories for which a corresponding will exists is smaller still. The habit of making an inventory of the estate became common only in the 1220s, and even afterwards it was by no means the rule to conduct an inventory. One notary, Enrico da Bisagno, evidently specialized in drawing up inventories; most other notaries seem to have avoided this time-consuming and tedious business. A proper inventory might take an entire day to complete, and a busy notary, not to mention the executors, may not have had this much time to spend on it. As usual in such matters, a shortcut was found. Most inventories are perfunctory acts. After stating that they wished to protect them-

201

selves and the heirs by making an inventory, the executors would record one or two important pieces of property, and then the notary would leave a large blank space in the cartulary. A concluding sentence would note that the space had been left in case the notaries found or remembered anything else later. This type of inventory met the legal requirements but for present purposes is worth very little. For example, the busy and important notary Maestro Salmone, two of whose cartularies survive, rarely participated in an inventory. When he did so, the inventory resembled the one Vassallo de Portali made of the estate of his late wife, Adalasia.[2] Vassallo noted that he had found a dowry instrument, which recorded that Adalasia had a L.100 dowry and a slave named Rodoano. That was all. A proper inventory would have recorded all of Adalasia's possessions—her clothes, jewels, furniture, commercial contracts—anything at all worth money. Some inventories contain page after page of just this sort of detail. However, most inventories take the form of Adalasia's.

The survival of a person's will and the inventory of his estate enhances our understanding of both, but for a variety of reasons these matches are very rare. Although many of the people making wills were ill, they might very well have survived, in which case no inventory would have been made. Unless an inventory was drawn up shortly after the will, by the same notary, the chance that both survived is slim. Only a small fragment of the Genoese notarial record still exists. If much time elapsed between the will and the inventory, or if the executors patronized another notary, the odds against both having survived increase. Another problem in finding these matches is that the executors did not always conduct an inventory. Sometimes the testators specifically stated that the heirs did not have to account for the estate. Many uncomplicated wills, which name only the principal heirs and a few charitable bequests, did not require an inventory. These wills do not even nominate any executors—a clear sign that no inventory would have been needed. Yet in the 1240s it became customary for some testators to stipulate that the executors should not pay any legacies until they had inventoried the estate.[3] The comparatively few extant inventories indicate that in only a minority of cases did the executors make the effort. As we shall see, some testators decided to make their own inventory while they were still alive, and they included this account in the will itself. While women were as likely to make wills as men, there are very few examples of inventories of a woman's estate. (The example cited above is one such rarity.) A woman's choice of heirs was more circumscribed, and rights to her property were already clearly established. Since women had less disposable wealth than men, their estates may simply have been less complicated. However, we have seen that Genoa had its share of wealthy women. The fact that almost all the extant inventories are of men's estates is puzzling, but this at least partially explains why inventories are not as numerous as wills.

There are four cases of a will and its corresponding inventory to consider.[4] Let us look at these examples in detail in order to determine the size and origin of the estate.

Oberto Barleta

Oberto Barleta made a will in his own home with the notary Niccolò Ferrario on October 9, 1220.[5] He left L.3 s.10 for his soul, and he requested Oberto Sicco and his son-in-law Anselmo Ferrario to distribute this money. Oberto left his wife, Margarita, beyond her rights, her clothes. His principal heirs were his daughters Ermigena and Sicheta. His other daughter, Giovanna, who was Anselmo's wife, was to share in the inheritance only if one of her sisters died without an heir. Anselmo, Margarita, and Oberto's son Giovanni Dietisalva were named as tutors. (The fact that Giovanni was not an heir was unusual, but since he was to be a tutor, we can assume that Oberto had previously emancipated Giovanni and settled some property on him.) Oberto then listed some of his outstanding commercial contracts. He had committed L.4 s.10 to his son on a voyage to Ceuta, and had L.9 "oltremare." L.3 of this last commenda belonged to Anselmo. Three people owed Oberto a total of L.1 s.13, and he owed a debt of two and a half solidi. Finally, Oberto had thirty-two hides in a partnership from Guglielmo da San Siro, of which he was entitled to one-third of the profit, after the capital had been deducted. This is a complete summary of Oberto's will. He was a typical Genoese testator, a mature man with an adult son and a married daughter. Oberto owned a house, and he had a few small commercial deals in progress. It is hard to pin down his principal occupation; he may have been a leather merchant. As usual in the wills, we have no idea how much the two daughters inherited.

By November 11, 1220, Oberto had died. On December 31, 1220 (1221 Genoese style) the notary Niccolò Ferrario recorded an inventory that the tutors Anselmo Ferrario, Margarita, and Giovanni had made of the estate on November 11 in the presence of five witnesses, all of them *ferrarii*—blacksmiths, iron workers. or merchants.[6] The first item the executors noted was the house in Fossato. The rest of the inventory consists of a long list of property in this house. The executors divided up this personal property into several obvious categories. They noted first that they had found L.10 s.10 in money. They had also found an *instrumentum*, a copy of a notarial act drawn up for a party to an agreement, against Amicuno de Castelleto for L.6, and another against Giovanni Dietisalva for L.4 s.10. The sums involved here are suspicious; the two debts amount to L.10 s.10, precisely the amount supposedly found in cash.[7] It is possible the executors considered these two debts to be as good as money, so they described the two documents in order to explain the L.10 s.10 'in money" they had found. Oberto had mentioned these two debts in the will, and the inventory reveals that he had a written commercial contract with his own son. The executors also noted that they had received L.18 s.6 d.3 ½ owing from another agreement; this sum may represent Oberto's share of the profits from his partnership with Guglielmo da San Siro. After accounting for these monetary matters, the executors turned their attention to describing the contents of Oberto's house. Most of the inventory consists of a painstaking list of his personal possessions. The executors obviously started in the kitchen, because the first items noted are pots and various cooking and fire implements. The next category consists of clothing and bed furnishings. The executors spent considerable time counting up Oberto's clothes, and they stopped taking an item by item list only when they came to the *roba minuta*. The last general category is furniture. Different kinds of chests and boxes are the expensive items. The house also contained several all-purpose "tables and tripods." These tables, evidently consisting of attached planks and two three-legged sawhorses, served a variety of uses. At night the Genoese put their mattresses on these tables; during the day they served as ordinary tables or were disassembled. Listed among the tables are four table knives, enough for Oberto, his wife, and the two daughters still living at home.

The last part of the inventory concerns some receipts and expenditures the executors encountered while winding up Oberto's affairs. The executors sold four sheets of metal for thirty solidi, and they paid someone seventeen solidi for two others. The executors spent L.4 s.10 for Oberto's soul, one lira more than Oberto had directed. The notary Niccolò received five solidi for his labors in drawing up the inventory; the two other notaries present, who served as official witnesses, received one solidus each. The major remaining debt was to Margarita, who was owed L.42 for her dowry. Oberto had mentioned his wife's rights but had not supplied the dowry's actual value. This was a sizable dowry for an artisan's family. Finally, two notaries and three smiths witnessed the notarial act on December 31, as opposed to those who had observed the actual inventory on November 11. Only the smith Oberto Sicco, who was a tutor, witnessed both. So together seven smiths had witnessed the inventory on these two days. This fact, and the presence of metal sheets in Oberto's home, suggest that the smiths were helping the family of a fellow guildsman. None of the tools associated with the craft are mentioned as having been found in Oberto's house, however, so there remains some doubt about his occupation. The principal heirs inherited the house and its contents, and from the inventory we learn that this was in fact the bulk of the estate.

Stefano Scriba

No doubt exists about Stefano's occupation; he was a notary. Stefano Scriba made a will with the notary Enrico da Bisagno on November 4, 1231.[8] Stefano left L.14 for his soul and then immediately turned to his business affairs. His brother Nicoloso owed him L.9, as in an instrument by the notary Guglielmo da Clavica, and his brother Ambrogio owed him L.20 in a *commenda* recorded by the notary Ansaldo da Piazzalunga. A notary might be expected to be this precise; however, he was not the only Genoese testator who put the name of the notary down as a way to identify an agreement.[9] Stefano owed five people a total of L.13 s.6, and he also owed the price of a suit made from white stanfort to a draper, whom he wanted to be paid. Nicoloso had paid Stefano's share of a dowry for their sister Sibilia, and Stefano wanted his share paid from the estate. Stefano also acknowledged that he owed his sister Giulietta L.10 for her dowry. He then declared that he had a *feudum* (some sort of annual income) in Acre. Stefano admitted that he had had a L.200 dowry from his wife, and he wanted her to have this sum. Stefano also wished his estate to pay one-half of the legacies left in his father's will. Since these legacies were still outstanding, we can assume that his father, the notary Giovanni di Guiberto, had died recently. Why Stefano should have assumed one-half of the burden and not one-third (since he had at least two brothers) is not clear. Perhaps he was paying one-half as a favor to his brothers, since he left them nothing. Stefano left his tenant Alessandro da Sestri the L.23 he owed for land rent, and furthermore permitted Alessandro to have the land for one year without rent. Stefano capped this generosity by directing that the actual rental document be returned to Alessandro. In other words, Stefano ended whatever arrangement he had had with his tenant by returning the contract and giving him one year's notice; but he also cleared Alessandro's debt. Stefano noted that he himself owed four solidi to Marino de Bulgaro, a promient and wealthy citizen who owned the house Stefano lived in. After all these business details that consumed most of the will, Stefano simply made his two daughters the principal heirs, and named his two brothers and mother-in-law, Giovanna, as curators.

Stefano was obviously a wealthy man. His wife's dowry and his landed wealth—worth L.23 a year—both point to this conclusion. The *feudum* in Acre indicates that Stefano had passed some part of his career in the Latin East, perhaps as the official notary for the Genoese commune in that city. In the first part of the thirteenth century Acre was the principal entrepot for the Eastern trade, and an astute notary might easily have made his fortune there. Whether Stefano had inherited or purchased his land, it is clear that he had diversified his wealth. Some of his money remained in commerce with his brothers as partners, and some was in land. Somewhat surprisingly, Stefano did not own his house in Genoa; he was certainly able to afford one.

Directly after drawing up Stefano's will, the notary recorded the inventory of his estate. Stefano may have died immediately after making his will, since the next act refers to him as deceased.[10] Nicoloso di Guiberto and Giovanna, the wife of the late Marino Carefico, tutors of the late Stefano's daughters, conducted the inventory. Stefano's other appointed tutor, his brother Ambrogio, was not present. As usual, the executors began to describe the estate by taking note of the landed property. Stefano owned land in Sestri Levante purchased from Alessandro, and lands in Sorlana and elsewhere held in common with his brother Ambrogio. From the will we know that Alessandro had continued to rent this land, now known to have originally been his own, from Stefano, whose apparent generosity now appears in a new light. Forgiving the rent of a person who had once owned the land was a charitable act, since society frowned on taking advantage of poverty. Stefano did not own a house anywhere. The executors did not record any of Stefano's commercial agreements. Instead, they next enumerated his furniture. The now familiar tables and tripods head the list. Again, though in this inventory the order is reversed, the executors lavished care on describing clothes. Stefano had a gown and a cloak decorated with pearls, and he seems to have favored the color red. Stefano had expensive clothing, befitting his wealth. The real proofs of this wealth appear at the end of the inventory, which tells us that Stefano had a silver belt and five silver spoons, a diamond, eighty-six North African bezants, and seven more in a purse of golden silk.[11] He also had two gold rings and five other jewels. The diamond justly receives pride of place, for it was a rare and precious possession. (The L.14 he left for his soul begins to appear rather small.) The executors concluded the inventory by recording some trade wares, including an ounce of brazilwood and a barrel of linen and cotton.

The inventory confirms that Stefano's daughters were able to count upon a rich inheritance. The "rest of the goods"—the share for the principal heirs—amounted to virtually everything that Stefano owned. The inventory also confirms the diversification of holdings seen in the will. We know from the will that Stefano was wealthier than even the inventory reveals. Stefano owned land, engaged in commerce as a silent partner and active participant, and had cash and valuable personal property that could easily be turned into cash if the need arose. Stefano also had his career as a notary and his annuity from Acre to produce a steady income, which he obviously put to good use.

Stefano the Shopkeeper

Stefano the shopkeeper made two wills.[12] His second will, made March 9, 1236, altered his wife's inheritance; this is the one to which I shall refer. Stefano left L.20 for his soul, specifying eighteen recipients and directing that his wife, Lombarda, give the remainder for masses and paupers. Stefano left his daughter L.10 and a silver vase. A former servant named Alia received L.3, and two other people inherited a total of L.3. Stefano left his niece Giacomina L.6, which was to go to paupers if she died without an heir. He freed his slave Manneto and left him forty solidi. Lombarda inherited his bed furnishings, her clothes, and the house for her lifetime, if she remained a widow, and also L.20 to spend as she pleased. Stefano named as his principal heirs his sons Ambrosino and Matteo. Lombarda was to be tutor so long as she did not remarry, and Stefano named the notary Opizone da Chiavari and his son-in-law Fulcone da Sori as her advisers.

Stefano's sizable pious bequests demonstrate that he was well-to-do. He left another L.44 in specific bequests and also owned a slave, though, as we have seen, people of comparatively modest means were able to afford a slave in Genoa.[13] Beyond stating the fact that Stefano was a shopkeeper *(mercerius)*, the will does not indicate what type of shop he kept. The will mentions no commercial agreements, so we know very little about how Stefano accumulated his wealth. Just how wealthy he was is also ambiguous. Stefano owned his house, but the exact nature of what the principal heirs inherited is, as is the case for most wills, a mystery.

On December 6, 1239, Opizone da Chiavari and Fulcone da Sori, curators for Ambrosino and Matteo, conducted an inventory of the estate of the late Stefano the shopkeeper and his late wife, Lombarda.[14] In this case over three years separate the will and the inventory, and two different notaries were involved. Bonovassallo de Cassino wrote the will, and Enrico da Bisagno did the inventory. The fact that the curators were the same two people named in the will strongly suggests that the 1236 will, or one like it, had remained in force. The inventory in fact mentions the testament of March 9, 1236, as one of the documents in Stefano's possession at the time of his death. Ironically, Lombarda, whom Stefano had tried to entice into remaining single after his death, did not remarry, but also did not survive him for long. Stefano had died, by all indications, not long after making his will. The executors began the inventory of this joint estate by taking note of Stefano's house, which was in the neighborhood of San Ambrogio. Stefano also owned a house and some land in Sori. The rest of the inventory mainly concerns various commercial agreements summarized in Table 13. Stefano made his last contract on March 18, 1236; from April 27 onward Lombarda handled the family business, and it seems likely that Stefano died between these two dates. The inventory lists only contracts still in force. Consequently there is no duplication of investments. The family had invested L.343, a considerable sum. Stefano's will did not reveal

Table 13. Commercial agreements of the shopkeeper Stefano and his wife, Lombarda, listed in inventory, December 6, 1239.

Date of contract	Type of contract	Partner	Amount of contract
August 11, 1239	*commenda*	Ambrogio Caldera	L.20
March 18, 1236	*commenda*	Pietro Barilarius	L.24
February 24, 1239	*commenda*	Niccoloso de Serrino	L.33
April 27, 1236	*commenda*	Guglielmo Tinca	L.50
August 26, 1237	*commenda*	Bongiovanni Bargalio	L.40
March 9, 1236	*commenda*	Fulcone da Sori	L.120
March 20, 1237	*societas*	Fulcone da Sori	L.50
November 20, 1236	*societas*	Benvegnuto Formarius	L.6
Total			L.343

Source: Robert S. Lopez, "Nota sulla composizione dei patrimoni privati," in *Studi sull'economia genovese nel medio-evo* (Turin, 1936), pp. 239–240. Text from Archivio di Stato di Genova, Cartolari Notarili, N. 11, notary Enrico da Bisagno.

this amount of wealth. Unfortunately, we do not know if the family invested cash or goods, or the exact nature of these enterprises.

The executors, after examining the commercial contracts and detailing them, then turned their attention to the household items and clothes. Unlike the two inventories discussed earlier, in this one the executors did not linger for long in the wardrobe. The executors did note that they had found L.20 in cash, and L.40 invested in knives, shears, and other merchandise ("in cultellis, cesuris, et alia mercaria"). This investment may reflect the kind of business Stefano had conducted in his shop. Last, the executors took note of some documents not related to commerce. There was an act of dowry and *antefactum* drawn up on February 19, 1211, probably just before Stefano and Lombarda were married. Again, the executors supplied no details, so we do not know the size of the dowry. The executors found a copy of Stefano's will, as noted above. They also found a record of a piece of land in Sori that Alda Portonario had sold to Ottone da Val de Tari in 1209, and another act dated 1234, when Ottone's widow had sold this land to Stefano. It is extremely significant that in land sales in this period the papers proving ownership—in fact deeds—were also transferred. Stefano could prove title to this land because he was able to produce his own purchase document and the original seller's as well. Hence he was able to show who had owned this land all the way back to 1209. Stefano and Lombarda were good record keepers. Two final documents reveal that Giovanni de Oliva had sold one-half of a wall, and the priest Guglielmo of San Giorgio a house, to Stefano.

The principal heirs received the bulk of Stefano's wealth. In his will he left a total of L.64 in specific bequests; his inventory reveals that he had L.343 in assets and two houses and their contents. At least 80 percent of Stefano's wealth passed to his two sons. Stefano had been married for about twenty-five years and therefore was at least in his late forties and most likely older. We cannot be sure how much he himself had inherited, although the land he held with his brother may have come from their father. Stefano had had a successful business career, and so had Lombarda. He had diversified his holdings in real estate and in his shop. The commercial contracts Stefano and Lombarda made reveal a similar diversity. Most of the contracts were *commendas*, in which one partner, in this case Stefano and Lombarda, supplied all the capital for a return of three-quarters of the profit. These *commendas* were spread around, and the family judiciously invested small amounts in a variety of ventures. The only partner entrusted with a comparatively large sum (L.70 in two contracts) was characteristically the son-in-law. Lombarda carried on her husband's enterprises for three years, and the evidence suggests that she did so successfully.

Bernardo de Nuxigia

Bernardo de Nuxigia, "sick in body," made his will in Rapallo with the notary Bonovassallo de Maiori on August 26, 1240.[15] Bernardo left L.2 s.7 d.4 for his soul and forty solidi to a nephew.[16] His wife, Giovanna, received, beyond her rights, her clothes, and Bernardo made her *domina* of his goods as long as she remained single and stayed with the children. Bernardo named as principal heirs two sons, two daughters, and his wife. He nominated as tutors his brothers Gaialdo and Giovanni; they were to have control until the sons were eighteen, and continue to conduct any business until the sons were twenty-six. Two of Bernardo's associates, Simone and Gandulfo, were to serve as advisers, and Simone was to serve as a tutor if one should die. Bernardo left the tutors twenty solidi apiece for their services. Finally, Bernardo listed three debts totaling L.3 s.12, and four people owed him L.2 s.2.

Bernardo's will does not tell us much about him. He left L.6 s.7 d.4 in legacies, and owed L.1 s.10 more than was owed to him. There is no sign of what Bernardo did for a living, and the only hint of any commercial activity is the unusual provision that the tutors continue to conduct the minors' business for eight years beyond their coming of age, for the boys, and considerably longer than that for the girls. What sort of business Bernardo expected the tutors to transact is not made explicit in the will. Bernardo's will is uninformative, and hence it is particularly fortunate that the inventory of his estate exists. Many Genoese wills resemble this one, and it is instructive for once to have the opportunity to see beneath the surface.

On September 17, 1240, Gaialdo de Nuxilia and Simone de

Corelia, tutors of the late Bernardo's four children, conducted an inventory of the estate with the same notary, Bonovassallo de Maiori.[17] The inventory mentions in pssing the late Giovanni Berino, Bernardo's brother, so the situation Bernardo had envisioned had occurred, with Simone substituting as a tutor. The first item the executors noted was some land with trees on it and a house in the village of Nuxilia, probably not far from Rapallo. As usual when describing a piece of property, the executors named the owners of the land at the four boundaries. The neighbors were: above, Guglielmo da Rapallo; below, a public road; to one side, Gandulfo and partners and Sarabaldo de Nuxilia; and to the other side, the heirs of Giovanni Berino. Next the tutors noted another plot of land in Nuxilia, bounded by a road and lands belonging to the tutors. The inventory continues, listing fifty-one other parcels of land Bernardo owned in his own village and the surrounding countryside. The notary ceased to record the boundaries of these holdings; if he had not, the inventory would have been an extremely tedious endeavor. These other fifty-one parcels had certain features worth discussing. In every instance Bernardo owned one-third or one-sixth of the piece in question. When he owned one-third, he held the land "indivisibly" with his brother Gaialdo and the heirs of his late brother, Giovanni. This arrangement probably came about when the three brothers had divided their father's estate. When Bernardo owned one-sixth, his partners were his two brothers and Simone de Corelia. These portions probably represented Bernardo' s father's share of his father's estate. If this assumption is valid, then Simone was Bernardo's first cousin (not an uncle, for the Genoese were careful about identifying uncles). After going through all these details about the landed property, the executors made a cursory list of the house's contents, concentrating on kitchen implements and tools. The executors concluded the inventory by noting the L.7 s.2 in debts owing to Bernardo, which they had not yet received.

Virtually all Bernardo's wealth was tied up in land. None of the diversity that characterized urban wealth is evident here. Bernardo's estate was scattered in tiny plots throughout the local countryside. It is not possible to place a value on these properties, but together they constituted the principal inheritance of Bernardo's four children. Typically, the will did not mention any land.

Generally, wills did not list real estate unless the testator left a specific piece of land to a beneficiary or his heirs. The Genoese practiced partible inheritance, at least through the thirteenth century. Bernardo's children would have listed one-twelfth and one-twenty-fourth of these same parcels, if they managed to keep them. Bernardo's father had started out with the tracts of land that the three brothers eventually divided into sixths of the original. This analysis rests on the plausible assumption that Bernardo's father had one sibling, and hence inherited one-half of the original land. The father, unfortunately nameless, acquired in his lifetime many other parcels, of which his sons inherited one-third each. The inventory reveals that, except for his house and one other piece of property, everything Bernardo owned came in thirds or sixths. Even the two undivided holdings in Nuxilia may represent Bernardo's clear share of his paternal inheritance. Bernardo was holding his own, but he was not able to acquire any additional properties in his lifetime. He was probably a small-time farmer, with no cash to invest in commerce. Perhaps Bernardo's lands were so divided up that they were no longer particularly profitable. However large this inheritance was, the details escaped notice in the will. Once again, the true size of the principal heirs' share of the estate, vague in the will, turns out to be worth more than the L.6 s.7 d.4 Bernardo left in specific bequests.

The inventory of Bernardo's estate also casts a new light on conditions in the Ligurian countryside. More than a century of comparative peace, and generations of reasonably healthy and prolific people, had created a bewildering and complex pattern of land holding. There is no sign of primogeniture in the wills. What were small pieces of land in the beginning were increasingly divided into smaller bits with every generation. While partible inheritance required a certain minimal level of family cooperation, it also had a tendency to atomize property and families. We have seen in Bernardo's will and inventory that he was able to rely on his nearest kin to administer his estate and raise his children. This kind of family solidarity had to continue over the years in order for the system of inheritance to work. With every generation the ties between members of Bernardo's descent group would become more tenuous, and cooperation more difficult. By contrast the death of childless heirs and subsequent land sales worked to reverse the tendency toward disorder in rural land holding; but marriage introduced new complications, and sales might inject total strangers into an already complex association of owners. All this makes one want to know more about Bernardo's father, for here was a man who reversed the trend toward partition and was able to thrive in this environment by putting back together scraps of land into productive blocks. Rural entrepreneurs like Bernardo's father were accomplishing on a smaller scale than their urban counterparts an agrarian commercial revolution.

The analysis of these four wills and their corresponding inventories enables us to answer the question raised at the beginning of this chapter: just how large was the share of the estate the principal heirs inherited? In all these cases the main heirs received the bulk of the estate. The wills did not indicate the actual size of the heirs' shares; the inventory alone supplies this information. The inventory also allows us to see how the testator accumulated and used his wealth. Any generalization based on four cases must remain tentative. Fortunately, there is another way to explore the size and origins of the estate. Occasionally, the testator attached a partial inventory to the will, and often the wills detail any business contracts still in progress. These two types of additional information, which I will call partial inventories, allow a broader segment of Genoese society to enter the study.

Partial Inventories

Giovanni Scriba, the first notary whose cartulary is extant, did not draw up any formal inventories made by the executors, although some of his clients did append to their wills lists of personal property or business deals still in force.[18] Other twelfth-century notaries, such as Guglielmo Cassinese, followed the same procedure.[19] The need for accurate lists of personal wealth preceded the taking of a formal inventory by the executors. This need arose for several reasons. When the heirs divided up the estate, a list greatly facilitated matters and helped ensure equitable division. Since many Genoese had much of their wealth tied up in commerce, the list of property often included, or was limited to, all the outstanding contracts. We have seen that the inventories also listed contracts. Depending on the type of contract, the testator either had money coming to him or owed his partners for their investments. An heir was responsible for paying and receiving the testator's debts, so he needed to know what the accounts were. Since the formal inventory had not yet developed in the twelfth century, if the testator foresaw a need for a list of property, he would have had to provide it himself.

An informative example of one of these early partial inventories concerns the will Guglielmo Scarsaria made on June 16, 1162.[20] Directly afterwards, on the same day, Giovanni Scriba transcribed a *commemoracio* (remembrance, memorandum) of Guglielmo's goods.[21] In his will Guglielmo alluded to his land holdings, but he limited this list of his goods to existing commercial contracts. Guglielmo had L.440 s.17 d.6 and 108 North African bezants invested in eight ventures. He also had commercial quantities of alum and pepper, and L.25 in cash, a silver cup, and a silver sword guard in his strongbox. Since Guglielmo's testamentary bequests amounted to only L.191, once again the principal heirs received most of his wealth.

During the thirteenth century executors began to take a formal inventory of the estate, and by the 1230s this process was standardized and fairly common. This development did not obviate the desire of certain people to include their own list in the will. Even if the executor knew that a formal inventory would be taken, it was still wise for the testator to mention his contracts. Documents might be lost; not all Genoese were as careful as Stefano and Lombarda, whose executors found an orderly estate. Often relatives striking deals among themselves did not have a notary draw up a formal contract. Testators, however, mentioned these oral arrangements in the wills. The Genoese also continued to note other transactions in their wills, which I shall consider shortly. Two kinds of testators were more likely than others to include their own inventory in the will. Foreign merchants in Genoa, who for reasons of prudence or illness needed to make a will, were likely to list what they had with them. Jacopo Riccardini of Florence, who left L.25 in Pisan money for his soul, listed L.293 s.2 in obligations to six Genoese.[22] Sinibaldo, from Poggibonsi in Tuscany, who was in the Hospital of San Giovanni in 1247 when he made his will there, listed the complete contents of his rented house.[23] He left everything he had in Genoa to the hospital. As I noted earlier, a foreigner was likely to feel comfortable with this familiar international order.[24] Sinibaldo seems to have specialized in luxury items; he had gold and silver jewelry and commercial quantities of silk and ivory in his house. The hospital had an interest in these commodities, and may have encouraged Sinibaldo to make the list.

The other group of testators who were likely to make their own inventory was women. A formal inventory of a woman's estate was a very rare occurrence. Women may have made their own inventories in order to compensate for this omission, and to retain a measure of control over the estate. Most of the women who attached a list of their goods to the will were widows, and hence heads of the household. Gaieta, the wife of Oberto Trasasco, whose husband was away, made a long list of the clothes, furniture, and kitchen utensils that she wanted safeguarded until his return.[25] In the same vein Sofia, the wife of the late Donato, whose son and heir was absent from Genoa on a voyage, wanted her administrator to assume control of her property.[26] Sofia had a significant quantity of cloth in her house; she may have been a weaver. If a woman's husband or heir were not present, making a list of property may have been the prudent course. Imegia da Vignamedia, a widow, was obviously the head of a farming household.[27] She took care to distinguish her livestock from her son Rubaldo's. These self-composed inventories are not as informative as the ones executors made, but they reveal more about the testator than do wills that lack them. This kind of inventory, largely made by foreign merchants and women, also confirms that the principal heirs received the bulk of the estate, and provides some clues about how the testator made a living.

Contracts in Progress

After formal inventories developed, the kind of *commemoracio* Guglielmo Scarsaria dictated was no longer used. The inventory of Stefano's estate, partially detailed in Table 13, reveals that individuals kept written records of agreements, which the executors would duly note. However, testators continued to refer to contracts in progress in their wills. As we shall see, not every Genoese wanted his executors to conduct an inventory, or expected them to do so voluntarily. The same reasons that prompted twelfth-century Genoese to include contracts in the will continued to be valid in the thirteenth century. The testators wanted oral agreements to be remembered; for some the ongoing ventures tied up most of their wealth, and it was important to describe where this wealth was. Notices of contracts in thirteenth-century wills are more specific than the earlier ones. They enable us to go beyond the usual constraints the will imposed as a source to see how the testator conducted his business over a period of time. Two recent studies have pointed out that women played an important part in Genoese commercial life.[28] Though men were more likely to mention business ventures in the will, some women also did so. Since the record lacks inventories of women's estates, where women mentioned business in progress, we have a comparatively rare glimpse of their activities.

The richness in detail of these thirteenth-century commercial notices is apparent in many wills. For example, Giovanni Cafaraina stated that he wanted L.70 returned to his partners, who had invested in a voyage he had planned to make to the Holy Land on the ship San Nicoloso, owned by Pietro Fallamonica.[29] In addition to supplying the names of the partners and the destinations, the wills often specified the type of merchandise involved. This level of detail made the wills even more informative than the inventories, which usually recorded only the size of the investment and the partner's name. Jacopo Urseto noted that Pagano di Rodolfo had given him in *commenda* L.130 invested in gall, a tanning agent, and mastic, an astringent resin.[30] These chemicals were still in Genoa in Pagano's shop, and Jacopo claimed that any amounts in excess of L.130 in value belonged to him. Women also provided clues to the commercial activities they had undetaken. Berta de Galla was in the wholesale cloth business, and she had several quantities of cloth "at sea."[31] Some testators actually left a contract in progress as a legacy. Jacopo the judge left his wife two-thirds of the capital and profit he had in a *commenda* with Enrico Dardella, and he left the other third to Enrico's wife.[32]

The last type of contract in progress concerned rural life. The Genoese were a city people, and most of the wills discussed here relate to city lfe. However, people from the countryside would come to town to make a will, and sometimes a city notary would make a tour of duty through the local villages. Commerce did not dominate rural life to the extent that it pervaded the city, but some of the methods of urban commerce were successfully transferred to the rural scene. Rents, of course, were paid everywhere, and people often noted that they owed rent for fields or city houses. These references to rent help to place the testator in the social hierarchy and also explain his relationship, which otherwise might only appear to be friendship, to the landlord. The commercial arrangement that most often found a role in the countryside was the *societas*, a form of partnership in which both parties contributed capital. In the rural setting the *societas* almost always involved livestock. Jacopo de Oliva's will provides many examples of this type of contract.[33] For example, he had in *societas* with Bulgaro one cow and one calf, and he was owed, before the capital was divided, twenty-four solidi. Altogether Jacopo owned four cows, two calves, two pigs, and nine piglets, with five different partners. Jacopo's partners were supposed to feed the animals, harvest the produce, and pay his share of the profit. Taking care of this valuable livestock was expensive and laborious. Jacopo stated that he and Zineto had one cow in *societas,* and in two years the cow would belong to Zineto; the profit would meanwhile be split. People in the countryside having surplus livestock to contract out to poorer neighbors were the elite of peasant society. Only the makers of these contracts, like Jacopo, made wills; the great majority of peasants did not. A person wealthy enough to rent land or livestock to others had a reason to make a will. We have seen two revealing patterns of rural life. Bernardo de Nuxigia's inventory portrays a static, conservative habit of holding on to scattered and increasingly tiny bits of land. Jacopo de Oliva represents the peasant as entrepreneur, who dealt in cows and pigs in much the same way as the city merchants handled more prestigious commodities.

We have thus far examined contracts in progress. Once a partnership had run its course, there was no reason for a testator to mention it. Only one social circumstance—usury—would prompt a testator to refer to previous business. If a testator felt remorse over instances of usury, the will was a last chance to make some sort of restitution. Genoa thrived on commerce, and most of its inhabitants were directly or indirectly engaged in profit-making enterprises. Only seven out of 632 testators mentioned usury. A little more than one percent of the sample expressed contrition on this subject. The church's attitude toward usury evolved over time and was never free from ambiguity.[34] No consistent view of usury emerges from the wills either. Sometimes usury clearly means interest on a loan. Perselda left twenty solidi to the parish for her profit (12.5 percent) on the L.8 she had lent to the archpriest of the parish.[35] These efforts to pay back interest on usury were counted as charitable bequests, but the lender often ran into the problem of not being able to find the victim. Alda left L.7 to pay anyone whom her late husband had charged usurious interest. If there were no such people, she wanted the money given away to benefit the souls of others.[36] Alda was doubly charitable; she was willing to give pious bequests, and also the spiritual merit of these bequests, to others. No one else went that far. A few testators identified the person or persons who had paid usurious gains and ordered a specific sum returned to them. One testator added a very unusual piece of information. Tommaso da Sestri, a caulker, wanted ten solidi "which I have from a certain Jew at Murcia from a certain loan that I made to him at the fortune of the sea" (a sea loan) to be given to paupers.[37] Tommaso had lent money to a Jew at a profit, but he felt some unease about the transaction. Theologians might debate whether this loan was usurious or not, but generally the idea of usury was confined to loans between coreligionists. Tommaso thought interest from a Jew was usury, but he did not order the money to be returned to the victim. Commercial contracts concealed interest and even the amount of profit, and this has been taken to mean that the church had some success in condemning usury, or at least driving it underground and making it disreputable. Few Genoese cared to admit that they had engaged in usury; however, their city prospered on interest, and certainly these seven cases are no complete index of commercial activity in Genoa.

The inventory and notices in the will of commercial contracts supply two kinds of important information. The inventories reveal that generally "the rest of the goods" was literally the bulk of the estate. The principal heirs—whether children, other relatives, or the church—inherited most of the testator's property. Both sources indicate how the testator accumulated his wealth. The will is not often clear about the actual size of the estate, but it provides clues about how the testator earned a living. The inventories and notices of contracts also contain the comparatively few instances of individual behavior. The standard will is a personal document couched in legal language and notarial style. The testator did not often explain things; Tommaso the caulker need not have mentioned that his usurious profit came from a Spanish Jew. Many executors did not bother to conduct a complete inventory, and those who did tell us things about the testator that we could learn from no other source.

All the hopes of the testator would come to nothing if the executors failed him. A person did not expect to carry out his last wishes; choosing someone to do this for him was almost as important and revealing as the choice of the principal heirs.

Executors

As we have seen, the Genoese selected tutors to be responsible for raising their children.[38] If the testator appointed tutors, these people were also the executors of the estate, and hence conducted the inventory. The tutors, as legal representatives of the heirs, paid all the other legacies. The Roman law on guardianship provided a framework for the tutor's responsibility as executor.[39] Many people who did not appoint or had no need for tutors nevertheless wanted someone to see that legacies were promptly and honestly paid. Testators who were childless, or who had children of age, appointed distributors, or fideicommissioners, whose duty it was to execute the terms of the will. In order to simplify the ensuing discussion, let us consider the tutors, distributors, and fideicommissioners as a single group—the executors. These executors, who might be the principal heirs or the beneficiaries of a bequest, were supposed to pay the legacies and settle all accounts. Many testators did not appoint executors, and there are some general reasons why they did not. When the testator left only a few small bequests, and everything else to an adult heir, no executor was required. As Tables 14, 15, and 16 reveal, women were less likely than men to name executors. The majority of women

male relative would distribute the estate. A minor making a will
had no need for an executor, since his own tutors would assume
that task too. These three categories of wills that do not name
executors account for the fact that less than half of the extant
wills name an executor.

What did the executors do? First, they had to determine that
the testator was in fact dead. Since some Genoese were abroad
when they died, the executors had to rely on news and verify it.
Their second obligation was often arranging the testator's burial,[40]
although some wills appointed a special set of distributors whose
only function was to oversee the charitable bequests, including
the burial expenses. Women and members of the clergy were often
entrusted with this important but clearly defined duty. More often
than not, though, the executors had the entire estate in their
hands. When the executors paid the legacies depended on when
and if they took an inventory. In the 1240s the testators began to
insist that no legacy be paid until the estate was recorded *in carta*—
that is, before a notary drew up an inventory.[41] In these cases the
executors probably undertook the inventory as soon as possible,
even though the testator usually allowed them to pay for the
funeral before the inventory. The rest of the legacies would be
paid after the inventory had been completed. In order to conduct
a proper inventory, the executors would gather witnesses and a
notary and then compile their list. Then they would take this list
to court, usually before the consul of justice—a judge the *podestà*
appointed—and register the act. The court appearance was the
closest the Genoese came to probate. The executors were now
legally obligated for the estate's contents and were expected to
fulfill the terms of the will. However, many inventories were quite
perfunctory and obviously not a complete list, so the comparison
to probate is by no means exact. Occasionally the testator specifically stated he did not want the executors to conduct an inventory.
Fulcone de Castello did not want anyone to constrain his wife to
account for his goods; Oberto Bonizo simply stated that he did
not want an inventory.[42] Personal motives prompted these decisions. Perhaps a public accounting of wealth was not always the
prudent course. When, for whatever reason, there was no inventory, the executors paid the legacies as they saw fit. Some testators
required them to pay the legacies within a year—the normal out-

side limit for paying legacies, whether there was an inventory or not.

Paying the legacies was not always a simple matter. Some testators had most of their wealth tied up in commercial contracts that could not be profitably terminated at once. The executors would have to wait for the right moment, or the expiration of an agreement, which might be years in the future. Probably in most cases, though, it was possible to wind up a person's affairs in a year. If the executors were also tutors, their responsibility might stretch ten or twenty years into the future. The tutors were supposed to do everything a good parent might do—invest the inheritance wisely, arrange marriages or apprenticeships, raise the minors well, and see that they had a decent start in life. These obligations were neither granted nor assumed lightly. Being a tutor was a long-term commitment; the testators recognized this when they arranged for substitutes if one of their nominees died or declined. Giovanni da Vilmercato the wool merchant noted in his will that he had L.22 of Lanfranchino's goods as his tutor, and L.7 s.10 of the sons of Maffeo, whose tutor he also was.[43] Giovanni supplied this information at the very beginning of his will, and he wished to make sure that the money would be returned to the minors. Gandolfo di Gotizone made his wife, Stefania, tutor for their children, and he imposed the condition that she take his place as tutor for the sons of his late brother.[44] The notarial cartularies contain many acts in which the tutors made contracts on behalf of the minors, or the beneficiary acknowledged to the executors that he had received the expected legacy. Any Genoese might find herself or himself in need of an executor or named as one in someone else's will.

Since more people appointed executors than named tutors, who were a subclass of executors, the sample is larger than that of tutors alone (see Chaper 3). Testators might appoint any number of executors, but one, two, or three usually satisfied them. Tables 14, 15, and 16 provide information about executors. The tables distinguish the testators by sex and the executors by number and by their relationship to the testator. Women rarely appointed tutors, and while they did not name executors as frequently as men did, they did so in numbers that make a comparison by sex possible. We should keep in mind that family situations differed, and

probably no testator had a complete set of potential executors—
that is, no one had father, mother, spouse, brother, and so on all
to choose from. Individual family circumstances dictated which
of these relatives, friends, or associates would come to mind as
suitable executors. The tables should be consulted with these qualifications in mind.

The tables reveal that most testators selected a single executor;
and Table 14 outlines these selections. About half the men selected
their wives as the sole executrix. No other choice came close to
rivaling the wife's position as the most likely executor. Close relatives such as siblings, children, or parents were chosen about as
frequently as in-laws or friends. Because men chose their wives
so frequently, the majority of men with a single executor chose a
woman, whether wife, mother, or some other relative. Women
choosing a single executor, however, did so in an apparently random fashion. Three categories stand out to some extent—hus-

Table 14. Sex of testators and executors in wills naming one executor.

Person named	Wills of—	
	79 male testators	48 female testators
Spouse	40	9
Father	0	2
Mother	5	2
Brother	7	3
Sister	1	2
Son	2	3
Daughter	0	2
Other relative[a]	4	3
In-law	8	3
Friend	8	11
Member of the clergy[b]	2	7
Notary[b]	2	0
Godparent	0	1
Total	79	48
Total female executors	50	11
Total male executors	29	37

Source: Archivio di Stato di Genova, Cartolari Notarili.
a. Uncle, aunt, nephew, niece, grandparent, or other blood relative.
b. Not a relative.

band, friend, and member of the clergy. Since we know that more females than males in Genoa were widowed, we should expect that the spouse would not figure as prominently as a choice for women as for men. Still, in the matter of choosing an executor women had more scope for choice than in almost anything else they did. Women were allowed to be executors, and yet women still mainly selected men for this task. Of the eleven friends women selected, eight were men, usually associates of the late father or husband, and only three were women. The women's choices indicate that no single type of relative or associate emerged as the clear favorite; depending on the circumstances, any of them might be chosen.

Table 15 contains the choices of testators who named two executors. The men reversed the pattern set by those who chose

Table 15. Sex of testators and executors in wills naming two executors.

0Person named	Wills of—	
	47 male testators	19 female testators
Spouse	13	3
Father	2	1
Mother	2	1
Brother	13	5
Sister	0	4
Son	9	1
Daughter	1	2
Other relative[a]	8	3
In-law	7	6
Friend	33	4
Member of the clergy[b]	6	8
Notary[b]	0	0
Godparent	0	0
Total	94	38
Total female executors	16	14
Total male executors	78	24

Source: Archivio di Stato di Genova, Cartolari Notarili.
a. Uncle, aunt, nephew, niece, grandparent, or other blood relative.
b. Not a relative.

only one executor. Forty-seven men chose two executors, for a total of ninety-four, of which only sixteen—thirteen wives, two daughters, and one mother—were women. These men more commonly selected other men to be their executors. The category that dominates here is that of friends, all of whom were men. The women choosing two executors commonly picked a relative and a friend. These choices are very different from those in Table 14. Many men overlooked their wives and chose other people to do the job, while in Table 14 the wife was the clear favorite. It seems that these tables distinguish the condition of marriages as well as the number of executors. Only nineteen women nominated two executors, and again their choices were random. When there were two executors, a woman was more likely to select at least one woman to be an executrix than at any other time. Perhaps women found it easier to appoint one female if they also named a male.

Table 16 contains the choices of testators who named three or more executors. In these cases friends were particularly important for both sexes. The common pattern was to select one relative and two other persons, whether friends or clergy, who were not relations. Men were much more likely than women to name three or more executors. In general, the wealthier a person was, the more inclined he was to want a number of executors. Complicated affairs required several stewards, and wealth taught some testators that perhaps three people were more likely to find the wisest course. I have previously discussed the importance of friends to the Genoese, who depended on these voluntary ties, built up over a period of years, and who drew on this credit when the need arose.[45]

The testators together chose 404 executors; men named 282, of which 200 were men and 82 were women. The women named 122 executors, of which 89 were men and 33 were women. On balance the proportion of male and female executors was roughly the same for all testators. But the number of executors, and to some extent their sex, are the important factors. Whether a testator chose one, two, or three executors tells us something about his family, and at one extreme his wealth. The same type of people—the nearest kin, some friends, and members of the clergy—who were the principal heirs also served as executors. However, usually the principal heirs and the executors were not the same

Table 16. Sex of testators and executors in wills naming three or more executors.

Person named	Wills of—	
	37 male testators	12 female testators
Spouse	13	0
Father	0	0
Mother	1	2
Brother	17	2
Sister	2	1
Son	7	0
Daughter	0	1
Other relative[a]	11	5
In-law	9	6
Friend	43	16
Member of the clergy[b]	5	2
Notary[b]	0	1
Godparent	1	0
Total	109	36
Total female executors	16	8
Total male executors	93	28

Source: Archivio di Stato di Genova, Cartolari Notarili.
a. Uncle, aunt, nephew, niece, grandparent, or other blood relative.
b. Not a relative.

people. In no category of executors were children prominent. What we see here is a common impulse to turn to the closest mature people to find an executor. The kind of people named help demonstrate the importance the Genoese attached to these selections. A testator placed his wealth and his trust in similar persons.

Upon investigation, the inventories reveal that the heirs did indeed inherit most of the estate when they were given "the rest of the goods." Inventories in their various forms and references to business contracts also enable us to see how the testator acquired his wealth, and this in turn supplies crucial biographical details not always found in the wills alone.[46] By making a will, a person hoped to influence a future he did not expect to see. The executors provided the testator with one last opportunity to ensure that his intentions would have some tangible future impact. The Genoese chose executors who were close to them, and gave some thought to how many executors there should be. We cannot reconstruct the reasoning by which the testator decided who his executors would be, yet the choices reveal that there were different strategies for approaching the problem. The nearest kin provided the majority of executors, but individual family circumstances determined just which relatives would be chosen. The inventories and executors remind us that family history is not merely the story of the family; it is also a bundle of personalized, often contradictory family histories. Almost every time I have examined these 632 families in aggregate, I have tried to give each one of them the individual attention that any family requires. The tension between the family and society has its counterpart within the family itself. If this study occasionally seems to emphasize the contradictions and varieties rather than the general conclusions, it is because families are often like that.

Conclusion

Any local history runs the risk of losing a sense of perspective. Conclusions based on the Genoese evidence have the potential of wider applicability if one keeps in mind city size, distance from Genoa, and purely local phenomena. Naturally, some evidence remains distinctly Genoese. A good example of this is the role large leper colonies played in the city's charitable concerns. The nature of the evidence suggests an important basis for comparisons. Although Genoa's notarial record forms a precious body of source material, its survival in Genoa was fortuitous. Other Italian cities, as well as areas of southern France and Spain, share a common background, in Spain enhanced by the literate Islamic culture, which stressed the legal importance of a written record. Beginning in the twelfth century, notaries increasingly played a fundamental role in making private records more economical and widely used, and in turn the growing volume of business created a need for more notaries. A broad segment of the urban population, and to a lesser extent the country people, utilized the services of notaries. A will was just one type of document that the notaries redacted. The themes developed in Chapter 1, principally how wills were drawn up and how the notary conducted his business, have a general validity that applies beyond Genoa. The unique nature of Genoa's source material allows one to examine the rise of the written word in the first century of its real advance.

I have concentrated on Genoese wills because they are relatively abundant and revealing, and represent a reasonably broad cross-section of Genose society. The reason for making a will, which in most cases seems to have been illness and a consequent fear of death, is also not limited to any particular city. The practical reasons for making a will, and the church's exhortations to make one as a last act of charity, were also widespread influences. Most wills were made at home, either before or after the business day. Illness, age, and the press of business helped to determine where and when wills were made. As early as the 1160s people of modest means were making wills, and over the course of the next century the habit of making wills continued to spread throughout the population. By 1250 it seems that social or economic position had little to do with the decision to make a will, since people having only a few lire found it worthwhile to make one. Women were as likely to make wills as men, and so testaments present one of the few balanced sources about medieval life. The Genoese had access to an independent and reliable means of preserving their last wishes, and any other piece of business they cared to record. Any more efficient way to preserve information will replace older ones, and the veritable explosion of paper in this century affected the way people conducted business, making the ability to read an important asset.

Conclusions about the family require a greater measure of caution. The medieval family was not the same throughout Europe, and Genoa may not have typified medieval urban life even in Italy. A millenium of human experience on a continental scale should offer some variety. There must be more local studies of family size and inheritance patterns before one can be certain about the regionality of the medieval family. Wills are an excellent source for family history because they provide the most complete view of individual family circumstances. Other sources, such as marriage contracts or records of the emancipation of sons, illuminate only one relationship within the family. The Genoese wills suggest that we look at the family as a descent group, a pool of potential heirs. The descent group has the additional advantage of pointing out that the family is a timeless institution, with ancestors and heirs. The choice of heirs was usually the will's most important feature. A person contemplating his own death was forced to examine the family in a new light—without himself. Those Genoese having children selected them as heirs. Childless persons turned to the nearest surviving kin—a spouse, sibling, or other close relative. The set of principal heirs closely conformed to the nuclear family. Extended families and the familial clan played a part in Genoese society, but in looking for these wider and more tenuous connections, one must not lose sight of the fundamental importance of the nearest kin.

Marriage united two people and two families, who all had a common objective—the well-being of any children born to the couple. The rights and obligations inherent in marriage were most strongly present in the arrangements to return the dowry, and the desire of nearly all husbands to prevent a wife's remarriage. A few wills illustrate the complications that could result from a second marriage. The number of widows in Genoa testifies to the age difference between husband and wife. Men tended to remarry very quickly; the number of widowers is minuscule. Men evidently thought that their remarriage was less dangerous to their children's status than that of a woman with children.

Roman and Lombard law, as well as local custom, provided a framework of rules for choosing heirs and settling marriage rights. The notaries had experience and legal expertise to offer their clients, and a collection of handbooks to consult if they had any problems. Other advisers—family members or lawyers—were also available. On one level the wills demonstrate a conformity to established customs, but at the same time they reveal that the testators had discretionary powers. If the law had prevented a significant number of people from doing what they wanted to do, the law would have been changed or ignored. The testament, as a legal way to convey property, allowed the testator to remember distant relatives and friends. A last will obligated the heirs and trustees to honor its terms, unless the will was blatantly defective or the testator insane. Most of the time the law ensured that the testator's intentions would be carried out, and did not pose any insurmountable barriers to his final wishes.

An idea of social charity evolved in Genoa and the rest of Italy, where there was an urban environment and a money economy to help shape its goals. From the beginning the church had taught that charity was blessed, and the commercial revolution created new social needs as well as the wherewithal to meet them. The will was a last chance to store up some merit in the next world, and such a business metaphor would not have been lost on the Genoese. The funeral and burial were at the heart of nearly everyone's charitable thoughts. The family, clergy, guildsmen, friends, and paupers who participated in the funeral all confirmed a person's social status in this world. The funeral also served as a step in the ritual that conveyed the individual from the family to the church. Burial itself was completely in the hands of the church. Anthropological models of rituals enhance our understanding of the poorly documented medieval funeral. In this age before the family tomb fully developed, the individual churches and monasteries controlled the churchyards and burial sites. The burial sites the Genoese selected reveal contemporary religious tastes and the levels of prestige the various institutions enjoyed.

The urban setting imparted a special urgency to the problems of the poor and the sick—needs that social charity tried to address. Poverty and disease were potentially serious challenges to the social order, but nothing in the experience of the medieval commune argued in favor of the idea of publicly funded charity. The social charities helped to preserve the stability of the family and community; by providing dowries for the poor, feeding and housing them, and ministering to the sick, the Genoese made their city a safer place for everyone. The new mendicant orders of the thirteenth century helped to spread the message of social justice and compassion. The Genoese continued to endow masses for the soul, and bequeathed money to churches and monasteries for strictly religious purposes. The new charitable ethos existed alongside these more established forms of charity. In time, however, the social charities consumed an increasingly larger share of what the Genoese were willing to spend on pious causes. Masses for the soul remained extremely popular, and so the burden of diminishing legacies fell mainly on the older local monasteries. The new orders encouraged this change in the goals of charity, and quickly adapted to the evolving sense of what constituted a meritorious gift. Wills are an excellent source for the history of charity because they reveal the range of charitable interests; other sources provide only a sporadic and partial view of actual giving. We cannot understand the history of charity only in the context of such prescriptive sources as theological works, sermons, and the law. The large sums of money devoted to social charities in Genoa demonstrate that social needs were perceived and a meaningful effort was made to meet them. The rich had the means to set the tone of charitable donations, and by their large gifts they influenced the course that the charitable impulse would pursue.

The history of charity in Genoa is the earliest known example in Europe of a city combining spiritual values and social concerns to support the existing social order.

The inventories prove that the principal heirs did indeed inherit the bulk of the estate. Estate inventories also enable us to see how the testator accumulated his wealth, and hence present a more complete picture of a person's life than a will alone does. Inventories are also quite informative about the range of contemporary business activity. The new entrepreneurs of Genoa invested in land and commerce, and they also often had a profession or engaged in wholesale or retail selling. Within the family itself there was a similar diversity; some members traveled, while others remained at home to oversee family business and investments. The executors were expected to continue these activities, manage the estate, distribute the legacies, and if there were children, responsibly give them a decent start in life. Again the testators turned to the nearest kin as persons worthy of trust, and friends also figure prominently as trustees. The choice of executors seems to have been one of the most independent and voluntary aspects of the will. Any Genoese might be asked to serve as an executor or tutor, and would eventually need others to perform this task for him.

The Genoese were able to put their personal stamp on a will. They attached conditions to legacies and appointments revealing their personal concerns and emotions. The wills are autobiographies in miniature, and they tell us about individuals whom standard histories generally omit or include as the faceless "people." The persons considered in this study emerge as distinct characters. Perhaps this is not the kind of attention they wanted from posterity, but their family pride and social attitudes lend a dignity to their city that, I hope, compensates for this intrusion.

Appendixes
Notes
Bibliography
Index

Appendix A

Testament of Oberto Lomellino
June 8, 1252
Bartolomeo Fornari, notary

Ego obertus lomellinus bone et sane mentis. timens dei iudicium comtemplacione ultime mee voluntas. rerum mearum talem facio disposicionem. corpus meum iubeo sepelliri apud ecclesiam Sancti teodori. pro anima mea iudico Lb. viginti quinque Ianue quorum decenum iudico operi Sancti laurencii. de quibus iudico predicte ecclesie pro misis canendis. annualibus et tretenis pro anima mea. Lb. decem. Alia vel sint in distribucione Ugonis grilli cognati mei et Symonis spinulle cognati mei et Symone uxoris mee. Item volo et ordino quod Symona uxor mea habeat et habere debeat de bonis meis Lb. quingentas Ianue dotium suarum et Lb. centum Ianue antefacti sui in pecunia numerata. Item lego predicte Symone uxori mee ultra predictas rationes suas docium et antefacti terram meam quam habeo in castelleto cum domo. instrumentis et omnibus superponitis suis. et omnia guarnamenta et ornamenta sua et vestes quibus utatur et utebatur cum tote furnite et cum omnibus paramentis tam camere quam domus et cum omnibus masariciis et utensilibus et ceteris omnibus rebus que sint in domo mea quam habeo exceptis armis et Guarnixonis de ferri de quibus lego miroaldo de turca osbergum unum cum pare uno caligarum ferri et corelum unum cum manicas quos ipse maluerit ex illis quos habeo. Item Gavino et petrino filiis Symone uxoris mee quos substulit ex daniele aurie quondam marito suo. lego de bonis meis cuilibet eorum Lb. quinqueginta Ianue quod implicantur in Sardineam in bestiis ad eorum utilitatem. consilio et voluntate petri grilli et Ingonis grilli cognatorum meorum et secundum quod eis videbitur. Item lego predictis Gavino et petrino pro anima mea quicquid mihi debeat et ab eis recipere debeo. pro eorum alimentis si de hac infirmitate decesero. et volo quod laudes quos habeo contra ipsos occasione dictorum alimentorum post meum decessum restituantur. Item lego cuilibet eorum corelum unum quos maluerint ex illis quos habeo deductis osberga et corelo quos lego miroaldo predicto. Item lego adalaxie sorori mee uxori Symonis spinulle cognati mei domum meam in quam dicti adalaxia soror mea cum dicto Symone spinulla cognato meo habitant. Item lego amico lomellino consanguineo meo domum meam quam habeo in carrubio drecta de peliparii et terram meam quam habeo in pelio tali modo videlicet quod dictus amicus predictam domum et terram per se vel alium non possit vendere nec alienare neque aliqua modo obligare aliqua termine. et si dictus amicus decesserit sine herede masculo legitimi coniugi ex se nato volo et odino quod Simone lomellinus. thomas lomellinus. Iohannes lomellinus et ansaldus lomellinus vel eorum heredes quilibet eorum pro quartam parte eidem amico in predicta domo et terra de pelio succedant et ipsos se in predictis statuo et ordino. supradicto heredes substituo. Item lego dicto amico omnes guarnixones meas ferri et arma mea deductis illis quos superius legavi miroaldo et Gavino et petrino predictis. Item andriole sorori dicti amici lego pro anima mea in vestibus Lb. quinque. Item symone sorori dicti amici lego pro anima mea in vestibus Lb. quinque. Item montanarie sorori dicti amici et uxori enrici de nigro lego pro anima mea Lb. quinque et remitto eidem Symone montanarie pro anima mea solidos viginti quos mihi debet ultra predictis Lb. quinque quos ei superius legavi. Item confiteor me debere dare Enrico Florentino de castello Lb. novem Ianue quos restant ad solvendum de dotibus Symone uxoris sue et neptis mee. Item confiteor quod frater marinus preceptor Sancti iohannis [256 verso] dicto enrico florentino Lb. tres Ianue quos promissus dare dicte simone uxori eius pro dotibus ipsius. quos volo quod solvantur de bonis meis si dictus frater marinus eas non solvit. Item statuo et ordino quod fredericus grillus socer meus habeat et habere debeat post meum decessum domum meam in qua habito pro precio sub extimatus precii librarum trescentarum Ianue. Salvo omni quod uxor mea stallum habeat in ipsa domo in vita sua dum steterit et stare in domo sine marito. Si autem maritabitur ipsam domum habeat dictus fredericus socer meus pro predictis Lb. trescentis ut predictum est. Item remito enriceto spinulle filio Symonis spinulle post meum decessum quicquid meis habeo contra ipsum circa eiusdem accomendam quam ei feci et tam satis finis fiat. Item lego Rubeo de turca et miroaldo eius filio Lb. triginta septem et solidos quatuordecem quos mihi debent et quod de questione et lite quam habeo cum dicto Rubeo fiat ei remisia et finis nec de cetero per heredes meos possit modo aliqua de dicta questione molestari. Item confiteor me dare debere Raimundete serviciali mee de suo feudo solidos triginta sex quos volo quod habeat de bonis meis. et eidem lego pro anima mea Lb. tres de bonis meis. Item lego ecclesie Sancte marie de vineis in misis canendis pro anima mea solidos quadraginta. confiteor cum me dare debere domino Rubeo priori monasterii sancte marie de vineis Lb. centum quinqueginta Ianue et ultra mutuum quem cum reperiretur in meo cartulo scriptum quod sint Gerardi et Iacobini filiorum quondam fulconis muasgerii quos volo quod habeant de bonis meis. Item lego altilie et Barbarine filiabus quondam willielmi lomellini cuilibet earum in vestibus Lb. quinque. Item operi madiolo solidos quadraginta. Item iacobe uxori willielmi de baiamonte Lb. quinque. Item lego adalaxie sorori mei uxori Symonis spinulle quicquid juris habeo et mihi competere contra quicumque seu quoscumque personis circa laudum seu sententiarum quos secutus sum et habeo contra omnibus personis. Salva terram quam supradictam est (et deductis debitis quam debere xxxxx.) Item confiteor me debere dare Symoni spinulle cognato meo Lb. decem Ianue quos mihi mutavit. reliquorum bonorum meorum omnium deductis debitis et legatis meis predictis mihi herede instituo amicum lomellinum predictum. Item demitto Symonem spinullam et Symonam uxorem meam distributores et pagatores legatorum et debitorum meorum de bonis meis. Salvis semper mutuis et collectis et honeribus comunis Ianue decetero prestandis de ipsis et statuo et ordino quod heredes meos seu illi quibus relictum est aliquod in mobilibus antequam possessionem habeant faciat scribi et super se in cartula posse comunis Ianue ad expendandum de ipsis in comuni Ianue. hec est mea ultima voluntas que si iure testamenti non tenet. saltim volo quod iure codicillorum alterius ultime voluntatis teneat et vim habeat. Actum Ianue in camera domini dicti oberti M CC Lii die viii junii post nonam. Testes petrus grillus. (Symon Spi) Symone lomellinus. thomas lomellinus. marinus ususmaris. Iacobus de vivaldo. Nicola baracerius. Iacobus grillus. et andriolus de turca.

I, Oberto Lomellino, of good and sound mind, fearing the judgment of God, with contemplation of my last will thus make disposition of my goods. I order my body to be buried at the Church of San Teodoro. For my soul I leave L.25 gen., of which I leave one-tenth to the works of San Lorenzo. Of the rest I leave to the said church L.10 for annual and monthly masses for my soul. The rest should be distributed by my in-law Ugone Grillo, my in-law Simone Spinola, and my wife, Simona. Item: I wish and order that my wife Simona should and ought to have from my goods L.500 gen. of her dowry and the L.100 gen. of her marriage gift in cash. Item: I leave the said Simona, my wife, beyond her said rights of dowry and *antefactum*, my land with a house that I have in Castelleto, and the instruments and everything on it, and all her garments and jewelry and clothes that she uses or has used, with all the furnishings and with all the accessories of her suite and also of the house, and with all the possessions, utensils, and all the rest of the things which may be in my house that I have, except my arms and pieces of armor made of iron. Of these I leave to Miroaldo de Turca a hauberk with a pair of metal greaves and a mail doublet with sleeves, which he himself shall choose from those I have. Item: I leave to Gavino and Petrino, sons of my wife, Simona, whom she had with her late husband, Daniele Doria, L.50 gen. to each of them from my goods, to be invested in Sardinia in livestock for their benefit, with the counsel and by the wish of my in-laws Pietro Grillo and Ingone Grillo, according to how it seems best to them. Item: I leave to the said Gavino and Petrino for my soul whatever is owed to me and whatever I should receive from them for their support, if I should die of this illness, and I want the decrees which I have against them for their support to be returned to them after my death. Item: I leave to each of them a mail doublet which they shall choose from those I have, minus the hauberk and mail doublet that I left the said Miroaldo. Item: I leave to my sister Adalasia, wife of my in-law Simone Spinola, my house in which the said Adalasia, my sister, lives with the said Simone Spinola, my in-law. Item: I leave to Amico Lomellino, my blood relative, my house which I have in the Furrier district, and land which I have in Pegli, in such a way, namely, that the said Amico cannot sell nor alienate nor obligate to any end, for himself or for others, the said house and land, and if the said Amico shall die without a legitimate male heir born in wedlock, I wish and order that Simone Lomellino, Tommaso Lomellino, Giovanni Lomellino, and Ansaldo Lomellino, or their heirs, each succeed Amico for one-fourth of the said house and land in Pegli, and I order that I substitute them for the said heir in the above. Item: I leave the said Amico all my armor of iron and my arms, saving what I left above to the said Miroaldo, Gavino, and Petrino. Item: I leave to Andriola, sister of the said Amico, for my soul in clothes L.5. Item: to Simona, sister of the said Amico, I leave for my soul in clothes L.5. Item: to Montanaria, sister of the said Amico and wife of Enrico de Nigrone, I leave for my soul L.5, and I remit to Montanaria for my soul twenty solidi which she owes me, beyond the L.5 I left her above. Item: I acknowledge that I ought to give Enrico Florentino de Castello L.9 gen. which remain to be paid for the dowry of his wife, my niece Simona. Item: I acknowledge that Brother Marino, preceptor of San Giovanni, owes the said Enrico Florentino L.3 gen. which he promised to give the said Simona, his wife, for her dowry, which I want to be paid from my goods if the said Brother Marino will not pay. Item: I decide and order that my father-in-law, Federigo Grillo, have and ought to have after my death the house I live in for a price and under the estimate of the price of L.300 gen., saving all, that my wife have an apartment in that house for her lifetime while she will stay and does stay in the house without a husband. If, however, she marries, the said Federigo, my father-in-law, should have the house for the said L.300 as is said above. Item: I remit to Enriceto Spinola, son of Simone Spinola, after my death whatever I have against him concerning a *commenda* which I made with him, and let there be a satisfactory end to this. Item: I leave to Rosso de Turca and his son Miroaldo L.37 s.14 which they owe me, and also, concerning the question and controversy that I have with the said Rosso, let there be a finish and an end and nothing further, and my heirs should not bother him on account of this dispute. Item: I acknowledge that I owe my servant Raimundeta for her pay thirty-six solidi, which I want her to have from my goods, and I leave her for my soul L.3 from my goods. Item: I leave the Church of Santa Maria delle Vigne for masses for my soul forty solidi. I acknowledge that I owe Lord Rosso, prior of the Monastery of Santa Maria delle Vigne, L.150 gen. for a loan, as contained and written in my cartulary, and this sum belongs to Gerardo and Jacobino, sons of the late Fulcone Muasgerio, and I want them to have this amount from my goods. Item: I leave Altilia and Barbarina, daughters of the late Guglielmo Lomellino, in clothes L.5 each. Item: to the works of the harbor mole forty solidi. Item: to Jacoba, wife of Guglielmo de Baiamonte, L.5. Item: I leave to my sister Adalasia, wife of Simone Spinola, whatever right I have or can be sought for me against anyone or whatever persons concerning cases or sentences that I have pursued, and whatever right I have against all persons, except for the above-mentioned land (and the debts I owe having been deducted). Item: I acknowledge that I owe Simone Spinola, my in-law, L.10 gen. which he loaned me. I make as my heir the said Amico Lomellino for the rest of all my goods, minus my said debts and legacies. I name Simone Spinola and my wife, Simona, as distributors and payers of my legacies and my debts from my goods, saving always the loans, obligations, and assessments of the commune of Genoa, and the rest of the loans from them. I order and decide that those to whom some movable property has been left ought to record the movables in writing in a cartulary of the commune of Genoa before they take possession of them, in order to make expenditures from them in the commune of Genoa. This is my last will, which if it does not hold by the law of the testament, at least I wish it by the law of codicils of another last will to hold and have force. Done in Genoa in the chambers of the said Lord Oberto, 8 June 1252, after nones. Witnesses: Pietro Grillo, (Simone Spi), Simone Lomellino, Tommaso Lomellino, Marino Usodimare, Jacopo de Vivaldo, Nicola *baracerius*, Jacopo Grillo, and Andriolo de Turca. [Words in parentheses were crossed out in the original document.]

Appendix B

Prices and Money

All the sums of money that appear in this work, unless otherwise stated, are in Genoese lire. The Genoese records refer to many other monetary systems, and the actual coinage in circulation further complicates the picture.[1] The Genoese lira consisted of 240 denarii (silver pennies), which equaled 20 solidi of twelve denarii each. This system of money, based on the pound, was widely used throughout Europe. In 1139 Genoa received the right to mint money, and it shortly began to produce silver pennies. Pisan coins continued to circulate in the city for some time, as did a wide array of other coins, most notably Byzantine and North African bezants. A commercial economy based on silver pennies faced considerable difficulties. From the first stages of the commercial revival money of account played an important role, because there was simply not enough hard currency in circulation. Money of account represented an abstract value that the parties to an agreement, or the marketplace, recognized as fair and accurate. Thus the L.100 invested in a commercial venture might reflect the value of merchandise, or some combination of goods and cash. The value of a dowry was fixed in lire, but the actual payment often consisted of land or some other property that the parties agreed was worth a certain amount. Genoese contracts and other documents often referred to "public estimators," whose job entailed fixing a fair monetary value to land or merchandise—in other words, creating money of account.

Besides relying on money of account, the Genoese found other ways to expand their money supply. Any form of bullion was easily assigned a lira value, and as we have seen, Genoese estates contained gold and silver objects which were perfectly acceptable liquid assets. In 1221 the city minted its first multiple of the silver penny—the silver grosso, originally worth four pennies, but by midcentury equal to a solidus, or twelve pennies.[2] In 1252 Genoa minted its first gold coin. Byzantine coinage, based on the gold bezant, later the hyperper, as well as North African gold and silver bezants, freely circulated in Genoa in the twelfth and thirteenth centuries. For example in 1222 eighty-eight Tunisian bezants were worth L.23 gen., and in this decade the price remained at a little over three bezants to the lira.[3] A dependable foreign currency was as good as any local one, and the banking profession was skilled at calculating the Genoese value of foreign currencies. Long-distance trade and the fairs of Champagne required an easy and tested way to exchange one currency for another. Exchanging coins was a relatively simple matter compared to figuring the exchange rates for monies of account. Bankers needed a sophisticated knowledge of European and Eastern markets to calculate what the Genoese lira would be worth in Troyes in six months, but their ability to do this created credit. Even within a growing money economy, barter continued to play a useful role that reduced to some extent the demands the Genoese economy made on its money supply.

The sums of money in Genoese wills might represent several systems of value besides cash. The occasional use of the expression "in pecunia numerata" (in counted money—cash) indicates that some legacies were paid in cash. Probably the most difficult job the executors had was to satisfy the beneficiaries, who received a legacy most often expressed in money of account. Presumably the executors were able to reach agreements as to what constituted a fair settlement of claims, and both parties might call on a public estimator to settle disputes. The executors may have used whatever cash they found in the estate to pay small charitable bequests and the immediate expenses of the funeral. The records do not reveal how the executors managed to pay the legacies or what form this payment took. Regardless of what the Genoese lira represented in any particular will, the reliance on money of account, and its implied consensus of value, means that we can compare the sums in different wills.

The value of money is not necessarily fixed over time, and so in comparing a sum from 1155 to one from 1253, one should consider any changes in prices. The Genoese records provide a formidable statistical base for examining over time the prices of key commodities like wheat, but unfortunately this work remains largely undone. Giovanni Pesce and Giuseppe Felloni have examined the purchasing power of Genoese money of account with respect to two key commodities—gold and silver. From 1154 to 1190 the price of an ounce of fine gold advanced from L.27 s.15 d.8 to L.34 s.5 d.6. After a gap in the record, from 1205 to 1253 the price increased from L.37 s.10 d.8 to L.47 s.11 d.7.[4] Fine silver exhibited a similar price rise, from L.3 s.10 d.7 per pound in 1162 to L.5 s.10 d.8 in 1253.[5] Gold was rising slightly more quickly in value than silver, but one must also consider how the gradual debasement of the silver currency in the thirteenth century affected these values. In terms of gold and silver, the purchasing power of the Genoese lira declined by about one-half during this period. It is necessary to know much more about the prices of other commodities before generalizing about any inflation between 1155 and 1253. Bigger markets and more efficient trade may have deflated some prices, and hence to some extent offset the increasing prices of gold and silver. We are still a long way from organizing the available sources into a sort of consumer price index for medieval Genoa. The price of any single commodity is no sure guide to general price levels. One must address the fundamental question of urban rents before even hazarding a guess about the rate of inflation. The economy undoubtedly experienced some inflation, probably much less than the increases in gold and silver prices alone might indicate. This study has not depended on comparing monetary values over time, since the rate of inflation remains uncertain.

Abbreviations Used in Notes and Bibliography

ASG	Archivio di Stato di Genova
ASLSP	*Atti della Società Ligure di Storia Patria*
B	*Bonvillano*
DSSCD	*Documenti e studi per la storia del commercio e del diritto commerciale italiano*
FSI	*Fonti per la storia d'Italia*
GC	*Guglielmo Cassinese*
GG	*Giovanni di Guiberto*
GS	*Il cartolare di Giovanni Scriba*
L	*Lanfranco*
M	Archivio di Stato di Genova, Sezione Manoscritti, ms. 102, *Diversorum Notariorum*
MS	*Maestro Salmone*
N.	Cartolari Notarili numero
OSI	*Oberto Scriba de Mercato (1186)*
OSII	*Oberto Scriba de Mercato (1190)*
RIS	*Rerum Italicarum Scriptores*
SMV	*Le carte di Santa Maria delle Vigne di Genova (1103–1392)*
SS	*Le carte del monastero di San Siro di Genova dal 952 al 1224*

Notes

1 The Sources

1. For an inventory of these primary sources, see Ministero dell'Interno, *Pubblicazioni degli Archivi di Stato, Archivio di Stato di Genova: Cartolari notarili genovesi*, vols. 22 and 41 (Rome, 1956 and 1961).

2. For some of the history of the Archivio di Stato di Genova (hereafter ASG), see Mattia Moresco and Gian Piero Bognetti, *Per l'edizione dei notai liguri del sec. XII* (Turin, 1938).

3. Arturo Ferretto, *Liber Magistri Salamonis Sacri Palatii Notarii 1222–1226* (cited hereafter as MS), *Atti della Società Ligure di Storia Patria*, vol. 36 (Genoa, 1906). Cited hereafter as ASLSP.

4. These collections appeared in the journal *Biblioteca della società storica subalpina* from 1906 to 1910. None of the wills he transcribed have been used here.

5. *Il Cartolare di Giovanni Scriba*, ed. Mario Chiaudano and Mattia Moresco (Rome, 1935). Cited hereafter as GS.

6. For the goals, methods, and problems of this endeavor, see Moresco and Bognetti, *Per l'edizione dei notai liguri.*

7. *Guglielmo Cassinese*, ed. Margaret W. Hall, Hilmar C. Krueger, Robert L. Reynolds (Turin, 1938); cited hereafter as GC. *Oberto Scriba de Mercato (1190)*, ed. Mario Chiaudano and R. M. Della Roca (Turin, 1938); cited hereafter as OSII. *Bonvillano*, ed. James E. Eierman, Hilmar C. Krueger, Robert L. Reynolds (Turin, 1939); cited hereafter as B. *Giovanni di Guiberto*, ed. Margaret W. Hall-Cole et al. (Turin, 1939); cited hereafter as GG. *Oberto Scriba de Mercato (1186)*, ed. Marion Chiaudano (Turin, 1940); cited hereafter as OSI. All these editions appeared in the series *Documenti e studi per la storia del commercio e del diritto commerciale italiano*, hereafter cited as DSSCD.

8. David Abulafia notes this omission in *The Two Italies* (Cambridge, 1977), p. 18.

9. *Lanfranco*, ed. Hilmar C. Krueger and Robert L. Reynolds (Genoa, 1951, 1952, 1953). Cited hereafter as L.

10. Two important church cartularies cited in this work are Gabriella Airaldi, *Le carte di Santa Maria delle Vigne di Genova (1103–1392)* (Genoa, 1969), cited hereafter as SMV, and Aurelia Basili and Luciana Pozza, *Le carte del monastero di San Siro di Genova dal 952 al 1224* (Genoa, 1974), cited hereafter as SS.

11. See bibliography for a complete list of the cartularies.

12. ASG, Cartolari Notarili, N. 19, 32r–36r. Hereafter the cartularies are cited by number (N).

13. N. 26 pt. 1, 203r.

14. For a more complete discussion of these technical terms, see Giorgio

Costamagna, "La triplice redazione dell'instrumentum genovesi," in his collected essays, *Studi di paleografia e di diplomatica* (Rome, 1972).

15. GS, N. 174.

16. N. 7, 126r.

17. SS, N. 164.

18. *Institutes*, bk. 2, title 10, trans. John B. Moyle (Oxford, 1889).

19. Marc Bloch, *Feudal Society*, trans. L. A. Manyon (Chicago, 1970), p. 125.

20. For the statement of some Genoese that they lived according to Lombard law, see the cartularies of San Siro and Santa Maria delle Vigne. For a good introduction to Lombard law, and an English translation of these laws, see Katherine Fischer Drew, *The Lombard Laws* (Philadelphia, 1973).

21. Giovanni Scriba mentioned some of his books in his will (GS, N. 174).

22. Drew, *Lombard Laws*, p. 146. Lombard law allowed minors to make pious bequests, recognized something akin to the *lex falcidia*, permitted testators to favor one child over others, and granted a husband the right to leave his wife usufruct for life to half the estate. Unfortunately, there are no Lombard wills from Genoa to study.

23. Giovanni Battista Palmieri, *Il "Formularium Tabellionum" di Irnerio* (Bologna, 1892). According to J. J. Murphy, *Medieval Rhetoric, A Select Bibliography* (Toronto, 1971), the attribution to Irnerius is incorrect. Ludwig Wahrmund, "Die Ars Notariae des Rainerius Perusinus," in *Quellen zur Geschichte des Römisch-Kanonischen Processes im Mittelalter*, vol. 3, pt. 2 (Innsbruck, 1917). Gianfranco Orlandelli, *Salatiele "Ars Notariae"* (Milan, 1961). Wahrmund, "Der *Ordo Iudiciorum* des Martinus De Fano," in *Quellen*, vol. 1, pt. 7 (Innsbruck, 1905).

24. Palmieri, *Irnerio*, pp. 86–87.

25. Wahrmund, *Martinus De Fano*, pp. 86–87.

26. Orlandelli, *Salatiele*, pp. 178–183.

27. Wahrmund, *Rainerius Perusinus*, pp. 176–177.

28. Palmieri, *Irnerio*, pp. 88–98.

29. For more on usury in wills, see Chapter 6.

30. Wahrmund, *Rainerius Perusinus*, pp. 187–192.

31. Orlandelli, *Salatiele*, p. 308.

32. Martino da Fano's sample will named the principal heirs at the beginning of the will and in general followed an idiosyncratic order of bequests. For more on this issue, see the comments on notarial style and use of formulas later in this chapter.

33. The Romans called oral wills nuncupatory wills. Some notaries considered a dictated will—which would include all 632 wills under study here—a nuncupatory will. No Genoese, not even a notary, so far as I know, drafted his own final will. For an example of this issue, see N. 16 pt. 1, and the wills written by Federigo da Sestri.

34. *Institutes*, bk. 2, title 18.

35. Ibid, bk. 2, title 22.

36. N. 5, 85v.

37. N. 7, 280v.

38. MS, N. 980.

39. For more on substitution and succession, see Chapters 3 and 4.

40. Wahrmund, *Rainerius Perusinus*, pp. 94–95.

41. Riccardo Filangieri di Candida, *Codice Diplomatico Amalfitano* (Naples, 1917). Charter of 1087, p. 132; will of 1099, pp. 154–156.

42. Raimundo M. della Rocca, A. Lombardo, *Documenti del commercio veneziano nei secolo XI–XIII*, in DSSCD vol. 1 (Turin, 1940), pp. 101–103.

43. Ibid., pp. 240–243, for 1172. Later examples in vol. 2.

44. Dina Bizzari, *Imbreviature notarili, II, Liber Imbreviaturarum Ildibrandini Notarii MCCXXVII–MCCXXIX*, in DSSCD, vol. 9 (Turin, 1938).

45. Antonino de Stefano, *Il registro notarile di Giovanni Maiorana (1297–1300)* (Palermo, 1943). Testament of Brachamo Ricio de Chalfano, April 14, 1299, p. 121.

46. Bloch, *Feudal Society*, p. 78.

47. ASG, Abbazia di Santo Stefano, Mazzo 1.

48. OSI, N. 289.

49. N. 7, between fols. 262 and 263.

50. OSI, N. 248.

51. B, N. 201.

52. "Et sic scribas, quecunque testator dixerit de predicta vel aliis quibuscunque, quia voluntas testatoris lex est." Wahrmund, *Rainerius Perusinus*, p. 185.

53. N. 20 pt. 1, 134r. Printed by Robert S. Lopez in his *Genova marinara nel Duecento: Benedetto Zaccaria, ammiraglio e mercante* (Milan, 1933), p. 243.

54. ASG, Sezione Manoscritti, Manoscritto N. 102, *Diversorum Notariorum*, 150v. Cited hereafter as M. 102.

55. N. 7, 100r.

56. N. 26 pt. 1, 130v.

57. N. 26 pt. 1, 169v.

58. N. 14, 4v.

59. N. 56, 85r.

60. Simone Barlaira, N. 7, 161r. Delomeda, N. 20 pt. 1, 11v. Jacoba Portonario, N. 11, 53r.

61. Ogerio Vento, GS, N. 1006 and N. 1047. Giulia, wife of Guglielmo Balbo, GG, N. 390, N. 20 pt. 1, 53r (notary Bonovassallo de Maiori). Antonio Rapallino, N. 4, 186r and 213v (notary Oberto Scriba). Guirardo de Verzellato, N. 16 pt. 2, 57r, and N. 26 pt. 2, 17v (notaries Urso and Bartolomeo Fornari). Contessa, wife of Oberto Balbo, N. 19, 52r and 60r (notary Niccoloso Beccaira). Stefano Scriba, N. 24, 59r and 77v (notary Bonovassallo de Cassino). Four of the six times the testator returned to the same notary.

62. GS, N. 1006, "Si ex hac infirmitate dominus me vocaverit."

63. GS, N. 1047.

64. N. 26 pt. 2, 17v, "Quod possim in vita mea dare et donare cui et quibus voluero et ut mihi placuerit de bonis meis et manibus propriis."

65. *Falcidia*, it should be recalled, was the minimum share of an estate to which a blood relative was entitled.

66. N. 24, 77v.

67. These acts appear in N. 7, fols. 1–20.

68. N. 19. Most of this notary's testators were in the hospital.

69. The wills state conditions in formulaic phrases, but each will had its own set of specific conditions. Other examples of formulas in wills are discussed elsewhere.

70. GS, N. 47, "Ego Raimundus Pictenadus iudico . . ." GS, N. 386, "Ego Leda Guidonis contemplacione ultima voluntatis iudico . . ."

71. GC, N. 1604, "Gisla de Castello sua ultima voluntate iudicat . . ."

72. GG, N. 1790, "Ego Symon Buferius maior mearum rerum disposi-tione[m] facere cupiens mea ultima voluntate judico . . ."

73. N. 11, 84r, "Ego Stephanus scriba filius iohannis de guiberto timens dei judicum mearum rerum talem facio dispositionem."

74. N. 26 pt. 2, 203r, "Ego Simon silvagius eger corpore sanus mente et intellectu bone memorie existens. divinum timens dei iudicium contemplatione mee ultime voluntatis rerum mearum talem facio disposicionem."

75. N. 20 pt. 1, 112v, "Ego Adalasia filia quondam Bonivassalli balbi no-laschi et cetera."

76. Genoa supported the papacy in this period, especially because Pope Innocent IV was a Fieschi from Lavagna. For details, see *Annales Ianuensis,* in *Annali Genovesi di Caffaro e de' suoi continuatori,* ed. Cesare Imperiale di Sant'Angelo, vol. 3, 1225–1250 (Rome, 1923). Hereafter cited as *Annales Ianuensis* by volume. (See bibliography for a complete list of volumes of this famous city chronicle.)

77. Giovanni Scriba, GS, N. 174. Niccolò Ferrario, MS, N. 1002. Stefano Scriba, N. 11, 84r. Oberto Marzano, N. 31 pt. 1, 107r.

78. N. 56, 137v–154v.

79 N. 17, 1–15v.

80. Robert S. Lopez, "Nota sulla composizione dei patrimoni privati," in *Studi sull'economia genovese nel medio-evo* (Turin, 1936).

81. Robert S. Lopez and Irving W. Raymond, *Medieval Trade in the Medi-terranean World* (New York, 1955). The authors present an English translation of one of the inventories Lopez published in 1936.

82. N. 7, 132r.

83. N. 56, 139r.

84. N. 56, 141r.

85. See note 53.

86. For more on inventories and their value as historical sources, see Chapter 7.

2   The Testament as an Act

1. Benjamin Z. Kedar, "Noms de saints et mentalité populaire à Gênes au XIVe siècle," *Le Moyen Age* 73 (1967): 443.

2. GG, N. 1790.

3. N. 5, 213r.

4. Robert S. Lopez, "Concerning Surnames and Places of Origin," *Medi-evalia et humanistica* 8 (1954) 8–9.

5. Ibid.

6. N. 13, 130r.

7. N. 31 pt. 1, 102r, 106v. Also printed in Robert S. Lopez, "Arte della Lana," in *Studi sull'economia genovese nel medio-evo* (Turin, 1936).

8. N. 20 pt. 1, 54r.

9. For this typical wage, see, for example, MS, N. 1598.

10. For more on this important motive, see Chapter 5.

11. Guglielmo Cassinese, Maestro Salmone (N. 14 and N. 15), Lanfranco.

12. All of Raimundo Medico's acts are in N. 5.

13. N. 16 pt. 2, 64r.

14. N. 19, 35r.

15. N. 18 pt. 2, 274r.

16. N. 18 pt. 2, 215r.

17. See Chapter 4.

18. N. 7, 50v.

19. GG, N. 1669.

20. GG, N. 1912; N. 5, 14v.

21. N. 7, 36v, 42v.

22. Pietro da Pavia, N. 31 pt. 1, 51v. For documents relating to the Crusade of Louis IX, see N. 26, 30r ff. Rainerio da Perugia's formulary taught the notary how to phrase the desire to go on pilgrimage. It is interesting to note that he also provided a list of destinations: the Holy Land, Santiago, Rome, and Monte Gargano.

23. N. 20 pt. 1, 29r, "Ego Iacobus de Alba infirmatus corpore et mee sane mentis . . ." N. 20 pt. 1, 23r. "Ego Viridis uxor quondam Simonis de sancto donato notarii in valida egritudine ponita timens iudicia dei in mea sana mente . . ."

24. For example, see N. 5, 85v.

25. OSII, N. 1512, N. 1545.

26. See Chapter 1

27. GG, N. 390, "Hec est sua ultima voluntas quam fecit in sua sanitate propter varia et instancia pericula que semper obstant humane vitae." (Note the use of the third person.) We know that she survived these perils for thirty-six more years at least.

28. N. 7, 55r, "Ego Bertolinus de Leo licet sim sanus corpore tam cogitans de futuris cum ex humana fragilitate homines cito deficiant . . ."

29. GG, N. 594–614.

30. David Abulafia, *The Two Italies* (Cambridge, 1977), p. 17.

31. N. 16 pt. 1, wills on 2r, 47v.

32. N. 25 passim.

33. GG, N. 1956.

34. The court appearance may have jogged the witnesses' memory since they were spending another Sunday, April 23, helping Anselmo's widow to prove her case. One other notary, Palodino de Sexto, who did not usually supply the day, once noted that he was writing a will on a Sunday; N. 21 pt. 1, 8v.

35. OSI and OSII, and GG. I am indebted to Maurice Herlihy for the computer program that calculates the day of the week for dates in the Julian calendar.

36. GG, N. 412.

37. See the annals of Giorgio Stella for 1353, in Stella, *Annales Genuenses*, ed. Giovanna Petti Balbi, vol. 17, pt. 2 (Bologna, 1975). Benjamin Kedar says that the clock did not arrive until 1354; see his *Merchants in Crisis* (New Haven, 1976), p. 169.

38. After Alain de Boüard, *Manuel de diplomatique française et pontificale* (Paris, 1929), p. 317, with changes.

39. After Gustav Bilfinger, *Die Mittelalterlichen Horen und die Modernen Stunden* (Stuttgart, 1892), with alterations.

40. OSI and OSII, and N. 4.

41. N. 102, 174r.

42. Bilfinger, *Mittelalterlichen Horen,* pp. 79–89.

43. Ibid., pp. 90–105.

44. "In nonis horis misit Deus ista timoris / Signa, potest signo quisque timere nouo. / Sidera quid poscant, quid nobis signa minentur, / Tempore pandetur per noua signa breui," *Annales Ianuenses,* vol. 3, p. 94.

45. Jacques Le Goff, "Merchant's Time and Church's Time in the Middle Ages," in *Time, Work and Culture in the Middle Ages,* trans. Arthur Goldhammer (Chicago, 1980), pp. 29–42. David S. Landes, in his recent *Revolution in Time: Clocks and the Making of the Modern World* (Cambridge, Mass., 1983), has adopted and extended part of Le Goff's suggestions on the usefulness of clocks in the urban artisanal and industrial society of late medieval Europe (pp. 71–73) Landes emphasizes the development of the mechanical clock, not the widespread interest in the measurement and effective use of time that is a distinctive feature of the first half of the thirteenth century. He notes that "the clock did not create an interest in time measurement; the interest in time measurement led to the invention of the clock" (p. 58). The Genoese merchant class in particular put sundials and the canonical hours to effective use; the rational use of time did not need to wait upon the arrival of the clock.

46. GG, N. 594–614.

47. GG, N. 615–635.

48. N. 19 passim.

49. *Annales Ianuenses,* vol. 1, p. 59.

50. *Annales Ianuenses,* vol. 5, p. 175.

51. *Annales Ianuenses,* vol. 2, for 1191, and in every subsequent year the names of the consuls were always supplied.

52. Robert Gottfried, *Epidemic Disease in Fifteenth Century England* (New Brunswick, N.J., 1978), pp. 159–161.

53. For example, see David Herlihy and Christiane Klapisch-Zuber, *Les Toscans et leurs familles* (Paris, 1978), p. 205, for age at marriage in Tuscany.

3   Family

1. This is his third sermon for the sixteenth Sunday after Trinity, and comes from the *Sermones de Tempore,* in the collection *Sermones de Tempore, de sanctis, et sermones quadrigesimales* (Lyon, 1491), n.p., indexed by subject. Unfortunately, no modern edition of his sermons exists. This particular sermon takes its theme from the passage, "And there was a widow," 1 Kings 17. Certain topical sermons, such as ones about the prophet Elijah or the massacre of the Holy Innocents, always mention children.

2. Proverbs 10.

3. M. 102, 250v.

4. On the clan, see Jacques Heers, *Le clan familial au moyen age* (Paris, 1974). This book relies heavily on Genoese evidence and discusses the *albergo,* a distinctive clanlike social institution that flourished in the fourteenth and fifteenth centuries. In the period under review here the clan lacked the formal structure it would later have. For the significance of the clan in this later period, see Diane Owen Hughes, "Kinsmen and Neighbors in Medieval Genoa," in Harry A. Miskimin, David Herlihy, and A. L. Udovitch, eds., *The Medieval City* (New Haven, 1977), pp. 95–111. Herlihy has shown that these late medieval clans varied in

their social and political importance over time, and the period 1150–1250 may have marked the low tide of their influence. See his "Family Solidarity in Medieval Italy," in David Herlihy, Robert S. Lopez, and Vsevolod Slessarev, eds., *Economy, Society, and Government in Medieval Italy* (Kent, Ohio, 1969), pp. 178–180.

5. N. 7, 55r.

6. GG, N. 1790.

7. MS, N. 469, "qui nondum baptizatus est nec christianus."

8. See Chapter 7 for more on tutors and the question of what constituted the bulk of the estate.

9. The will of Giovanna Pevere and related documents are discussed in detail later in this chapter.

10. N. 26 pt. 2, 39r.

11. N. 24, 44v.

12. GC, N. 1459.

13. N. 26 pt. 1, 176v.

14. N. 31 pt. 1, 149v.

15. N. 7, 55r.

16. Ibid., "Confiteor dictos filios me habuisse ex prefata lucentia concubina mea unica et sola et indubitate affectu mihi convincta ad quam solam naturalem consuetudinem habebam."

17. N. 27, 143r.

18. N. 26 pt. 1, 203r.

19. Ibid., "si bona mulier fuit de persona sua."

20. OSII, N. 277.

21. N. 4, 214v.

22. OSII, N. 609.

23. OSII, N. 52.

24. N. 56, 137v. A sample will is transcribed and translated in Appendix A.

25. N. 34, 23r. There are many lists of monks and nuns at particular religious houses. The members had to consent to different kinds of property arrangements, and these lists enable us to reconstruct the membership of various houses over time.

26. GG, N. 1790.

27. N. 20 pt. 1, 134r ff. Lopez published this inventory in his 'Nota sulla composizione dei patrimoni privati," in *Studi sull'economia genovese nel medio-evo* (Turin, 1936).

28. N. 26 pt. 1, 162v.

29. N. 3 pt. 1, 124r.

30. GS, N. 1047.

31. See Hughes, "Kinsmen and Neighbors," for more on clans in Genoa.

32. N. 22, 111r.

33. GC, N. 1512, "non valeret pati."

34. N. 26 pt. 2, 145r.

35. L, N. 1470, "Si autem filius meus Ido non bene neque sapienter se gesserit et stultus permanserit volo quod habeat solummodo introitus partis quam sibi perveniet de rebus meis quamdiu in stulticia permanserit, et proprietas sit alterius fratris sui."

36. *Institutes*, bks. 1, 13, and 23, for law on tutorship.

37. GG, N. 1697.

38. GG, N. 351.

39. N. 31 pt. 1, 107r.

40. L, N. 33.

41. M. 102 61r.

42. See Chapter 4 for more on remarriage and its consequences.

43. N. 14, 168r, also printed by Ferretto as MS, N. 1093, but his transcription is not reliable; he has the daughter's name as Nicolina and not Iacobina, as it really was.

44. *Annales Ianuenses*, vol. 3, p. 19.

45. N. 14, 298v; see also MS, N. 1486.

46. Ibid., "quos maritus meus noviter et recenter erat interfectus."

47. For Taraburlo's work for the Embrone, see, for example, N. 7, 247r.

48. Lopez, "Nota sulla composizione dei patrimoni privati," pp. 219–233. This inventory is from N. 7, 278v–279v. Lopez's transcriptions are always reliable.

49. *Annales Ianuenses*, vol. 3, p. 67, for 1232. For the survival of Sozo and Sorleone Pevere, see pp. 68 and 77, respectively.

50. Ibid., p. 95, "Eodem anno plurima matrimonia sive sponsalia contracta fuerunt in civitate Ianue inter tales personas que inter se habere credebantur et consueuerant odium potius quam amorem."

51. Ibid., "maxima pars bonorum hominum civitatis Ianue in admirationem et timorem deducta est."

4   A Good Wife without a Husband

1. A testator might leave the usufruct to the bulk of the estate to an heir to enjoy this legacy only for his lifetime. The person receiving ownership of the estate, and the reversion after the usufruct lapsed, was the principal heir.

2. Laura Balletto, "Cause matrimoniali a Genova nel 1236," *Archivio Storico Sardo di Sassari*, anno 4 (Sassari, 1978), p. 73 ff., and "Per la storia del matrimonio nella Liguria del Duecento (Sarzana, 1293)," *Atti dell'Academia Ligure di Scienze e Lettere* 32 (1975): 3 ff.

3. Salatiele, *Ars Notariae*, ed., Gianfranco Orlandelli (Milan, 1961), pp. 266–272.

4. The Genoese referred to this marriage gift as the *antefactum* or *donatio propter nuptias*. For a discussion of the way Roman and Lombard law treated the question of marriage gifts, see Manlio Bellomo, *Profili della famiglia italiana nell'età dei communi* (Catania, 1966), pp. 135–145. Unfortunately, no Genoese law codes survive for this period, and as Bellomo's work has demonstrated, there was considerable variety from city to city in municipal laws that regulated family matters.

5. Salatiele, *Ars Notariae*, p. 269.

6. In 1143 Genoese wives lost their traditional right to one-third of the dowry as a marriage gift, and from that time forward the exact size of the gift was basically negotiated by the two families involved in the marriage arrangements. The manuscript of Cafaro's chronicle of Genoa contains a famous illustration that shows some Genoese wives weeping over this loss. The printed edition of the chronicle effectively reproduces this informative drawing. See *Annales Ianuenses*, vol. 1, p. 31.

7. N. 18 pt. 1, 95v.

8. N. 18 pt. 1, 99r.

9. N. 21 pt. 1, 71r.

10. N. 7, 132r.

11. The word *parapherna,* used in legal sources, was applied to property beyond the dowry to which a wife had a right after her husband's decease. I have found no reference to *parapherna* in the notarial records. Legal theorists disputed the nature of these rights; for a summary see Bellomo, *Profili della famiglia italiana,* pp. 185–191. Here, I shall concentrate on ordinary practice with respect to these rights, using the wills as a guide to the prevailing customs.

12. MS, N. 1016. Michele left even his rights and actions against his wife to someone else.

13. N. 11, 168r, "donec lectum meum caste custodierit."

14. N. 4, 153r.

15. GS, N. 950.

16. N. 27, 125r.

17. GS, N. 761

18. SMV, N. 89.

19. M. 102, 93v.

20. L, N. 1351.

21. N. 19, 52r.

22. N. 7, 276r.

23. N. 7, 256r. Oberto Lomellino's will is transcribed and translated in Appendix A.

24. N. 4, 221r.

25. N. 5, 192r.

26. For Ansaldo, see MS, N. 584; for Berta, see N. 3 pt. 1, 126r.

27. N. 18, pt. 2, 115r.

28. N. 21 pt. 1, 10v.

29. *Barbanus,* occasionally used incorrectly, in some contexts clearly refers to a maternal uncle; see, for example, GG, N. 2066, and N. 5, 121v. It should be noted that the classical word for cousin, *sobrinus,* or *consobrinus,* was not used by Genoese notaries.

30. M. 102, 26v.

31. MS, N. 1513.

32. N. 4, 47v. Giovanni did not name any principal heirs.

33. N. 5, 196v. Adalasia named her daughter as principal heir.

34. N. 18 pt. 2, 306v.

35. N. 15, 309r.

36. GG, N. 351.

37. GC, N. 836.

38. M. 102, 146r.

39. GS, N. 174.

40. See Chapter 7.

41. N. 7, 36v.

42. N. 5, 138v.

43. M. 102, 212v.

44. ASG, Abbazia di Santo Stefano, Mazzo 1. Document dated September 26, 1204.

45. N. 2, 213r.

46. N. 27, 213r, "pro bona servicia."

47. N. 18 pt. 2, 24r, "bona mulier."

48. N. 16 pt. 2, 84r. Adalsia was clearly a servant, perhaps a companion.

49. See Chapter 6 for more on the question of Genoese slavery.

50. For more on the Fieschi family in the thirteenth century, see Alessandra Sisto, *Genova nel Duecento: Il capitolo di San Lorenzo* (Genoa, 1979), especially pp. 36–44, for the earlier history.

51. GS, N. 451.

52. N. 7, 64r.

53. N. 15, 144v.

54. N. 18 pt. 2, 351r.

55. OSII, N. 50. "Stays with me" in this context, refers to an apprentice. There was no sharp line between some kinds of apprentices and servants.

56. N. 7, 55v. The master was also the executor of the estate.

57. N. 11, 17v.

58. N. 31 pt. 1, 52v.

5   Charity

1. Jacobus de Voragine, *The Golden Legend* (New York, 1969), p. 437 ff. for life of San Lorenzo.

2. Arturo Ferretto, "I primordi e lo sviluppo de Christianismo in Liguria ed in particolare a Genova," ASLSP, vol. 39 (1907), pp. 177–178.

3. *Annales Ianuenses,* vol. 2, p. 13. See also *The Golden Legend* for the life of Saint John the Baptist.

4. Ibid., p. 28.

5. For one study among many, see Mario Falco, *Le disposizioni "pro anima"* (Turin, 1911).

6. Philippe Ariès, *L'Homme devant la mort* (Paris, 1977), pp. 155–157.

7. Robert Brentano, *Rome before Avignon* (New York, 1974), p. 272.

8. N. 16 pt. 1, 64v.

9. Aurelia Basili and Luciana Pozza, *Le carte del monastero di San Siro di Genova dal 952 al 1224* (Genoa, 1974), N. 164. Hereafter cited as *SS.*

10. OSI, N. 248.

11. The wills cited here are N. 14, 260r; N. 15, 41v; N. 4, 210v; N. 4, 31v; GC, N. 463. The five not discussed are N. 20 pt. 1, 226v; N. 15, 13r; GC, N. 311; N. 4, 140v; N. 3 pt. 2, 218r.

12. N. 4, 118v.

13. See Appendix B on prices.

14. M. 102, 13r.

15. Catherine Boyd, *Tithes and Parishes in Medieval Italy* (Ithaca, N.Y., 1952), p. 199.

16. Richard C. Trexler, "The Bishop's Portion: Generic Pious Legacies in the Late Middle Ages in Italy," *Traditio* 28 (1972): 397.

17. OSII, N. 101.

18. OSII, N. 299.

19. N. 11, 94v.

20. N. 20 pt. 1, 12r.

21. N. 16 pt. 1, 38v, "director and administrator of the works of San Lorenzo of Genoa." *Operarius* no longer meant "workman."

22. N. 5, 101r.

23. MS, N. 702.

24. N. 5, 232v, "si scandalum."

25. N. 7, 261r, "si posse."

26. N. 5, 7r, "si licet."

27. N. 5, 88v.

28. See Iacopo Doria, *La chiesa di San Matteo* (Genoa, 1860).

29. MS, N. 1070.

30. Basili and Pozza, *Le carte del monastero di San Siro*, p. vii.

31. *Annales Ianuenses*, vol. 1, p. 27.

32. For further information on the three monasteries discussed in this section, see Geo Pistarino, "Monasteri cittadini genovesi," in *Monasteri cittadini in Alta Italia dopo le invasioni saracene e magiare* (Turin, 1966), pp. 254–267.

33. N. 18 pt. 2, 304v, "si me monicaverit antequam moriatur libras tres, alioquin non."

34. Geo Pistarino, "Monasteri cittadini," p. 254.

35. David Herlihy, "Church Property on the European Continent, 701–1200," *Speculum* 36 (1961): 81–105.

36. See Introduction, Gabriella Airaldi, *Le carte di Santa Maria delle Vigne di Genova (1103–1392)* (Genoa, 1969). Cited hereafter as SMV.

37. *Annales Ianuenses*, vol. 1, p. 75.

38. *Annales Ianuenses*, vol. 2, p. 27.

39. For a general history of this order, see Jonathan S. Riley-Smith, *The Knights of St. John in Jerusalem and Cyprus, 1050–1310* (London, 1967).

40. For more on Genoese involvement in the politics of the Latin Kingdom, see Riley-Smith, *Knights of St. John*, and the chronicle of Genoa. The perennial ambitions of the marchesi of Montferrat, particularly Conrad at the time of the Third Crusade, tended to involve Genoa in local politics, usually as opponents of Pisan and Venetian interests.

41. For more on the Hospital of San Giovanni, see Chapter 6.

42. For this and the following, see Arturo Ferretto, "Annali storici di Sestri Ponente e delle sue famiglie (del secolo VII al secolo XV)," ASLSP vol. 34 (1904).

43. GS, N. 950.

44. N. 20 pt. 1, 237r.

45. MS, N. 1070.

46. M. 102, 250v.

47. San Lorenzo's necrology appears in "L'anno ecclesiastico e le feste dei santi in Genova nel loro svoglimento storico," ASLSP, vol. 48 (1917), pp. 283–347. For San Francesco see Vincenzo Promis, *Libro degli anniversarii del convento di San Francesco de Castelleto in Genova* (Genoa, 1876).

48. N. 31 pt. 1, 146r.

49. MS, N. 174; N. 5, 230r; N. 7, 67r.

50. See Arnold Van Gennep, *The Rites of Passage*, trans. Monika B. Vizedom and Gabrielle L. Caffee (Chicago, 1960), pp. 10–12.

51. Ibid., p. 146.

52. Richard Huntington and Peter Metcalf, *Celebrations of Death: The Anthropology of Mortuary Ritual* (Cambridge, 1979), p. 19.

53. Ibid., p. 14.

54. M. 102, 246r, "Scio quod dedi penitentiam."

55. N. 31 pt. 1, 246r.

56. Giorgio Stella, *Annales Genuenses,* ed. Giovanna Petti Balbi, vol. 17, pt. 2 (Bologna, 1975), p. 190, "ut moris est sepulture magnatum."

57. Ginevra Niccolini, "A Medieval Florentine, His Family and His Possessions," *American Historical Review* 31 (1925): 9.

58. N. 18 pt. 2, 306v, "si porro ibi portari."

59. I am grateful to Jean-A. Cancellieri, who allowed me to consult his unpublished thesis, *Gênes en Corse et en Sardaigne au XIII siècle,* volume 3 of which contains *Les Actes de Bonifacio, 1238–1262.* I quote his transcription of Orenga's will, "et si tenpus non esset quod possem ibi deferri, volo quod debeam sepelliri in quadam capsia quousque possem ibi esse delatam sive portatam," pp. 34–35. I am also grateful to him for allowing me to quote this passage.

60. N. 11, 16v, "pro . . . aliis negotiis faciendis."

61. N. 18 pt. 2, 257v, "pro mee funerationis officio faciendo et missis celebrandis et omnibus aliis que circa sepulturam meam fuerint necessaria faciendo."

62. GS, N. 843.

63. Ariès, *L'Homme devant la mort,* p. 167.

64. N. 31 pt. 1, 45r.

65. N. 11, 88v.

66. N. 56, 149r.

67. GG, N. 1937.

68. OSII, N. 50.

69. Ariès, *L'Homme devant la mort,* p. 161.

70. For what little there is on medieval confraternities in Genoa, see Domenico Cambiaso, "Casacce e confraternite medievali in Genova e Liguria," ASLSP, vol. 71 (1948), p. 82 ff.

71. It would be interesting to study ceremonies that used funerary rituals for other purposes. For example, in northern France there was a curious rite called "the separation of lepers." In some instances the community, led by the parish priest, would make lepers go through a funeral ceremony, which vividly persuaded the leper to stay away from everyone else. As far as the community was concerned, the leper was dead. There are other examples of mock funerals, a study of which would shed some light on what contemporaries actually thought about death in a metaphorical sense. The sources for the separation of lepers are in Edmond Martène, *De Antiquis ecclesiae ritibus,* vol. 2, bk. 2, ch. 10 (Antwerp, 1763), p. 358 ff.

72. Ariès, *L'Homme devant la mort,* p. 22. Jacques Chiffoleau has looked at cemeteries and what went on in them in his *Comptabilité de l'au-delà: Les Hommes, la mort et la religion dans la région d'Avignon à la fin du moyen age (vers 1320-vers 1480)* (Rome, 1980), pp. 155–165. Chiffoleau has made many interesting observations in this work about changing attitudes toward death in the later Middle Ages, but he could find little evidence about the period under review here for Avignon or the Comtat. One local custom worth noting is the placing of a pot (*pegau*) next to the head in the grave. (See figures 2 and 3 after p. 490). The contents of these pots are not known, but the existence of this probably pre-Christian custom is worth further examination.

73. N. 56, 102r.

74. N. 31 pt. 1, 160v, "in terra ante mastram portam."

75. For *ad sanctos* see Ariès, *L'Homme devant la mort,* pp. 37–40.

76. Peter Brown, *The Cult of the Saints: Its Rise and Function in Latin Christianity* (Chicago, 1981), p. 34. The whole chapter on the grave, "A Fine and Private Place," is filled with pertinent insights.

77. N. 56, 77v.

6   Social Charity

1. Jacopo da Voragine's sermons have not been printed since the eighteenth century. One of the best early editions, and the one principally used here, is *Sermones de Tempore, de sanctis, et sermones quadrigesimales* (Lyon, 1491), n.p., indexed by subject. Another useful edition is *Sermones Aurei* (Augsburg, 1760). This collection of sermons is organized by particular saints and feasts.

2. Luke 16:19.

3. Jacopo da Voragine, *Sermones quadrigesimales,* no. 31, "Primo eas [divitias] avare retinendo: quia nihil pauperi dare volebat. Hoc est enim proprium avari ut omnia sibi bona retineat et nihil alteri tribuat."

4. Ibid., "Quidem bona temporalia utiliter expendere cum sint non nostra sed a deo ad dispensandum nobis commissa ipsis pauperibus. quod enim non sint nostra propria patet in morte: quia nobiscum eas portare non possumus. quando enim canis duos homines sequatur cuius sit ignoratur. sed quando homines abinvicem separantur tunc canis dominum suum sequatur. sic quasi due persone sunt homo et mundus. et cuius sunt divitie hominis vel mundi in vita non apparet sed in morte. divitie remanent in mundo et homo nudus recedit de mundo. Et propterea dicitur Job. 1 Nudus egressus sum de utero matris mee: nudus revertar illuc."

5. Ibid., "Magnas enim temptationes patiebatur cum videret se non habere panem neque salutem."

6. Wilbur K. Jordan, *Philanthropy in England, 1480–1600* (London, 1959), p. 143.

7. Ibid., p. 144.

8. Giovanna Pevere claimed to be insane when she tried to get out of the Hospital of San Giovanni. See Chapter 3.

9. Rubaldo Galleta, N. 5, 7r. Oberto Bonizo, N. 7, 261r. Aimelina Galleta, N. 11, 113v. Contessa Braxili, N. 26 pt. 1, 206r.

10. For more on legacies to friends, see Chapter 4.

11. N. 16 pt. 2, 94r.

12. Jonathan S. Riley-Smith, *The Knights of St. John in Jerusalem and Cyprus 1050–1310* (London, 1967), p. 272.

13. For notice of the archbishop's work, and what follows on San Ugone, see Giacomo Bosio, *Dell'istoria della sacra religione et illustrissima militia S. Giovanni Gierosolimino* (Rome, 1620), pp. 567–570.

14. N. 26 pt. 1, 173r.

15. N. 5, 189r.

16. N. 5, 190r.

17. N. 5, 60r, 218v.

18. N. 5, 95v.

19. N. 5, 113v.

20. GS, N. 47 (1156); M. 102, 13r (1179); and MS, N. 1051 (1226).

21. GC, N, 836.

22. B, N. 148.

23. OSI, N. 341.

24. N. 16 pt. 2, 84v. Alda da Sori's will of 1217 confirms the existence of seven hospitals. SMV, N. 89.

25. In general, for one basic study in English, see Saul Brody, *The Disease of the Soul: Leprosy in Medieval Literature* (Ithaca, N.Y., 1974).

26. William of Tyre (Willermus Tyrensis archiepiscopus), *Historia rerum in partibus transmarinis gestarum*, in *Recueil des historiens des croisades*, vol. 2, pt. 2 (Paris, 1844), pp. 1004–1005.

27. Edmond Martène, *De antiquis ecclesiae ritibus* (Antwerp, 1763), p. 361 ff. For more on this ritual, see Chapter 5.

28. Jacopo da Voragine, *Sermones Aurei*, vol. 2, pp. 50–52.

29. Houghton Library, Harvard University, Manuscript Lat. 9, 23v, "Sicut eum leprosum corrumpit omnes sensus corporales item peccatum corrumpit omnes virtutes animae spirituales."

30. N. 16 pt. 2 57r, "ad vestiendum leprosos qui veniunt Janue de diversis partibus ad elemosinam petendam." For a general survey of leper hospitals in Italy, see Emilio Nassali Rocca, "Gli ospedali italiani di S. Lazzaro o dei Lebbresi," in *Zeitschrift der Savigny-Stiftung für Rechtsgeschichte*, 58. Band, Kan. Abt. 27 (1938), pp. 262–298.

31. The eighteenth-century Genoese antiquary Niccolò Perasso transcribed this document (now apparently lost) in the eleventh volume of his twelve-volume manuscript, *Chiese ed opere pie di Genova*, ASG, Sezione Manoscritti, N. 835–846.

32. N. 19, 34v.

33. N. 26 pt. 2, 127r.

34. B, N. 148.

35. Lester Little, *Religious Poverty and the Profit Economy in Medieval Europe* (Ithaca, N.Y., 1978), p. 28.

36. N. 31 pt. 1, 102r.

37. N. 26 pt. 1, 221r, and N. 16 pt. 2, 57r.

38. N. 5, 7r.

39. N. 26 pt. 2, 39r.

40. N. 5, 15v.

41. N. 26 pt. 2, 39r.

42. N. 22, 110v, "inutilatus manibus et pauper."

43. B, N. 148, and N. 16 pt. 2, 57r.

44. N. 56, 97r.

45. OSI, N. 341; GC, N. 1874; M. 102, 61r and 107v; N. 7, 34v.

46. The Genoese also left money for building projects. Two favored charities were the mole in the harbor and the Porta Vacca, one of the city's principal gates.

47. GG, N. 685.

48. GC, N. 384. For Genoa's involvement in the Third Crusade, see H. E. Mayer, *The Crusades* (Oxford, 1972), pp. 142–143.

49. N. 5, 153v.

50. N. 11, 88v.

51. N. 20 pt. 1, 12r.

52. N. 17, 113r.

53. For what follows, see Charles Verlinden, *L'esclavage dans l'Europe Médiévale*, vol. 2 (Ghent, 1977), pp. 445–446.

54. See Josiah Cox Russell, *Late Ancient and Medieval Population* (Philadelphia, 1958), pp. 109–114. Russell is justifiably cautious about population figures for medieval Genoa. His figure of twenty thousand for the thirteenth century may be too low.

55. Michel Balard, "Remarques sur les esclaves à Gênes dans la seconde moitié du XIIIᵉ siècle," *École française de Rome: Mélanges d'archéologie et d'histoire* 80 (1968): p. 650 for figures, and 679–680 for conclusions.

56. Domenico Gioffrè, *Il mercato degli schiavi a Genova nel secolo XV* (Genoa, 1971), p. 79.

57. N. 24, fols. 114–116, reveals the impact of Valencia's fall on the Genoese slave market.

58. Balard, "Remarques sur les esclaves," pp. 651–652.

59. GG, N. 1790.

60. N. 7, 36v.

61. GC, N. 239.

62. Balard, "Remarques sur les esclaves," p. 679.

63. N. 16 pt. 2, 84r, and MS, N. 1009.

64. N. 15, 66v.

65. *Annales Ianuenses*, vol. 3 (1229), p. 46.

66. Ibid. (1230), p. 53.

67 N. 16 pt. 2, 64v.

68. In Salimbene de Adam, *Chronica*, Ferdinando Bernini, ed. (Bari, 1942), see, for example, pp. 468–469. The friars were international orders, and individual Franciscans or Dominicans found themselves on the move quite frequently.

69. N. 26 pt. 2, 39r.

70. Giovanni Domenici, quoted in Iris Origo, *The Merchant of Prato* (New York, 1957), p. 367.

71. N. 15, 337r.

72. GG, N. 1461.

73. Table 12 supplies the average bequest in order to point out that the rich had a decisive impact on particular charities.

74. As was pointed out in Chapter 5, the Dominicans had been well established in Genoa for some two decades before the Franciscans had a church there. The burial preferences also confirm the idea that the Dominicans were more popular in Genoa.

75. Jacques Toussaert, *Le Sentiment religieux en Flandre à la fin du moyen age* (Paris, 1963), pp. 94–95.

76. For one recent survey of some of the issues concerning godparenthood, see John Bossy, "Padrine e madrine: Un'instituzione sociale del cristianesimo popolare in Occidente," in *Religioni delle classi popolari*, Carlo Ginsburg, ed., *Quaderni Storici* / 41 / (1979): 440–449. Jack Goody has also addressed the question of godparenthood in *The Development of the Family and Marriage in Europe* (Cambridge, 1983), pp. 194–204. Goody sees this institution of spiritual kinship

as another sign of "the power which the Church had to substitute alternative institutions in the domestic domain" (p. 203). This power over godparenthood represents to Goody part of the church's efforts to control the definition of kinship and marriage, at least partly in order to divert more legacies to the church. This note cannot do justice to the power of Goody's general arguments, but the Genoese evidence supports two main points that moderate Goody's conclusions about the role of the church. The Genoese were quite capable of devising strategies to protect the family's wealth in the face of spiritual demands, and a very large portion of charitable bequests, particularly the ones I have grouped together as social charity, were intended to strengthen the society in which families had to survive.

77. N. 7, 100r.

78. N. 11, 136r.

79. N. 24, 44v.

80. See note 23, Chapter 1.

81. N. 14 and N. 15. Parts of N. 14 have been edited by Arturo Ferretto, *Liber Magistri Salmonis: Sacri Palatii Notarii 1222–1226*, ASLSP, vol. 36 (Rome, 1906), but the transcription is not always reliable.

82. N. 7, 161r.

7   Inventories and Executors

1. For the pioneer work on inventories as historical sources, see Robert S. Lopez, "Nota sulla composizione dei patrimoni privati," in *Studi sull'economia genovese nel medio-evo* (Turin, 1936).

2. N. 15, 128r.

3. See, for example, the wills drawn up by Matteo de Predono in N. 31 pt. 1.

4. There are some other examples of extant wills and corresponding inventories, but the inventories are all perfunctory, and hence have limited value.

5. N. 56, 139r.

6. N. 56, 141r.

7. See Appendix B on prices for some comments on the role cash played in this society.

8. N. 11, 84r. See Chapter 1 for more on the wills of notaries, and this notary in particular.

9. The name of the notary would have led any interested party to the right cartulary. If, as I suggested in Chapter 1, a central notarial archive developed during the thirteenth century, the cartularies must have been catalogued by the notaries' names.

10. N. 11, 84v. The notary Enrico da Bisagno had the habit of leaving space after each act in his cartulary, perhaps to accommodate the many inventories he wrote. He may have left space for this inventory, which is not dated, after the will.

11. See Appendix B on prices for some evidence about the value of North African bezants.

12. For February 3, 1236, see N. 24, 59r. For March 9, 1236, see N. 24, 77v. See Chapter 1 for a discussion of these "double wills."

13. See Chapter 6 for more on slaves.

14. Transcription in Lopez, "Patrimoni privati," pp. 239–240.

15. N. 3 pt. 2, 172r.

16. Among his charitable bequests, Bernardo included L.1 for his church to buy a book, an unusual intention.

17. N. 3 pt. 2, 175r–175v.

18. See, for example, GS, N. 47

19. See, for example, GC, N. 1451.

20. GS, N. 950.

21. GS, N. 951

22. N. 4, 53r.

23. N. 3 pt. 2, 230v. Another will made by a foreign merchant, Rubaldo da Cremona, is in N. 26 pt. 1, 169v.

24. For more on the Hospitallers, see Chapter 6

25. N. 26 pt. 2, 76r.

26. MS, N. 707.

27. N. 3 pt. 2, 145r.

28. Georges Jehel, "Le Role des femmes et du milieu familial à Gênes dans les activités commerciales," *Revue de l'histoire economique et sociale* 53 (1975): 210, and Geo Pistarino, "La donna d'affari a genova nel secolo XIII," in *Miscellanea di storia italiana e mediterranea per Nino Lamboglia* (Milano, 1962), p. 157.

29. N. 26 pt. 1, 176v.

30. N. 143, 158v.

31. L, N. 1079.

32. N. 7, 140v.

33. N. 5, 180v.

34. See John T. Noonan, *The Scholastic Analysis of Usury* (Cambridge, Mass., 1957), pp. 133–153, for the scholastic analysis of partnerships, and pp. 193–195, for a brief but incisive summary of the debates on usury in the central Middle Ages.

35. N. 7, 31v.

36. N. 18 pt. 2, 109v.

37. N. 31 pt. 1, 45r, "quod habeo a quodam iudeo apud murciam de quodam mutuo quod ei feci ad fortunam maris."

38. For more on tutors, see Chapter 3

39. See *Institutes*, bk. 1, titles 13–15, for the basic Roman law of guardianship and appointment by will.

40. See Chapter 3 for an analysis of one set of tutors' expenses.

41. See, for example, N. 31 pt. 1, Matteo de Predono, and N. 21 pt. 1, Bartolomeo de Fornari.

42. N. 7, 132r and 261v.

43. N. 18 pt. 2, 313r.

44. GS, N. 286.

45. For more on friends and friendship, see Chapter 4.

46. For examples of the usefulness of inventories as historical sources, see the papers in *Probate Inventories: A New Source for the Historical Study of Wealth, Material Culture and Agricultural Development*, A. A. G. Bijdragen 23, ed. Ad Van der Woude and Anton Schuurman (Wageningen, Netherlands, 1980).

Appendix B

1. For a succinct note on coinage, weights, and other technical terms, see Robert S. Lopez and Irving W. Raymond, *Medieval Trade in the Mediterranean World* (New York, 1955), pp. 10–16. Throughout the work the authors discuss the meaning of many technical terms, and the book has a useful bibliography and index.

2. Giuseppe Felloni, *Profilio economico delle monete genovesi,* from the volume by Felloni and Giovanni Pesce, *Le monete genovesi—storia, arte ed economia delle monete di Genova dal 1139 al 1814* (Genoa, 1975), p. 234.

3. For 1222, see MS, N. 180, and for a reference in 1225, see L, N. 1721.

4. Felloni, *Profilio economico delle monete genovesi,* p. 223.

5. Ibid.

Bibliography

Manuscripts

GENOA

Archivio di Stato di Genova, Cartolari Notarili (Cartularies catalogues by traditional attributions)

Cart. N. 2	Lanfranco et al.
Cart. N. 3 pt. 1	Lanfranco et al.
Cart. N. 3 pt. 2	Lanfranco et al.
Cart. N. 4	Lanfranco et al.
Cart. N. 5	Lanfranco, Raimundo Medico, et al.
Cart. N. 7	Pietro Rufo et al.
Cart. N. 11	Giovanni Enrico de Porta
Cart. N. 14	Maestro Salmone
Cart. N. 15	Maestro Salmone
Cart. N. 16 pt. 1	Federigo de Sigestro
Cart. N. 16 pt. 2	Federigo de Sigestro and Ugone de Quinto
Cart. N. 17	Oberto de Marzano, Simone Flacono, et al.
Cart. N. 18 pt. 1	Giannino de Predono
Cart. N. 18 pt. 2	Giannino de Predono
Cart. N. 19	Nicoloso de Beccaira
Cart. N. 20 pt. 1	Giovanni Vegio
Cart. N. 20 pt. 2	Giovanni Vegio
Cart. N. 21 pt. 1	Palodino de Sexto
Cart. N. 22	Palodino de Sexto
Cart. N. 24	Bonovassallo de Cassino
Cart. N. 26 pt. 1	Bartolomeo de Fornari
Cart. N. 26 pt. 2	Bartolomeo de Fornari
Cart. N. 27	Bartolomeo de Fornari
Cart. N. 31 pt. 1	Matteo de Predono
Cart. N. 34	Domenico Durante
Cart. N. 56	Giovanni de Amandolesio
Cart. N. 143	Federigo de Sigestro

For a partial catalogue of these manuscripts, see Ministero dell'Interno, Pubblicazioni degli Archivi di Stato, *Archivio di Stato di Genova: Cartolari notarili genovesi*, vols. 22 and 41, Rome, 1956 and 1961.

Sezione Manoscritti

N. 102	*Diversorum Notariorum*
N. 835–846	*Chiese ed opere di Genova di Nicolò Perasso*

Abbazia di Santo Stefano
Mazzo I
Mazzo II

HOUGHTON LIBRARY, HARVARD UNIVERSITY, CAMBRIDGE, MASSACHUSETTS
MS Lat. 9, Jacobus de Voragine, *Sermones dominicales per circulum anni*

Primary Sources

GENOESE DOCUMENTS

Airaldi, Gabriella. *Le carte di Santa Maria delle Vigne di Genova (1103–1392)*. Genoa: Fratelli Bozzi, 1969.

Basili, Aurelia, and Pozza, Luciana. *Le carte del monastero di San Siro di Genova dal 952 al 1224*. Genoa: University of Genoa, 1974.

Bonvillano. James E. Eierman, Hilmar C. Krueger, and Robert L. Reynolds, eds. Turin: Editrice libraria italiana, 1939.

Ferretto, Arturo. *Liber Magistri Salmonis Sacri Imperii Notarii 1222–1226*. ASLSP, vol. 36. Genoa: Sede della Società, 1906.

Giovanni di Guiberto. Margaret W. Hall-Cole, Hilmar C. Krueger, Robert G. Renert, and Robert L. Reynolds, eds. 2 vols. Turin: Editrice libraria italiana, 1939.

Guglielmo Cassinese. Margaret W. Hall, Hilmar C. Krueger, and Robert L. Reynolds, eds. 2 vols. Turin: S. Lattes, 1938.

Il cartolare di Giovanni Scriba. Mario Chiaudano and Mattia Moresco, eds. 2 vols. Rome: Nella sede dell'Instituto storico italiano, 1935.

Lanfranco. Hilmar C. Kreuger and Robert L. Reynolds. eds. 2 vols. Genoa: Società ligure di storia patria, 1951–1953.

Oberto Scriba de Mercato (1186). Mario Chiaudano, ed. Turin: Editrice libraria italiana, 1940.

Oberto Scriba de Mercato (1190). Mario Chiaudano and R. M. Della Rocca, eds. Turin: Editrice libraria italiana, 1938.

CHRONICLES AND OTHER SOURCES

Annales Ianuenses, Annali Genovesi di Caffaro e de' Suoi Continuatori
Vol. 1, FSI N. 11. 1099–1173. Luigi Tommaso Belgrano, ed. Genoa: Tipografia del R. instituto sordo-muti, 1890.
Vol. 2, FSI N. 12. 1174–1224. Luigi T. Belgrano and Cesare Imperiale di Sant'Angelo, eds. Genoa: Instituto storico italiano, 1901.
Vol. 3, FSI N. 13. 1225–1250. C. Imperiale di Sant'Angelo, ed. Rome: Instituto storico italiano, 1923.
Vol. 4, FSI N. 14. 1251–1279. C. Imperiale di Sant'Angelo, ed. Rome: Instituto storico italiano, 1926.
Vol. 5, FSI N. 14 bis, 1280–1293. C. Imperiale di Sant'Angelo, ed. Rome: Instituto storico italiano, 1929.

Bizzari, Dina. *Imbreviature notarili: Liber imbreviaturarum ildibrandini notarii MCCXXVII–MCCXXIX*. Turin: S. Lattes, 1938.

De Adam, Salimbene. *Chronica*. Edited by Ferdinando Bernini. Bari: G. Laterza e Figli, 1942.

De Stefano, Antonino. *Il registro notarile di Giovanni Maiorana (1297–1300)*. Palermo: Presso L'Instituto di storia patria, 1943.

De Voragine, Jacopo (= Varagine, Varazze). *Cronaca Civitatis Ianuensis ab origine a 1297*. Edited by Giovanni Monleone. FSI N. 84, 85. Rome: Instituto storico italiano, 1941.

——— *Sermones de Tempore, de sanctis, et sermones quadrigesimales*. Lyon: Jean Trechsel, 1491.

———— *Sermones Aurei.* Augsburg: C. Bartl, 1760.

———— *The Golden Legend.* Translated by Granger Ryan and Helmut Ripperger. New York: Arno Press, 1969.

Della Rocca, Raimondo M. and Lombardo, A. *Documenti del commercio veneziano nei secoli XI–XIII.* Turin: Libraria italiana, 1940.

Drew, Katherine F. *The Lombard Laws.* Philadelphia: University of Pennsylvania Press, 1973.

Filangieri di Candida, Riccardo. *Codice diplomatico amalfitano.* Naples: Typografico Silvio Morano, 1917.

The Institutes of Justinian. John B. Moyle, trans. Oxford: Oxford University Press, 1889.

Martène, Edmond. *De Antiquis ecclesiae ritibus.* Venice: J. B. Novelli, 1763.

Palmieri, Giovanni Battista. *Appunti documenti per la storia dei glossatori: Il "Formularium Tabellionum" di Irnerio.* Bologna: Libraria Fratelli Treves di P. Virano, 1892.

Promis, Vincenzo. *Libro degli anniversarii del convento di San Francesco di Castelleto in Genova.* Genoa: Tipografia del R. instituto sordo-muti, 1876.

Salatiele. *Ars Notarie.* Edited by Gianfranco Orlandelli. Milan: Giuffrè, 1961.

Stella, Giorgio. *Annales Genuenses.* Edited by Giovanna Petti Balbi. Vol. 17, pt. 2. Bologna: N. Zanichelli, 1975.

Wahrmund, Ludwig. *Quellen zur Geschichte des Römisch-Kanonischen Processes im Mittelalter.* Vol. 1, pt. 1. *Der "Ordo Iudiciorum" des Martinus de Fano.* Innsbruck: Wagner, 1905.

———— Vol. 3, pt. 2. *Die "Ars Notariae" des Rainerius Perusinus.* Innsbruck: Wagner, 1917.

William of Tyre (=Willermus Tyrensis archiepiscopus). *Historia rerum in partibus transmarinis gestarum.* In *Recueil des historiens des Croisades.* Paris: Institut Académie des inscriptions et belles-lettres, 1844.

Secondary Works

Abulafia, David. *The Two Italies: Economic Relations between the Norman Kingdom of Sicily and the Northern Communes.* Cambridge: Cambridge University Press, 1977.

Ariès, Philippe. *L'Homme devant la mort.* Paris: Editions du Seuil, 1977.

Bach, Erik. *La Cité de Gênes au XIIe siècle.* Copenhagen: Gyldendalske boghandel, 1955.

Balard, Michel. "Remarques sur les esclaves à Gênes dans la seconde moitié du XIIIe siècle." *Mélanges d'archéologie et d'histoire,* 80 (1968): 627–680.

Balbi, Giovanna. "La schiavitù a Genova tra i secoli XIIe XIII." *Mèlanges offerts à René Crozet.* Edited by Pierre Gallais and Yves-Jean Riou. Vol. 2. Poitiers: Société d'études médiévales, 1966.

Balletto, Laura. "Cause matrimoniali a Genova nel 1236." *Archivio storico sardo di Sassari.* 4 (1978): 73–84.

———— "Per la storia del matrimonio nella Liguria del Duecento (Sarzana, 1293)." *Atti dell'academia ligure di scienze e lettere* 32 (1975): 3–13.

Bellomo, Manlio. *Profili della famiglia italiana nell'età dei communi.* Catania: Giannotta, 1966.

Bloch, Marc. *Feudal Society*. Translated by L. A. Manyon. Chicago: University of Chicago Press, 1970.

Bosio, Giacomo. *Dell'istoria della sacra religione et illustrissima militia di S. Giovanni Gierosolimino*. Rome: G. Facciotto, 1620.

Bossy, John. "Padrine e madrine: Un instituzione sociale del cristianesimo popolare in Occidente." *Quaderni storici* 41 (1979); 440–449.

De Boüard, Alain. *Manuel de diplomatique française et pontificale*. Paris: A. Picard, 1929.

Boyd, Catherine. *Tithes and Parishes in Medieval Italy*. Ithaca, N.Y.: Cornell University Press, 1952.

Braudel, Fernand. *The Mediterranean and the Mediterranean World in the Age of Philip II*. Translated by Sian Reynolds. New York: Harper and Row, 1976.

Brentano, Robert. *Rome before Avignon*. New York: Basic Books, 1974.

Brody, Saul. *The Disease of the Soul: Leprosy in Medieval Literature*. Ithaca, N. Y.: Cornell University Press, 1974.

Brown, Peter. *The Cult of the Saints: Its Rise and Function in Latin Christianity*. Chicago: University of Chicago Press, 1981.

Cambiaso, Domenico. *L'anno ecclesiastico e le feste dei santi in Genova nel loro svolgimento storico*. ASLSP 48 (1917).

——— "Casacce e confraternite medievali in Genova e Liguria," ASLSP 71 (1948), pp. 79–111.

Chiffoleau, Jacques. *La Comptabilité de l'au-delà: Les Hommes, la mort et la religion dans la région d'Avignon à la fin du moyen age (vers 1320–vers 1480)*. Rome: École française de Rome, 1980.

Clanchy, M. T. *From Memory to Written Record: England, 1066–1307*. Cambridge, Mass.: Harvard University Press, 1979.

Cocito, Luciana. *Anonimo Genovese: Poesie*. Rome: Edizione dell'Ateneo, 1970.

Costamagna, Giorgio. *Studi di paleografia e di diplomatica*. Rome: Il centro di ricerca editore, 1972.

Falco, Mario. *Le disposizioni "pro anima."* Turin: Fratelli Bocca, 1911.

Felloni, Giuseppe. *Profilio economico delle monete genovesi dal 1139 al 1814*. Genoa, 1975.

Gioffrè, Domenico. *Il mercato degli schiavi a Genova nel secolo XV*. Genoa: Fratelli Bozzi, 1971.

Goody, Jack. *The Development of the Family and Marriage in Europe*. Cambridge: Cambridge University Press, 1983.

Gottfried, Robert. *Epidemic Disease in Fifteenth Century England*. New Brunswick, N.J.: Rutgers University Press, 1978.

Heers, Jacques. *Gênes au XVe siècle*. Paris: SEVPEN, 1961.

——— *Le Clan familial au moyen age*. Paris: Presses universitaires de France, 1974.

Herlihy, David, *Pisa in the Early Renaissance: A Study of Urban Growth*. New Haven: Yale University Press, 1958.

——— "Church Property on the European Continent, 701–1200." *Speculum* 36 (1961): 81–104.

——— "Family Solidarity in Medieval Italian History." In *Economy, Society, and Government in Medieval Italy*. edited by David Herlihy, Robert S. Lopez, and Vsevolod Slessarev, pp. 173–184. Kent, Ohio: Kent State University Press, 1969.

Herlihy, David, and Klapisch-Zuber, Christiane. *Les Toscans et leurs familles*.

Paris: Presses de la Fondation Nationale des Sciences Politiques, 1978.

Hughes, Diane Owen. "Kinsmen and Neighbors in Medieval Genoa." In *The Medieval City*. H. Miskimin, David Herlihy, and A. L. Udovitch, eds., pp. 95–111. New Haven: Yale University Press, 1977.

———— "Urban Growth and Family Structure in Medieval Genoa." *Past and Present* 66 (1975): 3–28.

Huntington, Richard, and Metcalf, Peter. *Celebrations of Death: The Anthropology of Mortuary Ritual*. Cambridge: Cambridge University Press, 1979.

Jehel, Georges. "Le Rôle des femmes et du milieu familial à Gênes dans les activités commerciales." *Revue de l'histoire economique et sociale* 53 (1975): 193–215.

Jordan, Wilbur K. *Philanthropy in England 1480–1600*. London: Allen and Unwin, 1959.

Kedar, Benjamin Z. *Merchants in Crisis: Genoese and Venetian Men of Affairs and the Fourteenth-Century Depression*. New Haven: Yale University Press, 1976.

———— "Noms des saints et mentalité populaire à Gênes au XIVᵉ siècle." *Le moyen age* 73 (1967): 431–445.

Landes, David S. *Revolution in Time: Clocks and the Making of the Modern World*. Cambridge, Mass.: Harvard University Press, 1983.

Le Goff, Jacques. *Time, Work, and Culture in the Middle Ages*. Translated by Arthur Goldhammer. Chicago: University of Chicago Press, 1980.

Little, Lester. *Religious Poverty and the Profit Economy in Medieval Europe*. Ithaca, N. Y.: Cornell University Press, 1978.

Lopez, Robert S. *The Commercial Revolution of the Middle Ages, 950–1350*. Cambridge: Cambridge University Press, 1976.

———— "Concerning Surnames and Places of Origin." *Medievalia et humanistica* 8 (1954): 6–16.

———— *Genova marinara nel Duecento: Benedetto Zaccaria, ammiraglio e mercante*. Milan: G. Principato, 1933.

———— *Studi sull'economia genovese nel medio-evo*. Turin: S. Lattes, 1936.

———— *Su e giù per la storia di Genova*. Genoa: University of Genoa, 1975.

———— and Raymond Irving W. *Medieval Trade in the Mediterranean World*. New York: Columbia University Press, 1955.

Moresco, Mattia, and Bognetti, Gian P. *Per l'edizione dei notai liguri del sec. XII*. Turin: S. Lattes, 1938.

Murray, Alexander. *Reason and Society in the Middle Ages*. Oxford: Oxford University Press, 1978.

Nasalli-Rocca, E. "Gli Ospedali italiani di S. Lazzaro o dei Lebbrosi." *Zeitschrift der Savigny-Stiftung fur Rechtsgeschichte* 27 (1938): 262–298.

Niccolini, Ginevra. "A Medieval Florentine, His Family and His Possessions." *American Historical Review* 31 (1925): 1–19.

Noonan, John T. *The Scholastic Analysis of Usury*. Cambridge, Mass.: Harvard University Press, 1957.

Origo, Iris. *The Merchant of Prato*. New York: Knopf, 1957.

Pistarino, Geo. "La Donna d'affari a Genova nel secolo XIII." In *Miscellanea di storia italiana e mediterranea per Nino Lamboglia*. pp. 157–169. Milan, 1962.

———— "Monasteri cittadini genovesi." In *Monasteri cittadini in Alta Italia dopo le invasioni saracene e magiare*. pp. 239–281. Turin: Deputazione subalpina di storia patria, 1966.

Riley-Smith, Jonathan S. *The Knights of St. John in Jerusalem and Cyprus, 1050–1310.* London: Macmillan, 1967.

Russell, Josiah Cox. *Late Ancient and Medieval Population.* Philadelphia: Transactions of the American Philosophical Society, 1958.

Sisto, Alessandra, *Genova nel duecento: Il capitolo di San Lorenzo.* Genoa: University of Genoa, 1979.

Tangheroni, Marco. *Politica, commercio, agricoltura a Pisa nel trecento.* Pisa: Pacini Editore, 1973.

Toussaert, Jacques. *Le Sentiment religieux en Flandre à la fin du moyen age.* Paris: Plon, 1963.

Trexler, Richard C. "The Bishop's Portion: Generic Pious Legacies in the Late Middle Ages in Italy." *Traditio* 28 (1972): 397–450.

Van Gennep, Arnold. *The Rites of Passage.* Translated by Monika B. Vizedom and Gabrielle L. Caffee. Chicago: University of Chicago Press, 1960.

Verlinden, Charles. *L'Esclavage dans l'Europe médiévale.* Ghent: Ryksuniveriteit te Gent, 1977.

Vitale, Vito. *Il commune del podestà a Genova.* Milan: Ricciardi, 1951.

——— *Storia di Genova.* Genoa: Società ligure di storia patria, 1955.

Index

Abulafia, David, 51
Acre, 206
Adalasia de Portali, 202
Adalasia, wife of Giordano, 20
Alberto de Fontana, 75
Alexander III, pope, 179
Amalfi, wills, 14
Anita de Carmadino, 88
Anniversaries, 152, 154. *See also* Masses
Anonymous of Bologna, 9
Antefactum, 109–110. *See also* Dowry
Archbishop of Genoa: elections of 1163
    and 1188, 149
Ariès, Philippe, 137, 159, 160–161, 162,
    165

Balard, Michele, 190, 191
Balbo, Contessa, 28
Balbo, Giulia, 27
Baldoino de Pavero, 89–90
Baldwin IV, king of Jerusalem, 180
Balleto, Laura, 103
Barleta, Oberto, 36, 203–205
Bed, as a bequest, 107
Bequests: conditions on, 84–88; of land,
    86–87; to family members, 120–122.
    See also Legacies
Bernardo de Nuxigia, 211–214
Bertolino de Leo, 48, 70; children of, 75–
    76
Bilfinger, Gustav, 55
Bisagno, river, 186
Blacksmiths, 204
Bloch, Marc, 5, 16
Bonovassallo de Cassino, notary, 23
Bonovassallo de Maiori, notary, 31
Bonvillano, notary, 2
Boyd, Catherine, 142
Braxili, Contessa, 173
Brentano, Robert, 137
Bridges: as charity, 186–187; economic
    significance, 187
Brown, Peter, 164
Buferio, Simone, 191; children of, 41;
    heirs, 70, 80

Burial: sites, 144–150, 164; church rights
    over, 144–145; responsibility for, 151;
    cost, 151, 153, 162; location in cemetery
    or church, 163–164; payment for, 165–
    166. *See also* Funerals

Cafaro, Genoese historian, 62
Captives: ransoms as charity, 187
Carta iudicamenti, 16–17
Cartularies: survival, 1; *notula*, 18–19. *See*
    also Notaries
Castello, Giulia de, 48
Charity: to friends, 126; spiritual founda-
    tions, 136–137, 167–168; absence of,
    138–139; scope, 140–141, 199–200; so-
    cial function, 169–170, 194–196; by
    economic status, 171–172, 174; level of
    bequests, 176–178; notarial influence
    upon, 198–200. *See also* Bridges; Cap-
    tives; Friars; Hospitals; Lepers; Poor;
    Slavery
Chiaudano, Mario, 2
Children: attitudes toward, 67–69; as
    heirs, 70–76, 81–84; ages, 71; illegiti-
    mate, 72, 75–77; sons and daughters,
    82–84; posthumous, 84. *See also* Family
Churches: influence and reputation, 149;
    charitable role, 169–170. *See also* Mon-
    asteries
Clergy: heirs of, 119; at funerals, 160;
    charitable donations by, 194
Climate, in Genoa, 51
Clock, in Genoa, 53
Codicils, 22
Coffin, 156, 158
Commerce: family activities in, 209–210;
    contracts, 216–220
Crociferi, religious order, 179
Crusades, Genoese involvement in, 187–
    189

Death, 156–157. *See also* Burial; Funerals
Dictation, errors in, 22–23. *See also* Re-
    daction
Dietisalva, Enrico, 77–81

Harvard Historical Studies

Out of Print Titles Are Omitted

88. *Angeliki E. Laiou.* Constantinople and the Latins: The Foreign Policy of Andronicus, 1282–1328. 1972.
89. *Donald Nugent.* Ecumenism in the Age of the Reformation: The Colloquy of Poissy. 1974.
90. *Robert A. McCaughey.* Josiah Quincy, 1772–1864: The Last Federalist. 1974.
91. *Sherman Kent.* The Election of 1827 in France. 1975.
92. *A. N. Galpern.* The Religions of the People in Sixteenth-Century Champagne. 1976.
93. *Robert G. Keith.* Conquest and Agrarian Change: The Emergence of the Hacienda System on the Peruvian Coast. 1976.
94. *Keith Hitchins.* Orthodoxy and Nationality: Andreiu Şaguna and the Rumanians of Transylvania, 1846–1873. 1977.
95. *A. R. Disney.* Twilight of the Pepper Empire: Portuguese Trade in Southwest India in the Early Seventeenth Century. 1978.
96. *Gregory D. Phillips.* The Diehards: Aristocratic Society and Politics in Edwardian England. 1979.
97. *Alan Kreider.* English Chantries: The Road to Dissolution. 1979.
98. *John Buckler.* The Theban Hegemony, 371–362 BC. 1980.
99. *John A. Carey.* Judicial Reform in France before the Revolution of 1789. 1981.
100. *Andrew W. Lewis.* Royal Succession in Capetian France: Studies on Familial Order and the State. 1981.
101. *Robert E. Sullivan.* John Toland and the Deist Controversy: A Study in Adaptations. 1982.
102. *William Hunt.* The Puritan Moment: The Coming of Revolution in an English County. 1983.
103. *Steven Epstein.* Wills and Wealth in Medieval Genoa, 1150–1250. 1984.